Impressionism
Paint and Politics

John House

Impressionism
Paint and Politics

Yale University Press
New Haven and London

Designed by Gillian Malpass

Printed in Singapore

Library of Congress Cataloging-in-Publication Data

House, John, 1945–
  Impressionism : paint and politics / John House.–1st ed.
      p. cm.
Includes bibliographical references and index.
  ISBN 0-300-10240-2 (cl : alk. paper)
  1. Impressionism (Art)–France. 1. Title.
  ND547.5.I4H684 2004
  759.4'09'034–dc22
                                          2003018956

A catalogue record for this book is available from
The British Library

ILLUSTRATIONS Dimensions are given in centimetres, height before width.
Where known, the titles given are those originally given to the pictures by the artist;
wherever relevant, alternative and subsequent titles are also indicated.
All works are oil on canvas unless otherwise stated.

FRONTISPIECE Claude Monet, *The Boats, Regatta at Argenteuil*
(*Les Barques, Régates à Argenteuil*), *c.* 1874, Musée d'Orsay, Paris (detail of pl. 74)

Contents

Acknowledgements

THE WORK OF OTHER SCHOLARS IN THE FIELD has been of central importance to my thinking, as the historical study of Impressionism has diversified since the 1970s, opening out a range of issues ignored by the orthodoxies of high Modernism. My Coda explores these developments in the field. I cannot, of course, claim to have read everything that has been published on Impressionism in these years, but I hope that my notes and bibliography acknowledge adequately the rich and thought-provoking work that has been done, without which this book would not have been possible.

I am indebted to the British Academy for the award of a Research Readership in 1988–90. Although *Impressionism: Paint and Politics* is not the book that was originally planned to emerge from this period of leave, that extended interlude without teaching responsibilities allowed me to begin the broader reconsideration of approaches to nineteenth-century painting that underpins this book.

I am most grateful to Luuk van der Loeff and Piet de Jonge of the Kröller-Müller Museum, Otterlo, for sending me, at the last moment, a transparency of the freshly cleaned Pissarro that adorns the book jacket in its new-found splendour.

On a personal note, it has been my pleasure and privilege to talk about art and its histories with many friends, colleagues and students over the years, sometimes in the semi-formal context of lectures, symposia, seminars, conferences and art museums, and – happily – often in the more informal and expansive setting of a café, restaurant or wine bar, or a private home. I should like, particularly, to acknowledge what I have learned from Richard Brettell, Elizabeth Childs, Richard Hobbs, Richard Kendall, Richard Shiff and Martha Ward; and I owe a special debt to those friends who, in addition, have read longer or shorter chunks of the book itself: Kathleen Adler, Kate Flint, Hope Kingsley, Suzanne Glover Lindsay, Nancy Rose Marshall and Elizabeth Prettejohn. My thanks, too, to Linda Goddard and Harriet Hornby for vital last-minute help, and to Sue Adler for preparing the index. I should also acknowledge my sons, Adam and Joe, without whom this book would have been just the same, but the rest of my life very different.

At Yale University Press, I am indebted to Delia Gaze for her scrupulous and sympathetic editing, and especially to Gillian Malpass, whose patient encouragement hastened the completion of this book, and whose design skills have made it what it is.

facing page Paul Cézanne, *View of the Surroundings of Auvers (Auvers-sur-Oise, vu des environs)* (detail of pl. 160)

Introduction

THE STUDY OF IMPRESSIONISM HAS CHANGED ENORMOUSLY since the 1970s. A whole range of historical perspectives has been brought to bear on the art of the late nineteenth century, perspectives that have opened out many fresh ways of viewing the art of the Impressionists. Recent work has focused, variously, on style and technique, on subject matter and imagery, on the institutional and commercial contexts of the Impressionists' careers, on the critical responses to their art, and on the social, political and ideological values that their art expressed.

All of these are fundamental to a historical understanding of Impressionism (the contributions of individual scholars are discussed below, in the Coda). Yet in the recent historical writing each approach has tended to be treated in isolation. The result has been a fragmentation, a loss of coherence. The central question that we need to ask about any work of art is what it meant to make a work in that way, at that date, and in, and for, that particular context. In seeking to answer this question, we have to take account of all these perspectives.

The present book seeks to bring these issues together, and to explore the ways in which each may illuminate the significance of the others. They cannot be melded into a single seamless account; but they are all part of a single, larger history: all need to be taken into consideration in assessing the historical position of Impressionist painting. The chapters that follow range from an examination of the position of Manet and his associates in the late 1860s to an analysis of the breakup of the Impressionist group around 1880, with a central focus, in four chapters, on the key aspects of their art of the 1870s, examining in turn the issue of sketch and finish, the imagery of the environs of Paris and of the city itself, and the changing status of the Impressionist brushstroke. Taken together, they seek to do full justice to these different facets of the broader history of Impressionism, although individual chapters place more emphasis on some factors than others.

My arguments start from a number of basic tenets. Any such analysis must be grounded in a sustained examination of the physical appearance and make-up of the works themselves. It was their visual form – their style and treatment, as much as their content – that generated the meanings that they carried for their first viewers; the central challenge for the historian today is to develop a nuanced and wide-ranging historical understanding of the ways in which form generated meanings. These forms cannot be discussed separately from wider questions of values. Much of the initial criticism of Impressionism focused on questions of technique – on the seeming incoherence and lack of resolution of the pictures. Yet the tone and the urgency of these critiques shows that more was at stake – that the Impressionists' art offered a more far-reaching challenge to accepted values.

facing page   Camille Pissarro, *Spring at Louveciennes* (*Printemps à Louveciennes*) (detail of pl. 137)

Here, the issues need to be defined within two types of historical framework. First, I shall be insisting that their art must be viewed within its immediate political contexts: it is no coincidence that their most experimental and controversial work coincided with the social and political repression of Marshal MacMahon's 'moral order' regime of the mid-1870s, or that the group effectively broke up with the installation of the 'opportunist Republic' of the early 1880s. But, beyond this, the Impressionist vision of the world belongs to a longer history, of the emergence of a secular world view, and correspondingly of notions of vision that depended on sense experiences alone, repudiating the authority of prior abstract knowledge, and more specifically rejecting a view of the natural world that depended on divine providence. These two histories cannot be separated – the issue of secularisation was a crucial underlying factor in the social and political controversies of the 1870s; but our understanding will be limited if either the political specifics or the wider questions of belief are neglected.

It was these contexts that gave meaning to the three labels that were applied to the painters of the group in the years of their early exhibitions: 'independent', because they rejected the state-organised, institutional structures of the art world by organising their own exhibitions; the explicitly political term 'intransigent', because their attack on the dominant values of the art world could so readily be seen as an attack on the values of the 'moral order' regime; and 'impressionist', because their vision depended on sensory experience alone.

We must, though, never lose sight of the specificity of the medium – that we are dealing with paintings that were created as 'fine art' and exhibited or sold in 'fine art' forums. In the nineteenth century, distinctive values were attributed to 'fine art', in contrast to other types of visual imagery; we cannot ignore the ways in which artists positioned their works in relation to the expectations and conventions of 'fine art' painting and the debates they aroused – whether they were working within, or against, those conventions. This is not to endorse the idea that 'fine art' had, or has, any transcendent value, but rather to insist that we must reckon with the values that were attributed to the medium in the nineteenth century.

Beyond this, we should not treat the art of the Impressionists in isolation. Throughout, my analysis depends on the belief that any grounded historical understanding of their art must view it in relation to the wider patterns of artistic production of the period. Although the artists did at times work closely together and act as catalysts for each other's experiments, they were also making art with the active determination that it should be viewed in the public forum of a Parisian art exhibition. Most obviously, this applies to paintings designed to be shown at the Salon. Manet's major canvases, throughout his career, were expressly designed to find their meanings when viewed at the Salon alongside pictures that treated similar themes in very different ways. It was by contrast with their neighbours on the crowded Salon walls that his paintings gained their impact and forged his reputation; the implications of the Salon as a display forum will be a central theme in the first chapter. The Impressionists' group exhibitions of the 1870s, too, were inseparable from wider critical debates in the art world, and were inevitably assessed and judged by critics and viewers whose criteria of evaluation were forged primarily at the Salon. For those who saw the Salon as the only surviving bastion defending true quality, the Impressionists' shows were a threat to the nation's cultural values, whereas they seemed a breath of fresh air to those for whom the Salon was an outmoded forum full of mediocre art.

Any such analysis must avoid the pitfall of treating Salon art as a coherent body of work. Throughout the period, critics emphasised the extraordinary range of painting at the Salon. From an academic standpoint, this diversity was widely viewed as marking a loss of shared purpose and self-belief in the art world; but other critics celebrated it as a sign of healthy creativity. In 1995–6, in the exhibition *Landscapes of France* at the Hayward Gallery in London, shown as *Impressions of France* at the Museum of Fine Arts, Boston, I was able to present a group of Impressionist landscapes alongside a selection of landscape paintings shown at the Salon in the same years. This show stressed the variety of Salon landscape, but the comparison also highlighted the ways in which, during the 1870s, the Impressionists challenged and subverted contemporary expectations about the aims and methods of landscape painting. The present book is in a sense a development of this project, but, in treating the Impressionists' activities as a whole, it seeks to present a fuller and more nuanced argument than was possible in the confines of an exhibition.

I shall be placing great emphasis on the issue of artistic agency. The notion of intentionality has had a bad press in recent years, and certainly it is impossible, both theoretically and in practical terms, to give a comprehensive account of an artist's aims and motivations. Yet much is lost if historians restrict themselves to analysing the reception of finished works of art and the frameworks and contexts within which their viewers found meanings in them. Artists were vividly aware of the contexts, both physical and critical, in which their paintings would be viewed (indeed, Monet kept a press-cuttings file during the 1870s), and, whatever the immediate contexts of their work, the decisions they took – ranging from the size and subject matter of their pictures and their material technique to the outlets that they sought for their work – must be discussed in terms of conscious, deliberate strategy, and viewed as considered, self-aware interventions into the wider frameworks of the art world.

Finally, my insistence on the necessity of close analysis of the visual qualities of the paintings can effectively be fulfilled only by examining the works themselves. Colour reproduction has expanded immeasurably since the 1970s, but no reproduction, however accurate, can stand in for the experience of the physical object. Any analysis of the processes of making or of the effect of the finished painting depends on access to the original, and on having the space and time to explore it visually. The proliferation of temporary exhibitions in the Impressionist field has made still more works accessible (the impact of these exhibitions is discussed in the Coda), but in the long term it is the permanent collections of museums and galleries that enable us to explore pictures at leisure and – generally – in favourable viewing conditions. Most pictures discussed in the present book are in major museum collections; this has allowed me to examine and re-examine them in recent years, and will enable my readers to gain access to them as circumstances permit. However well one feels one knows a painting, there are always more meanings to find in it and more to learn from it about its making.

1   The *Ecole des Batignolles*: Oppositional Painting in the Late 1860s

Edouard Manet's artistic project in the early 1860s was dominated by the problem of reconciling the past with the present. He was seeking to create a type of exhibition painting that dealt with issues that were explicitly contemporary and often controversial, whilst legitimising itself by demonstrating the artist's wide-ranging knowledge and appreciation of the art of the past. Some of his exemplars were from the Italian Renaissance, some from seventeenth-century Spain, some from French art of the seventeenth and eighteenth centuries; sometimes his citations of past art were direct, sometimes generic; in some cases his appropriations seem to be acts of homage, but at times they seem more ironic, parodic even. At the same time he tackled the principal themes and genres of traditional 'high art' – the female nude, the life of Christ, the pastoral. Throughout these years, for all its diversity, his art was consistent with this Janus-like project of dovetailing a critical interrogation of the art of the past with a central concern for the modern. It is this phase of his career – up to around 1866 – that has most closely engaged historians of art, who have for many years pursued Manet's 'sources' and debated their implications.[1]

After 1866, echoes of past art remained in Manet's art, but only very rarely is it possible to pinpoint specific sources, specific paintings with which he was seeking to set up a dialogue. His chosen subject matter, too, became less overtly provocative – with one significant exception, *The Execution of the Emperor Maximilian*. Abandoning traditional 'high art' themes, he focused primarily on subjects that, by contemporary criteria, would have been classified as genre painting – the representation of everyday life.

It was in the later 1860s, too, that Manet became for the first time the central figure in a loosely knit grouping of artists, many of them younger than himself, who were all pursuing broadly similar goals in their search to become painters of modern life.[2] Genre paintings of fashionable bourgeois interiors, by artists such as Auguste Toulmouche, Charles Baugniet and Alfred Stevens, were already commercially very successful, marketed through dealers such as Adolphe Goupil. But critics and theorists regarded them as a trivial form of art, with their mundane subjects and their preoccupation with the detailed depiction of lavish decor and fashionable female dress. The challenge was to create a type of exhibition painting that engaged uncompromisingly with the scenes and events of contemporary Parisian life.

* * *

Two paintings can stand as the visual manifestos of this grouping: Henri Fantin-Latour's *A Studio in the Batignolles* (pl. 1), exhibited at the Paris Salon in 1870, and Frédéric Bazille's *Studio in the Rue de la Condamine* (pl. 2); yet the two present the group in

facing page   Edouard Manet, *Luncheon (Le Déjeuner)* (detail of pl. 4)

1 Henri Fantin-Latour, *A Studio in the Batignolles* (*Un Atelier aux Batignolles*), 1870, 204 × 273.5, Musée d'Orsay, Paris

very different guises, and invite contrasting readings of their position and their project. Fantin-Latour's canvas shows Manet painting his friend the critic Zacharie Astruc, with a group of onlookers: the painters Otto Scholderer, Pierre-Auguste Renoir, Bazille and Claude Monet, and the novelist and critic Emile Zola. It is a formal grouping, solemn even, reminiscent of Dutch seventeenth-century group portraits, and one that focuses on Manet as the master, the orchestrator of the group around him. This effect is heightened by the intent gaze of Renoir, his head framed by the secular halo of the gilded but empty picture frame, while Zola, turned away from Manet, poses as his interpreter, his mediator. Bazille's *Studio in the Rue de la Condamine*, by contrast, is a scene of informal symbiosis. Manet still occupies a central place, seemingly giving his opinion of Bazille's canvas while the painter himself listens respectfully, with another friend (perhaps Astruc) looking on; but two other figures (either Zola and Renoir or Monet and Alfred Sisley – the authorities cannot agree[3]) ignore the main group as they chat by the staircase, and the musician and writer Edmond Maître plays the piano, seemingly oblivious to his companions.

6

2 Frédéric Bazille, *The Studio in the Rue de la Condamine* (*L'Atelier de la rue de la Condamine*), 1870, 98 × 128.5, Musée d'Orsay, Paris

Of these men, only Manet was at this point widely known – as a notorious rebel against accepted practices in painting; the others were generally viewed as Manet's supporters and followers. Together, they were seen as forming a distinct group, separate from and in opposition to the mainstreams of Salon painting. The critic Edmond Duranty had already labelled this group the 'école des Batignolles' in his review of the Salon of 1869,[4] naming it after the quarter of north-western Paris where they met and where many of them had their studios. Discussion of this grouping has often been conflated with the history of Impressionism, and presented as the pre-history of the group who came together to mount the independently organised exhibition in 1874, most notably in John Rewald's *The History of Impressionism*.[5] For a number of reasons, this is misleading.

First, the show of 1874 presented itself as an alternative to the Salon, whereas in the late 1860s the artists still considered the Salon the appropriate outlet for their most ambitious work. This much affected the nature of the work they produced: in the late 1860s their primary focus was still on individual, large-scale pictures, rather than the smaller, more informal canvases that were typical of the group exhibitions of the 1870s. Certainly, the first known plan for an alternative exhibition involving members of the later group does date from 1867, the year when their work was most consistently rejected by the jury,[6] and they were also painting smaller pictures in the late 1860s (see Chapter Two); Bazille's *Studio* was one such work. But the Salon remained their main focus of attention.

Secondly, the two groups were operating in entirely different political situations. The exhibitions of the mid-1870s emerged during the savage political repression of the first years of the Third Republic, when articulate protest was wholly suppressed after the bloody overthrow of the Paris Commune of 1871. At the same time, State arts policy was in the deeply conservative hands of the Marquis de Chennevières, and was dedicated to the renewal – or revival – of traditional history painting.[7] By contrast, the late 1860s was a phase of ostensible liberalisation, as Napoleon III responded to an increasingly articulate Parisian political opposition by a sequence of political concessions, which restored a semblance of free public speech and political activity. Historians have come to stress the limitations of these reforms, and have seen the so-called liberal empire as more veneer than reality, but certainly it seemed at the time as if there was a real space for political and cultural opposition, which might lead to meaningful reform.[8]

Thirdly, it was not the same group of painters who were involved on the two occasions. From the hindsight of the 'Impressionism' of the 1870s, Rewald concentrated his discussion of the late 1860s on the artists who were part of the later group, virtually ignoring the evidence that his chosen band had other artistic and personal links, with artists outside the charmed circle.[9] A problem here is the scarcity of surviving biographical material – particularly for the early years of the artists' lives, when their reputations did not yet lead people to preserve letters and other documents. But even what has survived reveals that their circle was wider than generally realised. Fantin-Latour is one case in point, playing a central part in the former group, but never participating in the later group shows. Another example is the portrait of Monet by Carolus-Duran of 1867, inscribed 'A l'ami Monet/Carolus', which entered the Musée Marmottan in the Monet family bequest in 1971.[10] Monet's friendship with Carolus, at the moment when Carolus was embarking on a successful career as a fashionable portraitist, suggests fresh perspectives on Monet's own work; these will be explored below.

Likewise, the circle who gathered at the legendary Café Guerbois, the group's meeting place just to the north of the Place de Clichy in the Batignolles quarter, cannot be viewed as a sort of proto-Impressionist laboratory. Certainly Manet played a central part in the social network that met there, but many different viewpoints were represented, and the gatherings were doubtless vigorously argumentative.[11] The interplay of personal contacts in these years is significant, but this biographical mode cannot be used on its own. Personal friendship may have little to do with aesthetic position: friends may have very different views about their art, and others outside a particular circle may hold many of the same values.

Further valuable indications of artistic groupings are offered by the way in which critics at the time classified young artists in their reviews of the Salon. Salon reviews were habitually organised according to the genre of the work under discussion, but increasingly other forms of categorisation cut across this thematic system. Certain individuals, notably Gustave Courbet, were regularly singled out for separate consideration from the early 1850s, and by the 1860s 'the realists' was a relatively common category in reviews, which focused as much on the way that the artists treated their material as on the subjects they chose.

By the later 1860s, critical reviews quite often wrote about 'la jeune école' or some such grouping, before Duranty's public naming of the 'école des Batignolles' in 1869. The work of the Guerbois/Batignolles group was consistently singled out by the critics who were themselves associated with the group – Astruc, Philippe Burty, Duranty, Théodore Duret and Zola. They discussed their work together, and sometimes included less-expected artists, such as Eugène Boudin, Paul Guigou, Antoine Guillemet and Gustave Colin.[12] But certain other critics, with no such insider interest, also made similar groupings. Not many did this, and many wholly ignored these pictures, but the fact that it happened at all shows that there was some wider awareness of the social and/or artistic links between them. Jules Castagnary, for example, in 1868 grouped together Edgar Degas, Renoir, Monet and Bazille along with Manet.[13] In these accounts we do certainly have the core of the later group, but the presence of the other artists and the very different political and institutional circumstances mean that we cannot simply regard the earlier group as a prefiguration of the later one.

*   *   *

An analysis of the *école des Batignolles* in its original contexts needs to explore the frameworks for which the works were made and within which they were seen. These frameworks were both institutional and socio-political. They involved critics', artists' and viewers' expectations of canvases designed for the Salon, and more generally of paintings designed to be viewed as fine art. But these cannot be separated from the wider social and discursive contexts in which subject matter and its treatment were viewed. We shall first examine a group of major works by the members of the group, most of them designed specifically for the big public forum of the Salon, in relation to the norms and criteria against which paintings were generally judged in these years. But we must also ask what was the scope of the group's opposition. Should this be discussed primarily in relation to the artistic authorities of the moment, or did it engage with wider political and social issues? And, if so, in what sense and from what standpoints? We shall move on to consider these issues, seeking to bring together the visual and the conceptual, and to make historical sense of the artists' pictorial practice.

The distinctive characteristics of the art of Manet and his associates in these years emerge from two groups of paintings executed between 1866 and 1870 – multi-figure genre scenes and single figures in contemporary dress. These pictures may be contextualised in two ways. The painters in the group were well aware of each other's work, and, as we shall see, some paintings seem to be direct or indirect responses to canvases by their friends and associates. But at the same time the artists themselves, like the viewers and critics of their paintings, located their paintings within a wider context – by reference to other pictures of comparable types and subjects at the Salon, executed by artists of quite different aesthetic persuasions. The distinctiveness of the paintings of the Batignolles group emerges most clearly by comparison with works in which conventional norms are observed.[14]

The artists themselves well knew that it was in relation to these conventions that their works would be viewed, categorised and judged – it was not only the critics who recognised these norms as points of reference. In Manet's case, especially, critics often

3 Charles Baugniet, *The Happy Mother* (*L'heureuse mère*), c.1865, size and present whereabouts unknown (reproduced from a photograph published by Goupil and Co.; Witt Library, Courtauld Institute of Art, London)

described his approach explicitly in terms of the rejection of norms. In 1869 Marius Chaumelin, a republican critic but not a supporter of the Batignolles group, noted that Manet's canvases had 'scandalised the lovers of neat, tidy, sentimental bourgeois painting' through their lack of 'expression, sentiment and composition'.[15] Duranty in 1870 viewed this rejection positively:

> Against refined, artful painting Manet opposes a systematic *naïveté* and a scorn of all seductive devices. He places his figures against a dull slate-grey background, as if he were puritanically protesting against the *trompe-l'oeil* curtains and bric-à-brac furnishings that the greater and lesser *toulmoucheries* . . . heap up for fear of being taken for paupers.[16]

It is particularly the work of Toulmouche, Baugniet and other fashionable genre painters (see pls 3, 10 and 24) that helps us to define what made the work of Manet and his associates appear so difficult and so provocative to their first viewers.

Castagnary's discussion of *The Balcony* and *Luncheon*, the two paintings that Manet exhibited at the Salon of 1869 (pls 7, 4), offers a particularly revealing insight into the standard criteria by which genre paintings were assessed; this text combines detailed comments with broad declarations of principle:

In looking at this *Luncheon* . . . I see, on a table where coffee has been served, a half-peeled lemon and some fresh oysters; these objects hardly go together. Why have they been put there? . . . Just as M. Manet assembles, merely for the pleasure of astonishing, still lifes that should be mutually incompatible, so he arranges his people at random without any reason or necessity for the composition. The result is uncertainty and often obscurity of thought. What is the young man of the *Luncheon* doing, the one who is seated in the foreground and who seems to be looking at the public? . . . Where is he? In the dining room? If so, having his back to the table, he has the wall between himself and us, and his position is inexplicable. On this *Balcony* I see two women, one of them very young. Are they two sisters? Is this a mother and daughter? I don't know. And one is seated and seems to have taken her place solely to enjoy the spectacle of the street; the other is putting on her gloves as if she were just about to go out. This contradictory attitude baffles me . . . A feeling for functions, for fitness are indispensable. Neither the painter nor the writer can abandon them. Like characters in a comedy, so in a painting each figure must be in its place, play its part, and so contribute to the expression of the general idea. Nothing arbitrary and nothing superfluous, that is the law of every artistic composition.[17]

Castagnary's text reiterates Manet's failure to observe artistic convention, yet his message is wider than this. Manet has failed to inject real life into his subjects; wilfully or not, the pictures transgress social as well as artistic norms; what we see are disorderly pictures, but we are also viewing disorderly behaviour.

Castagnary's strictures on Manet are especially significant because he was a committed republican, writing in an opposition newspaper, *Le Siècle*, and also an advocate of a politically engaged art that dealt with contemporary social issues.[18] He recognised in Manet a fellow opponent of authority who was equally committed to a painting of modern life, but felt that Manet's acts of defiance were fundamentally misconceived. The explanation that he gave for what he called Manet's 'arbitrariness' was his feeling for the 'tache colorante' – the touch or patch of colour.[19] Manet excelled in rendering inanimate objects, but this exclusive concern was at the expense of the indispensable 'feeling for functions and fitness'. The aesthetic dimension, we might say, overrode the social. In 1869 Paul Mantz, too, accounted for the oddities of Manet's art in similar terms: 'Let us admit that it is a question of the combination of colours.'[20] A 'high modernist' critic, too, might accept this characterisation of Manet, but with a different verdict, seeing his privileging of the aesthetic as a matter for celebration, not censure. We shall return to this issue, arguing that such an account is not adequate to account for the disquiet that Manet's art aroused.

As Castagnary's comments show, various things were expected of a well-put-together picture. It needed an intelligible subject, treated on a scale appropriate to its significance; it required an intelligible viewpoint, which involved both the physical, spatial position constructed for the viewer by the picture and a clear moral or ethical standpoint; it should have intelligible, legible characters, whose relationships with each other and role in the whole scene are unambiguous; any action should contribute to the overall subject; and details should contribute to the whole.

Castagnary's comments show how comprehensively Manet's *Luncheon* flouted the rules. The subject is not consistent – is it before or after lunch? – and certainly not significant enough for a canvas of this size. The question of viewpoint leads Castagnary

4 Edouard Manet, *Luncheon (Le Déjeuner)* [now known as *Luncheon in the Studio*], 1868, 118.3 × 153.9, Bayerische Staatsgemäldesammlungen, Munich, Neue Pinakothek

to his odd comment about the front wall of the room – something that is of course absent in all standard pictures, as in the theatre. But somehow the boy's pose, looking into our space, brings the convention of the absent front wall into uncomfortable consciousness, and violates this unspoken barrier.[21] As for characters, we have no indication of the relationship between man and boy, either in narrative or social terms. In terms of action, why is the boy standing up with his back to the table? And many details are puzzling: the oysters together with the coffee, and also the cat washing itself and the armour (Manet himself titled the picture *Le Dejeuner*, not the title by which it is now generally known, *Le Déjeuner dans l'atelier*). Comparison with Carolus-Duran's *The Merrymakers* of 1870 (pl. 5) highlights the thematic incoherence of Manet's picture; here the focuses of attention are absolutely clear, as the servant – her status carefully differentiated by dress and physiognomy – demonstrates the paper bird to the baby, protectively framed by the two laughing *bourgeoises*.

The apparent narrative incoherence of Manet's canvas is complemented by its treatment. Highlights and focal points are scattered across the picture, seemingly disregard-

5   Carolus-Duran, *The Merrymakers* (*Les Rieuses*), 1870, 90 × 139, The Detroit Institute of Arts, Founders' Society Purchase, Robert H. Tannahill Foundation Fund

ing the expected hierarchy of significance among the elements within it. The boy's collar is a particularly intense highlight, as are the coffee cup on the far side of the table and the handle of the weapon at bottom left; the cup is also viewed in sharp focus, in marked contrast to the blurring of other elements in the same spatial plane, such as the hand of the man seated at the table and the servant with the coffee pot she holds. These scattered points of visual emphasis – quite unrelated to any potential thematic focuses – further dislocate the viewer's experience of the picture.

In the winter of 1868–9 Monet, too, painted a *Luncheon* (pl. 6), probably without knowing about Manet's project. He did not send it to the Salon of 1869, presumably to avoid competition with Manet, but submitted it to the jury in 1870, when it was rejected.[22] At first sight it is even less conventional than Manet's canvas. It is on a huge scale for a genre painting, and with a vertical format (odd for such a subject), and its forms are cut off at the picture's margins: these are the outward trappings of oppositional picture-making. But thematically it is wholly coherent; we are witnessing a mealtime, with a servant and a bourgeois visitor in the room, and there is even a place at the table laid for the artist, ready for him (and us) to step into from our viewpoint. The action is unambiguous, and even the casual details, such as the doll and the ball on the floor, contribute to the overall image of an informal but nuclear modest bourgeois family and household. In Manet's picture, by contrast, the relationship between the figures was unclear, but the figures themselves did not raise any very problematic social issues. One reviewer called the boy a 'petit crevé', a stock and rather disreputable Parisian type;[23] but the relationship and situation invited no wider anxiety.

This was not the case with Manet's other exhibit in 1869, *The Balcony* (pl. 7). As Castagnary noted, its subject was puzzling: one woman is seated seemingly to enjoy the view, another is putting on her gloves; and there is a man smoking a cigar. Our viewpoint is very uncertain: we are in front of the balcony, perhaps too close to it to imagine ourselves on another balcony on the opposite side of the street; and are we to consider ourselves as a part of, and party to, the scene, or as complete outsiders? And, as Castagnary again noted, the relationship between the two women is very uncertain (are they sisters, or mother and daughter?), as are their relationship to the man and the significance of their actions. Nor do the dog and ball contribute to the subject as clearly as the doll and ball do in Monet's *Luncheon*.

6   Claude Monet, *Luncheon (Le Déjeuner)*, 1868, 230 × 150, Städelsches Kunstinstitut, Frankfurt

7 Edouard Manet,
The Balcony
(*Le Balcon*), 1868–9,
170 × 124.5, Musée
d'Orsay, Paris

Another painting by Monet makes a revealing comparison here – *Women in the Garden* (pl. 8), rejected at the Salon of 1867. Monet's subject is very insignificant for so huge a picture, but at least it is coherent: women in a garden. In Monet's picture, too, our viewpoint is uncertain – we are half on the path and half on the grass, and apart from the young women. Here there is an action of a sort, taking place at the centre of the picture: one woman is picking a rose. But this action is wholly trivial and relegated to the background; and moreover it is actually masked from our view by the tree-trunk. It is a travesty of a focal point in a composition that markedly lacks a clear-cut focus. The detail is largely invisible, because of the breadth of the *taches* with which everything (including figures and faces) is treated, but the edging on the dress of the seated figure stands out crisply; this decoration, rather than any more significant feature, is first to catch the eye. The technique, like the composition, is a blatant defiance of academic precept.

The wider social connotations of these subjects raise more complex issues than the *Luncheon* pictures. Both deal with the margins between public and private spaces:

9   James Tissot, *The Secret* (*Confidence*), 1867, 86.5 × 72, Ishizuka Collection, Tokyo.

8 (*left*)   Claude Monet, *Women in the Garden* (*Femmes au jardin*), 1866–7, 255 × 205, Musée d'Orsay, Paris

Monet's scene is set out of doors, but in the security of a garden (probably a private garden, a *hortus conclusus*, though a rather unkempt one), Manet's, on a balcony where a private residence gives onto the public street. To some extent Monet touches on concerns that were recurrent in contemporary social debate: on questions of young women's vanity, idleness and gossip, and the form that girls' education should take.[24] Subjects of idle young women, morally imperilled by vanity or dreams of romance, were common in the fashionable genre painting of the period, as for instance in James Tissot's *The Secret* (pl. 9), shown in the Salon of 1867 from which Monet's painting was excluded, and, like the Monet, set in a park or a garden. But, in comparison with this, *Women in the Garden* makes little of such associations. The paraded technique of broad coloured *taches* in Monet's picture seems systematically to defuse the sort of thematic reading that the other pictures invite.

Manet's *The Balcony* trespasses on many more problematic areas. As Castagnary implied, the scene could be interpreted as a visit, but the uncertain relationships in it are quite unlike stock treatments of the theme, such as Alfred Stevens's *The Visit* (pl. 10), shown at the Exposition Universelle of 1867, in which two women are depicted in close communication in a lavish, secluded interior. In *The Balcony*, the presence of a man, particularly playing so unclear a role, adds a disruptive, risqué note. Male figures were extremely rare in fashionable genre paintings of modern life in France in the 1860s. Where they do appear, their roles are made very explicit and conform closely to stock gender stereotypes, as in Eugène Feyen's *The Honeymoon* (pl. 11), in which, even at this tender moment, the man is seen working at his desk, and turning to kiss his wife's temple, as she dutifully sits behind him sewing.

In a few scenes, moral perils are overtly presented, but these again highlight the ambivalence of Manet's image. In Fritz Paulsen's *Promenade of the Girls' Boarding School* (pl. 12), the men are presented as potential temptations to the watchfully guarded boarding-school girls. One of the men is smoking, a regular sign of moral laxity in the imagery of the period. The male figure in *The Balcony* is smoking too, but, beyond this, no clue is given that allows the viewer to deduce his status. Yet several reviewers of the picture were disturbed by this male figure; two call him a *gandin*, one an *Arthur* – both terms that designated men of outward fashion but dubious morality[25] – but in Manet's composition he is cast neither as potential client nor as potential seducer.

Paulsen's picture introduces a further area of moral debate, since in the later 1860s girls' boarding schools were under repeated attack for teaching only the *arts d'agrément*, fuel for female vanity and likely to make girls morally vulnerable, and for neglecting to encourage moral values by educating the spirit.[26] However, there is nothing in the way in which Manet's female figures are treated that raises such issues.

Yet these figures do both break fundamental pictorial codes, and codes that had moral associations: one looks out at the street, the other directly at the viewer. Indiscriminate looking, or *curiosité*, was widely seen as a threat to moral values, and such *curiosité*, in a public space, was especially inappropriate for a woman (we shall return to this issue below). In subject paintings, direct eye contact with the viewer was considered appropriate only in a very few subjects. When it appeared, it was used in unambiguous ways: in many images of beggars, the begging figure looks directly out from the picture, thus casting the viewer in the role of charitable donor (e.g. pl. 125). Manet himself had

11 (*above*) Eugène Feyen, *The Honeymoon* (*La Lune de miel*), 1870, size and present whereabouts unknown

10 Alfred Stevens, *The Visit* (*La Visite*), 1867, size and present whereabouts unknown

12   Fritz Paulsen, *The Promenade of the Girls' Boarding School* (*La Promenade du pension-nat*), 1868, size and present whereabouts unknown (reproduced from a photograph published by Goupil and Co.; Witt Library, Courtauld Institute of Art, London)

already explored the disruptive potential of a gazing female figure in his *Déjeuner sur l'herbe* of 1863 (Musée d'Orsay, Paris), in which the clothed men alongside her naked-ness made the immoral connotations inescapable.[27]

The virtual absence of male figures in genre paintings raises wider questions about the depiction of contemporary life in fine art painting. The fact that they regularly appeared along with female figures in illustrations in magazines such as *La Vie parisi-enne* shows that this absence was not primarily a question of moral propriety but rather a matter of artistic decorum. Many critics attributed it to the un-picturesqueness of modern male dress.[28] However, it seems likely that there was more at issue than this. In contemporary social theory, the bourgeois man was regarded as the quintessence of indi-viduality; conventional genre painting, by contrast, depended on typecasting. The proper province of the individualised image was the portrait, and the most appropriate subject for portraiture was the adult male. Writing in 1857, Jules Castagnary argued that por-traiture was inappropriate for children, since their identities were still unformed, and also excluded women from true individuality because their appearance was the result of vanity and cosmetics, rather than the expression of their true selves.[29] Artists may well have been reluctant to seek ways of reconciling notions of male individuality with the stereotyped scenarios of genre painting.

Besides their inclusion of male figures, Manet's genre paintings of the late 1860s (but not Monet's) are notable for the degree of individualisation of the female figures. The markedly contrasting physiognomies of the two women in *The Balcony* are a far cry from the stereotypical faces in paintings by artists such as Toulmouche and Baugniet (see pls 3 and 24). Much has been made of the identity of the models in Manet's genre paintings (in this case Berthe Morisot and the violinist Fanny Claus), but his genre paintings appeared at the Salon with generic and generally very uninformative titles, and few viewers would have been able to identify the figures depicted. It was the distinctiveness of their appearance, rather than their specific identities, that made them so unlike the stock images of the period.

Similar issues are raised by the sequence of single-figure paintings produced by Manet and his circle in the same years. From the start of his career, Manet painted canvases of individual figures that belonged to the long-standing tradition of representing 'types' – of using an image of an individual to stand for a stereotype; such types had been the focus of extensive literary and pictorial treatment since the 1830s in a long series of publications of *Physiologies*.[30] Paintings such as *The Absinthe Drinker* of 1859 (Ny Carlsberg Glyptotek, Copenhagen) and *The Street Singer* of 1862 (Museum of Fine Arts, Boston) adopt conventions very close to these precedents.[31]

However, around 1866, he and his associates began to explore a more elusive vision of modern woman, not grounded in the conventional forms of classification that the 'types' represented. In these paintings, the artists were clearly responding to the challenges and stimuli posed by each other's paintings; but at the same time the solutions that they sought show that they remained acutely aware of the conventions of fashionable Salon painting. The oppositional tactics that they adopted and their rejection of stock formulae depended on their own awareness of these formulae and on their recognition of the critical criteria by which their works would be classified and judged.

The sequence begins with two paintings intended for the Salon of 1866. Manet's own *The Fifer* (Musée d'Orsay, Paris), rejected by the jury, still belongs in the lineage of *Physiologies*, despite the remarkable economy of its technique. By contrast, Monet's *Camille* (pl. 13) cannot be so readily categorised. The figure seems to be moving rapidly past the viewer, her head momentarily turned as she adjusts her neck-scarf. In later years, Monet insisted: 'I did not intend to make it precisely a portrait, but only a figure of a Parisian woman of that period...'.[32] Crucial here is the title that Monet chose: to name a female sitter by her Christian name alone was to place her beyond the pale of respectable portraiture; deprived of a family name, she was presented as either a model or a mistress, but at the same time the specificity of the title and of the model's face emphasised that the picture represented a unique individual, not a generic type.

Manet took up this challenge in a painting executed later in the same year, and shown in his one-artist exhibition in 1867 with the title *Young Lady in 1866* – the canvas now generally known as *Woman with a Parrot* (pl. 15). The original title, with its strange emphasis on a specific date, shows that Manet, like Monet in *Camille*, was seeking the epitome of the contemporary Parisian woman. However, the specific motif that he chose, of a woman standing beside a parrot on a stand, suggests that his principal stimulus was another canvas shown at the Salon of 1866, Gustave Courbet's *Woman with a Parrot* (pl. 14). Although given a contemporary frisson by the discarded crinoline on the floor, Courbet's sprawling nude, set off against curtains and columns, evidently belonged to the tradition of reclining Venuses and odalisques; as Zola said sarcastically in reviewing the Salon, 'he has painted something pretty'.[33] Manet, by contrast, presented his demure young woman as a truly contemporary figure, unlike Courbet's neo-Renaissance extravaganza. Manet exhibited the canvas again in 1868 at the Salon with the title *A Young Woman*.

13 (*right*) Claude
Monet, *Camille*, 1866,
231 × 151, Kunsthalle,
Bremen

14 (*below*) Gustave
Courbet, *Woman with
a Parrot (Femme au
perroquet)*, 1866,
129.5 × 195.6,
The Metropolitan
Museum of Art,
New York, H. O.
Havemeyer Collection,
Bequest of Mrs. H.O.
Havemeyer, 1929.
(29.100.57)

15   Edouard Manet, *Young Lady in 1866 (Jeune dame en 1866)* [now known as *Woman with a Parrot*], 1866, 185.1 × 128.6, The Metropolitan Museum of Art, New York, Gift of Irwin Davis, 1889. (89.21.3)

16 (*right*) Charles Marchal, *Phryne*, 1868, size and present whereabouts unknown (reproduced from an engraving by Huot; Witt Library, Courtauld Institute of Art, London)

17 (*far right*) Charles Marchal, *Penelope*, 1868, 110.5 × 49.5, The Metropolitan Museum of Art, New York, Gift of Mrs. Adolf Obrig in memory of her husband, 1917. (17.138.2)

Manet's figure makes direct eye contact with the viewer, but this is more quizzical than flirtatious. She is shown indoors and in unambiguously private clothing – a housecoat; but this is wholly unrevealing and without any enticing elaboration. Like *The Balcony*, *Young Lady in 1866* also transgressed the accepted conventions of genre painting in the degree of individuality given to the figure – clearly a distinctive individual, not the stock fashionable type of a Toulmouche. In this sense, the painting trespassed on the territory of portraiture; yet, as the title tells us, the figure was not presented as a portrait.

Another pair of pictures shown, with *A Young Woman*, at the Salon of 1868 throws light on the distinctiveness of Manet's treatment of the subject. Charles Marchal's *Phryne* and *Penelope* (pls 16, 17) presented two contemporary feminine stereotypes with names from Classical mythology – Phryne the courtesan who acted as model for the sculptor Praxiteles, and Penelope the faithful wife who embroidered as she awaited the homecoming of Odysseus. The eye contact in *Phryne* amplifies the woman's role as a prostitute, also clearly indicated by her lavish attributes; this is a programmatic contrast with the demure profile and modest surroundings of the *Penelope*.[34] The contrasting physiognomies of Marchal's two figures also correspond to contemporary stereotypes,

18 Alfred Stevens,
The Morning Visit
(*La Visite matinale*),
c.1868, 73 × 60, present
whereabouts unknown
(sold Brussels, Galerie
Royale, 17 December
1923, lot 51)

setting the puffy, indulged features of Phryne against the finely drawn, ascetic profile of Penelope.

Unlike Marchal's canvases, Manet's picture gives us no information about the setting in which the figure is placed. However, Manet's attributes, like Marchal's, are very explicit, but his combination of details is puzzling: the bird and the citrus fruit; the eye-glass, and the bunch of violets. But how should these be read? The picture has been interpreted as a modern version of the five senses (with touch represented by the hand on the string),[35] but this seems inappropriately programmatic. Indeed, a story recorded by Manet's friend Antonin Proust testifies to the artist's scorn of just such legible details. Proust recalled his mocking interpretation of such an element in a picture by Alfred Stevens (see pl. 18): 'Alfred Stevens had painted a picture of a woman drawing aside a curtain. At the bottom of this curtain there was a feather duster that played the part of the useless adjective in a fine phrase of prose or the padding in a well-turned verse. "It's quite clear," said Manet, "this woman's waiting for the valet". Alfred Stevens was clearly very irritated by this comment.'[36]

Manet's subversion of the conventions of legible detail must have been deliberate. This is suggested, too, by the puzzling elements in *Luncheon*; but the clearest example

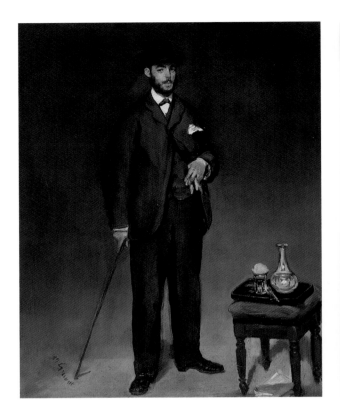

is his *Portrait of Théodore Duret* of 1868 (pl. 19), and the account that Duret himself
gave of its completion. When the figure appeared to be finished, Manet asked Duret to
pose again, and added, successively, the stool, the book beneath it, the tray and uten-
sils on top of it, and finally the sharp yellow note of the lemon.[37] These apparently
incongruous elements and illegible details may well have been a deliberate provocation
– a challenge to seemingly 'natural' processes of reading images. A further parodic
element in the Duret portrait is its actual size – the figure is presented full-length, as for
a grand, formal portrait, but the picture itself is tiny.

Another male portrait of 1868 treats its subject in a totally different way, revealing
how unsystematically Manet approached his subjects – the *Portrait of Emile Zola*
(pl. 20), shown with *A Young Woman* at the Salon of 1868. Stéphane Mallarmé in 1876
emphasised Manet's determination to conceive every picture afresh and never to repeat
himself: 'Each work should be a new creation of the mind.'[38] In the Zola portrait, there
is nothing incongruous about the sitter's surroundings – these are appropriate attributes
of an ambitious young writer;[39] but critics felt that the picture concentrated on these
attributes at the expense of the human essence of the sitter. Reviewing the Salon, the
critic Théophile Thoré wrote:

> When [Manet] has placed on the canvas 'the touch of colour' which a figure or an
> object makes on its natural surroundings, he gives up. Do not ask him for anything
> more, for the moment. But he will sort this out later, when he decides to give their
> relative value to the essential parts of human beings. His present vice is a sort of pan-
> theism that places no higher value on a head than on a slipper . . . which paints every-
> thing almost uniformly – furniture, carpets, books, costumes, flesh, facial features.[40]

19 (*facing page left*)
Edouard Manet, *Portrait of Théodore Duret*
(*Portrait de Théodore Duret*), 1868, 46.5 × 35.5,
Musée du Petit Palais,
Paris

20 (*facing page right*)
Edouard Manet, *Portrait of Emile Zola (Portrait d'Emile Zola)*, 1868,
146.5 × 114, Musée
d'Orsay, Paris

21 (*left*) Pierre-Auguste
Renoir, *Lise*, 1867,
184 × 115, Museum
Folkwang, Essen

The two pictures present very different puzzles: the illegible details in the *Duret*, and the de-humanising 'pantheism' in the *Zola*. But significantly both Duret's comments and Thoré's critique pursue similar interpretations. Duret assumed that the additions to his portrait were made simply to offset the dominant brown-grey tonality of the rest of the picture, and Thoré focused on the 'touch of colour'. As we have seen, it was in just these terms that both Mantz and Castagnary viewed the *Luncheon* and the *Balcony* the following year. We shall return to the implications of these readings.

At the Salon of 1868, in which Manet exhibited *Zola* and *A Young Woman*, Renoir showed *Lise* (pl. 21). Like *A Young Woman* and Monet's *Camille*, this should be viewed as a generic image of a modern young woman, though it is set in a very different context. The figure is standing in a wood beside a tree on which lovers' initials are carved; we can imagine that she is waiting for her lover, but the picture itself gives no clear anecdotal details. As with *Camille*, the Christian-name title indicates that it should not be viewed strictly as a portrait, though again the figure is highly individualised. Astruc's review of it made it clear that she could not be seen as a respectable bourgeois woman, but characterised her at length as 'a likeable Parisian girl', whose 'eyes express clearly her native mischievousness and her incisive working-class perceptiveness'.[41]

Similar studiedly informal poses were also adopted for paintings conceived explicitly as portraits, such as Monet's commissioned *Portrait of Madame Gaudibert* of 1868 and Carolus-Duran's *Portrait of Madame ****, a portrait of the painter's wife, shown at the Salon in 1869 (both Musée d'Orsay, Paris). Monet's friendship with Carolus-Duran, and the similarities between these two pictures, force us to reconsider traditional views of the polarity between academic and avant-garde in the late 1860s. Indeed, Carolus-Duran's portrait seems to be in some sense a response to Monet's *Camille* of 1866,

22 Carolus-Duran,
Portrait of Madame * * *
[Portrait of Madame
Feydeau] (*Portrait de
Madame* * * * [*Portrait de
Madame Feydeau*]), 1870,
230 × 164, Musée des
Beaux-Arts, Lille

though lent decorum by its title, which specified that this was a portrait of a respectable woman. Carolus-Duran's follow-up at the Salon of 1870 was a commissioned portrait of the wife of the fashionable playwright Ernest Feydeau (pl. 22). These two portraits seemed to many critics to be the epitome of modern woman, not only because of the figures' fashionable clothes, but also, it seems, because their gestural language tallied so closely with current notions of high fashion. In the Feydeau portrait, Marius Chaumelin noted that Carolus-Duran had not individualised the head enough, but insisted that the overall appearance of the figure and her costume were 'frankly modern'; for Duret, she was 'a real type, a living woman, the woman of our time'.[42] Comments such as these show how far the criteria for judging portraits and genre paintings might intersect: a picture presented as a portrait might be viewed as the image of a type. However, the category of the portrait – as signalled here by Carolus-Duran's titles – remained distinct, and raised none of the same uncertainties about social identity and moral status as Monet's *Camille*, Manet's *Young Lady in 1866* and Renoir's *Lise*.[43]

These issues come into focus particularly clearly in another canvas by Manet, probably painted in 1870 – the picture exhibited at the Salon of 1873 as *Repose* (pl. 23). This title makes it clear that it should not be viewed as a portrait of its model, Berthe Morisot. Manet was very probably referring to this picture when he wrote to Morisot's mother in 1871 asking for her permission to send it to the Salon: 'This painting is not at all in the character of a portrait, and in the catalogue I shall call it an *étude*'.[44] Again, the critical responses when it was finally exhibited in 1873 are revealing: for Théodore de Banville, it had 'an intense character of modernity'; but for Ernest Duvergier de

23 Edouard Manet, *Repose (Le Repos)*, *c.*1870, 147.8 × 111, Museum of Art, Rhode Island School of Design, Providence

Hauranne it was 'an indecent and barbarous smear'.[45] We have to ask how the picture could be viewed in these terms.

Everything in *The Balcony*, *Young Lady in 1866* (*Woman with a Parrot*) and *Repose* disrupted standard patterns of reading and finding meanings: the lack of clear relationships between the figures; the poses and activities of the individual figures; their attributes, and their very individuality; and also the technique, which prevented the viewer from finding clear focal points in the composition.

But what was the significance of this disruption? What did it mean to paint like this in the late 1860s – in the last years of Napoleon III's Second Empire? A number of distinct answers to this question were given by critics in the late 1860s. One explanation was, simply, that Manet did not know how to draw or paint. Such comments do not get us very far, but this blanket refusal to address his art must itself be seen as a marker of the threat that it posed. But was this threat merely artistic – a threat to academic values – or did its implications spread further?

Beyond this, as we have seen, many critics attributed Manet's rule-breaking to his love for the coloured *tache*, and argued that he sacrificed all other values – drawing and composition – in favour of the *tache*. Other writers were more uncomfortable about his imagery, and some, including Castagnary, encompassed both his imagery and his love of the *tache*. The interweaving of questions of technique and meaning emerges especially clearly in Thoré's comments of 1868 quoted above, in which he criticised him for treating everything in equally weighted *taches*, and attributed this to a form of 'pantheism' – a refusal to deploy the conventional hierarchies of focus and detail as a means of according transcendent value to the human subject.

This linkage is of central importance to our argument: the *tache* could be seen at one and the same time as an aestheticised unit and a socially disruptive element. Such a conjunction stands in marked contrast to the categorical distinction between form and content in the criticism of the modernist tradition, which has until recently dominated Manet studies.[46]

Related arguments are found, too, in the first sustained attempts to forge a critical language to justify Manet's pictorial vision – by his friends Zola, Duranty and Astruc between 1867 and 1870. They associate his technique with the fleeting experience of scenes glimpsed in passing in the modern city. In his essay on Manet of 1867, Zola imagined inviting an *amateur* to stand at a distance from *Music in the Tuileries Gardens* (National Gallery, London), in order to see 'that these *taches* are alive, that the crowd is talking'.[47] Reviewing *The Balcony* in 1869, Duranty argued that the treatment of the picture conveyed the impression of a scene viewed quickly, in passing, and in 1870 he stressed Manet's fascination with 'the violent effect of nature, the intense crudity of its appearance, of its contrasting accents', describing how his pictures jumped out from those around them on the walls of the Salon.[48] In the same year, Astruc noted how, in such surroundings, Manet's work could look 'barbarous, preserving that crudity that is his very own, that conveys the energy and profundity of his vision. When he treats things in movement, he invests them with his dazzling verve, fixing crowds and deploying a range of tones of an extraordinary distinction.'[49] 'Barbarous', for Astruc, was clearly a positive term – in marked contrast to Duvergier de Hauranne's comments about *Repose*.

Common to all these accounts is the critics' insistence that Manet's technique and subject matter were inseparable – that the seeming incompleteness and incoherencies in his art had to be seen, not as artistic failings, but as the expression of a vision of the modern world, and of the experience of vision in that world. Critical analyses such as these define Manet's vision in terms of a particular notion of modernity – a modernity concerned with the contemporary world, but also with a particular way of viewing that world. This vision needs to be analysed in two ways, within two frames. First, it represented an artistic project, since, as we have insisted throughout, his principal paintings were designed to be viewed in relation to other paintings at the Salon and to gain their meanings in that forum. But, beyond this, as these commentaries suggest, Manet's pictorial language could be interpreted as representing a world view – an approach to the world of lived experience that was inescapably both social and political.

*   *   *

In order to bring together these two frames, the artistic project and the world view, we need to step back from the pictures themselves and their immediate contexts. This broader framework can be explored in two distinct ways, following two very different models of historical analysis. Viewed synchronically, it can be analysed in terms of rival notions of modernity, rival ways of making sense of the everyday experience of a rapidly changing world, in the context of the social debates and political constraints of the last years of the Second Empire. But these developments can also be viewed diachronically, as part of a linear historical narrative, in terms of notions of progress, both artistic and socio-political. Modernist art history in the mid-twentieth century favoured this diachronic perspective, according Manet a central position in the genesis of the avant-garde and of what has come to be known as 'modern art'. By contrast, more recent accounts have focused primarily on the notion of modernity, and on the immediate contexts within which and for which the paintings were made. Both of these models are sanctioned by the critical writing of the period. As we shall see, the issue of modernity was much debated in these years, and the idea of progress in art, together with the emerging notion of the 'avant-garde', formed an alternative focus of critical analysis.

The concept of the 'avant-garde' offers a revealing starting point for an exploration of the broader context and significance of the work of Manet and the *école des Batignolles* in the later 1860s. The historical justification for this lies in part in the title of a book. When in 1885 Théodore Duret reprinted his art criticism, he gave the volume the title *Critique d'avant-garde*, and placed his review of the Salon of 1870 at the start. The rest of the book includes reprints of Duret's later essays on the Impressionist painters, together with his writings on Japanese art, Wagner and Schopenhauer.[50] The title *Critique d'avant-garde* does not overtly label the artists he discusses as 'avant-garde'; rather, it claims that Duret's own critical position is avant-garde in supporting them – the title is best translated as *Avant-Garde Criticism*. However, the book does explicitly associate these artists with the notion of the 'avant-garde' and presents Duret's own appreciation of them as an 'avant-garde' position. His friend James McNeill Whistler responded very positively to Duret's title: '. . . what a perfect title – *L'Avant-Garde! C'est ça – voilà qui est bien trouvé!* For let us never forget that you were always to the fore, while the others were left behind in the dim distance of doubt and stupidity.'[51]

The history of the term 'avant-garde' has been surprisingly neglected in the recent art-historical literature. Some intellectually sophisticated texts have used it as if its meaning and implications are self-evident,[52] while another tells us that the term was not current in art criticism of the 1880s and 1890s – and this despite the title of Duret's book.[53]

The starting point of the term 'avant-garde' is of course military, referring to the advance party that leads the way and marks out the path that the main force will follow. A central element in this usage is that it implies movement or progress towards some goal; it is teleological, identifying some end in view in the future. The same applies to the implications of the term when it came to be used metaphorically. 'Avant-garde' was also being used in a broadly political sense by the mid-nineteenth century, to indicate a smaller group who were leading where others would follow; in this sense, it was generally applied to reformist or radical groupings.[54]

It was in a broadly political context, too, that the term made its first traced appearance in nineteenth-century discussions of the field of art. It appears in two often-quoted passages from the radical utopian philosophers of the earlier nineteenth century, used once by a follower of Saint-Simon in 1825, once by a follower of Charles Fourier in 1845. In both of these texts, the argument is that art as a whole should act as an 'avant-garde' to society at large, through its superior vision – that is, that art could guide and lead society towards a new world.[55]

Nicos Hadjinicolaou has pinpointed a crucial shift between these texts and the senses in which the term came to be used later in the century, when it came to characterise distinct groups *within* the art world that were seen as ahead of, and also opposed to, the dominant values in that world.[56] This is the familiar model of the 'modernist' avant-garde – an artistic grouping that takes an oppositional stance that the mass initially rejects but later accepts and then follows. This is very different from the original military usage. Clearly the avant-garde of soldiers are not in conflict with the main army over the path to follow: both are under a single command, and the avant-garde is entrusted with leading ahead of the rest, but in the same direction. The utopian texts of the early nineteenth century follow this: art as a whole is entrusted with the role of pioneering the path that the whole of society will follow. However, the shift to the avant-garde as splinter group has clearly been made in Duret's book title in 1885.

Before we ask whether the notion of the 'avant-garde' is implicit in the work and position of the group around Manet, and, if so, in what sense, a number of questions about the history and usage of the term need to be refined. Here, further examples of its early use will help us to clarify the issues, and to trace the emergence of the idea of the avant-garde as oppositional. So few such examples have been found that it is worth looking at each in turn, in order to assess the range of assumptions that the term embraced.[57]

Hints of the avant-garde as a splinter group begin to emerge in mid-nineteenth-century texts. The first example is from a literary text, but the grouping described is political, not cultural. In *Les Comédiens sans le savoir*, one of the novels in Honoré de Balzac's *La Comédie humaine*, a text first published in 1846, one character talks about 'communists, humanitarians and philanthropes' as 'our avant-garde', who, when the right moment comes, will light the fire of social and political revolution.[58]

Yet the utopian vision of the avant-garde leading society in a seamless flow of progress continued alongside this. It appears in a particularly interesting context in one of the long passages of social philosophising in Victor Hugo's *Les Misérables* of 1862:

The encyclopedists, led by Diderot, the physiocrats, led by Turgot, the philosophes, led by Voltaire, and the utopists, led by Rousseau, these are the four sacred legions. The immense advance of humanity towards the light is due to them. They are the four avant-gardes of humankind as it marches towards the four cardinal points of progress – Diderot towards the beautiful, Turgot towards the useful, Voltaire towards truth, and Rousseau towards justice.[59]

This text is significant for us in three ways. First, it is quite explicit about the links between the avant-garde and notions of progress; second, it defines 'progress' in fascinatingly wide-ranging terms – towards four quite distinct 'cardinal points', beauty, utility, truth and justice; and third, it explicitly presents a model for an avant-garde in the cultural sphere – Diderot leading humanity towards the 'beautiful'. This 'beautiful' in Hugo's formulation should not be seen as exclusively a matter of aesthetics, but should rather be read in terms of *le beau* as defined in Victor Cousin's vastly influential book *Du vrai, du beau et du bien*, in which *le beau* is a fusion of the moral and the aesthetic faculties – the product of a marriage between reason and the senses in which reason takes the dominant role.[60] We shall return in this chapter to the question of progress, and, later in the book, to the values attributed to the senses.

The term 'avant-garde' was also used in connection with one of the most long-running debates in French culture – the so-called quarrel between the ancients and the moderns. This was a dispute between those who upheld absolute and ahistorical notions of value in literature, claiming that the writers of classical antiquity presented a model and a standard that could never be bettered, and those who believed that the arts changed in different historical circumstances, and that subsequent developments could improve on antique models, or needed to be judged by different criteria. A central element in the argument of the 'moderns' was the notion of progress.

It is in this context that by far the earliest cultural use of the term 'avant-garde' has been traced – in a text of about 1600 by Etienne Pasquier, in which he describes the poets who are 'waging war against ignorance' as the 'avant-garde' – in other words 'the fore-runners of the other poets'. The metaphorical language in this passage is clearly military, and the phrase 'war against ignorance' suggests parallels with contemporary scientific debates; but Pasquier's concern is emphatically about quality in poetry, and it is explicitly couched in terms of progress.[61] At the opposite end of the history of the quarrel between the ancients and the moderns, and more immediately relevant to our argument, is a discussion of the quarrel by C.-A. Sainte-Beuve published in 1856, in which he celebrates the 'modern' critic and theoretician the Abbé de Pons, who wrote in the early eighteenth century, as being 'à l'avant-garde' and manifesting the 'zèle d'avant-garde'.[62]

The final text is of a different order – one of Charles Baudelaire's aphoristic notebook entries from the early 1860s, published after his death as *Mon coeur mis à nu*. He mocks the current fashion for military metaphors, and lists these, including among them 'les poètes de combat' and 'les littérateurs d'avant-garde'.[63] The distinction that he is making here evidently belongs within the literary field, between 'avant-garde' *littérateurs* and other *littérateurs*; but it is not clear in this context whether they are claiming to be 'avant-garde' in their politics or in their approach to the literary arts.

The earliest uses of 'avant-garde' in relation to contemporary painting that have so far been traced date from the 1870s. In 1874 Théophile Silvestre described Octave Tassaert, who had recently committed suicide, as 'artiste d'avant-garde de l'Art moderne, who through his knowledge remained faithful to the great tradition, with his spirit open to all sorts of innovatory inspiration'.[64] The Impressionists were characterised in similar terms by Jules Claretie in his Salon review of 1875, in which he described them as 'fighting *à l'avant-garde*'; despite his criticisms of their technique, Claretie praised their pursuit of the 'new', and speculated that some master might be able to build on their methods and achieve 'some absolute progress'.[65] 'Jacques', reviewing the third Impressionist group exhibition in 1877, described the exhibitors, *en bloc*, as 'les peintres d'avant-garde'.[66] In 1880, in a retrospective survey of the Exposition Universelle of 1878, Tullo Massarani wrote of the universal enthusiasm for the art of Camille Corot: 'Even the most audacious avant-garde, the one that has baptised itself the legion of Impressionists, does not repudiate him as a mentor. This is only a small bold group, forming a sect of their own.'[67] The term was used again in 1883 by an anonymous critic in relation to Monet, viewing him both as pioneer and as potential victim before others claimed the rewards of his enterprise,[68] and once by Félix Fénéon in 1886, after the publication of Duret's *Critique d'avant-garde*, when he described the Neo-Impressionists as 'à l'avant-garde de l'impressionnisme'. This phrase in Fénéon's essay generated heated discussions among Georges Seurat's friends, which shows that the usage was wholly familiar to them.[69]

No example has yet been found of the term 'avant-garde' used to describe the group around Manet in strictly contemporary writing of the late 1860s, though one may well exist among the mass of verbal material that the period has left for us. But even the absence of a written example would not prove that the notion was not current in artistic circles. Even in an age that generated so many printed words, many things that were often spoken may have left no lasting trace.

These examples show that the use of the term 'avant-garde' in the nineteenth century was grounded on assumptions about linear development and progress, assumptions that have remained fundamental to the subsequent uses of the term. Such claims to being a vanguard may have a wider social and political dimension, but equally they may not, and indeed they may repudiate any notion that art had, or should have, any social role.

In some sense, the idea of the 'avant-garde' must necessarily involve notions of novelty or innovation as a defining characteristic, although it would be possible to be innovative without claiming to be avant-garde. However, in nineteenth-century terms, an avant-garde position did not necessarily imply active opposition to the dominant modes, but might just be a correction, an extension, a development, as in Hugo's text. Also, an avant-garde position was inevitably in some way an elite, minority position, since only later would the mass follow where the pioneers had led, but at the same time it seems to be appropriate only to group enterprises, rather than to the 'eccentricity' of the unique individual.[70]

The notions of avant-gardeness and of progressive art were central to the rhetoric surrounding many types of art in the later nineteenth and twentieth centuries, both in the ambitions that went into the making of particular works of art, and in the meanings that they bore for their first viewers. It is in these terms – as rhetoric – that these ideas must be analysed, rather than being used as a template for our own historical narrative. To take this rhetoric at face value implies accepting a linear, progress-based account of the development of art. Any such linear account is inevitably teleological, since it implies that changes in art have an ultimate goal in view; yet any such goal can only be defined retrospectively, through hindsight. Linear histories also prise the movements apart from the contexts from which the oppositional positions grew and within which they set themselves up, although it was these contexts that gave them their initial meanings and urgency.

We must now return to the artistic situation in the late 1860s, to see how the activities of Manet and the *école des Batignolles* relate to the notions of the 'avant-garde' that were then current. Two questions are central here. First, how relevant was the notion of 'progress' to their artistic projects? and second, how can the position they assumed within the art world be characterised? Should it be seen as pioneering, or corrective, or oppositional? These questions will lead us to consider the issue of modernity, and the various meanings that were ascribed to the idea during the 1860s.

The issue of progress in art was inescapable at the period. Inspired by the far more tangible notions of progress in scientific, technological and social fields, commentators consistently asked, in their reviews of the Salon, whether that year's exhibition marked an advance over the last. However, the notion of progress in art proved tricky to define, and a number of very different notions of 'progressive' art were proposed.

At one extreme was Courbet's friend the philosopher Pierre-Joseph Proudhon, whose answer, as published in 1865, was straightforward. Art's function, he repeatedly insisted, should be 'the physical, intellectual and moral perfecting of humanity', as part of his overall project 'to educate the people, to give them, together with a taste for knowledge, an understanding of history and philosophy and a respect for justice, the true joys of labour and of society'.[71] At the opposite extreme was Hugo's vision in 1862, in which he insisted that the 'beautiful', as pioneered by Diderot, belonged to a distinct sphere of progress, one that was categorically distinct from utility, truth and justice.

This contrast resumes the critical debate of the 1830s between Théophile Gautier's notion of 'l'art pour l'art' and Thoré's 'l'art pour l'homme' – between the aesthetic and the social missions of art.[72] At the other end of the historical spectrum, the same polarity was explored again in Clement Greenberg's celebrated essays of the late 1930s, 'Avant-Garde and Kitsch' and 'Towards a Newer Laocoon', in which he upheld the 'art for art's sake' tradition, by defining the true avant-garde as lying in the maximising of the intrinsic qualities of painting itself, in contrast to his notion of Kitsch – propagandistic art deployed for political ends.[73]

By the 1860s a third option was clearly in place, which viewed progress in terms of a commitment to the direct observation of nature and rejection of the conventions of the academy. This ambition could be couched in both political and ostensibly apolitical terms. For Castagnary this return to nature was in a sense an extension of 'l'art pour l'homme'; it had an explicitly political dimension, as part of society's march towards democracy that was, he believed, beginning to be realised by the reforms of the last years of Napoleon III's Second Empire.[74] Duranty's essay of 1876, *La nouvelle peinture*, also defined the goal of the young artists in terms of a return to nature as the means of ridding painting of academic conventions, but he viewed this in less explicitly political terms, instead emphasising the artists' independent vision. The essay does not directly invoke the idea of progress, but ends by very nearly using the term 'avant-garde'. Duranty asks whether the Impressionist group will themselves be the 'primitives' of the 'artistic resurgence' or rather 'cannon fodder . . . the front-line soldiers' who are killed before the main army appropriates their initiatives and gains the victory.[75] This *topos* of the pioneers who open the way for others to reap the rewards recurs in the anonymous comment of 1883 on Monet where the term 'avant-garde' is used: 'the soldiers of the avant-garde are always those who have the least chance of being there when the flag is planted on the citadel and the medals are distributed'.[76]

In contrast to these visions of progress through the study of nature, Eugène Fromentin, also writing in 1876, insisted that progress in art depended on turning the tide back against the formlessness and lack of finish of modern landscape painting, and on a return to the discipline and careful execution of traditional methods.[77] However, there was another very different idea of looking back to the arts of the past that played a crucial role in the history of 'modernist' art: the notion of going back in order to go forward. Fromentin's idea of progress demanded a return to traditional artistic values. Yet by far the more powerful current, from the early nineteenth century onwards, involved the reassessment of types of art from the past that lay outside the academic canon, such as Italian art of the fourteenth and fifteenth centuries, the French seventeenth-century peasant painters the Le Nains, French popular woodblock prints and, from the 1860s, the arts of Japan. In all of these cases, the motivation was a search for a form of art that seemed purer, less rule-bound and less conventionalised. These anti-academic examples acted as a catalyst that helped artists to find ways to renew their vision.

How far can these encounters be characterised as avant-garde? The central issue here is the question of novelty. Some such movements – for instance, aspects of the Gothic revival – were primarily seeking to go back to what was seen as a healthier state of society in the past. This cannot be regarded as an 'avant-garde' position; nor can Fromentin's revitalised academicism. By contrast, those movements that used the re-examination of the past as a basis for renewal and novelty may meet our criteria. Although, in military terms, they were leading the troops backwards, this might be a prelude to striking off in new directions and inviting the rest to follow. Later in the century, Maurice Denis's manifesto of the Nabi group of 1890, entitled *Définition du Néo-Traditionnisme*, is a fine example of this.[78]

Thus the notion of progress in art was widely discussed, and in very varied terms, in the cultural context in which Manet played a central part. Indeed, in 1869 the *Journal officiel* published a treatise titled *Progrès de la France sous le gouvernement impérial*, in which a chapter was devoted to progress in the fine arts, defining this in terms of the sums of money that the government had spent on the arts, the number of works it had purchased, and the expansion of the Salon exhibitions, with the intention of 'arousing zeal and competitiveness among young artists'.[79]

However, there were some dissenting voices. In the entry on 'Progress' in his great *Dictionnaire*, Pierre Larousse was very uncertain about the concept of progress in the visual arts, concluding that the idea did not make sense if used qualitatively, in terms of improvement in the practice of the arts, but only if it was understood in terms of the introduction of new ideas and ways of thinking that had not been available to the ancients.[80]

More directly relevant to Manet's position are the views of Baudelaire and Zola. Baudelaire's aesthetics were based on a notion of modernity that was rooted in the present – in understanding the changing world around the viewer. He felt that the artist had to engage with this transitory modern world, and that the defining characteristic of his art should lie in that act of engagement, in the here-and-now, and not in its place in any chronological line of development. In his first essay on the Exposition Universelle of 1855, he voiced his scepticism about the promise of constant material progress, and declared that the idea of progress in the sphere of the imagination was a 'gigantic absurdity': 'in the field of poetry and art, innovators rarely have precursors'.[81]

At first sight, Zola's position looks rather different. In many ways he followed lines that we have already encountered. In 1866 he argued that those who are persecuted today will be tomorrow's masters, insisting that Manet was one of these 'masters of tomorrow' and that the movement of the day was 'realist, or rather positivist'; his notion of positivism clearly encompassed ideas of progress. But at the same time he adamantly denied that he was praising 'the painting of the future', insisting instead that we could never anticipate the art of the future, since it would be the product of societies that had not yet come into being.[82] His arguments here closely follow Hippolyte Taine's theories of 'race, milieu et moment' – that all cultural production is dependent on these factors within the society that produces it, and thus must be analysed synchronically. For our purposes, it is important that Zola so strongly opposed teleological readings of the development of art.

Where should we place Manet in relation to these debates? In the preface to his one-man exhibition of 1867, there is no hint of ideas of artistic progress. He insisted that he did not want to protest against traditional methods; rather, his aim was to paint 'sincere' works. He was seeking only to 'render his impression'; it was this sincerity that had led others to protest against him.[83] This rhetoric of 'sincerity' and, to use Zola's key term, 'temperament', was a crucial element in Manet's declared position: each artist had to be true to his or her unique personal experiences of the world.

In Zola's essay on Manet of 1867, this project is described in terms of 'forgetting'. In order to achieve this personal vision, artists had to try to forget what they had seen and learned in the museums and from their teachers.[84] The notion of forgetting was also central to Baudelaire's aesthetic in these years,[85] and, as Joel Isaacson has emphasised, it played a major role in Mallarmé's and Duranty's essays of 1876 on the Impressionists as well.[86]

One of the most potent myths of the modernist tradition has been the 'innocent eye'. We must stress that this is a myth, since the very concept of innocence presupposes knowledge. Notions such as *naïveté* and the innocent eye demand historical definitions; they must be viewed as reactions against, and as the antithesis of, the conceptions of knowledge that are dominant in a particular society and culture. Each such quest for the 'innocent eye' can be understood only in terms of the values and conventions that it seeks to reject, and represents a process of unlearning. As Nelson Goodman so eloquently put it: 'The eye comes always ancient to its work, obsessed by its own past and by old and new insinuations of the ear, nose, tongue, fingers, heart and brain.'[87] The quest to shed this accumulated knowledge is just as calculated, just as much the product of knowing artifice, as the conventions that are being rejected. Yet this must not lead us to ignore the potency of the myth. The idea of a renewed, cleansed vision has acted as a strong, enabling metaphor for creativity within modernist artistic practice.

The notions of sincerity and *naïveté* define only the starting point – the notional innocence of the eye confronting the external world. Manet's preface of 1867 did not go on to define what this eye was looking for in that world or how it viewed what it saw. Reviewing Manet's one-artist show in 1867, Hippolyte Babou, an associate at the Café Guerbois, had no time for the sincerity argument in Manet's preface, since, taken literally, it would mean that everyone's sincere impressions should be considered equally valuable. Intelligence was needed, over and above sincerity, and this, Babou insisted, Manet had: 'This intelligence has already been much exercised by curiosity, meditation and study; this alert intelligence pleases me, because it escapes further and further away from that thoughtless carelessness that so often passes for originality . . . , and because its nature is essentially suggestive.'[88] Babou's emphasis on Manet's 'study' was a pointed rebuttal of the recurrent litany of hostile critics that Manet's art was the product of a slapdash, lazy practitioner. The terms 'curiosity' and 'alert' raise issues to which we shall return.

Further hints of the way in which this 'new' vision was characterised can be found in the commentaries on Manet's art that we have already examined, by Zola, Duranty and Astruc, his friends and associates in these years. The question of progress in art plays little part in these accounts. They all seek to define Manet's art in terms of a distinctive way of viewing the world that he saw around him, and all characterise it in part by reference to his painting technique (see above, p. 28). Babou repeated the regular criticism that painting everything by *taches* diminished the human content of the pictures, but felt that Manet was moving beyond this in pictures like *Young Lady in 1866* (*Woman with a Parrot*).[89] Zola, Duranty and Astruc saw his use of coloured touches as an integral part of his pictorial vision.

As we have seen, it was possible for critics to isolate the *tache* from its context, and view it as Manet's sole concern. For Castagnary in 1869, Manet's reason for combining incongruous elements was his highly developed 'sense of the coloured *tache*'. In the same year, Mantz wrote about *The Balcony*:

> In this painting without thought [*pensée* – i.e. without any idea or values behind it], you would search in vain for the accentuation of a type or the characterisation of a sentiment or an idea. Let us admit that it is a question of a combination of colours, and let us look at it as we would look at the extravagant arabesques of a Persian vase, the harmony of a bouquet of flowers, or the decorative brilliance of wall-paper.[90]

For both critics, Manet's art was disconcerting because he reduced the figure to the status of still life.

Similar arguments appear, but here harnessed in Manet's favour, in a celebrated passage in Zola's essay of 1867, in which he sought to defuse the significance and shock value of Manet's subject matter, in pictures such as *Olympia* (1863; Musée d'Orsay, Paris). Although the public had sought out an obscene intention in it, for Manet a picture was simply a pretext for analysis: 'You needed a naked woman, and you chose Olympia, the one nearest to hand; you needed some light and luminous *taches*, and you put in a bouquet; you needed some black *taches*, and you placed in a corner a negress and a cat.'[91]

But should we take such readings at face value? In the light of Zola's fascination with torrid and scandalous subjects in *Thérèse Raquin* of 1866, it seems implausible that he considered that coloured *taches* were the only significant element in Manet's art. Rather, Zola emphasised this facet of Manet's work at the expense of others for a particular reason at this particular moment – at the end of 1866. His essay was part of an unsuccessful campaign to get a significant group of Manet's paintings accepted at the Paris Exposition Universelle of 1867,[92] and Manet's chances might be enhanced by a bold claim that pictures such as *Olympia* were not meant to be provocative.

On one occasion, too, Manet himself tried to use an appeal to 'artistic' values as a means to pre-empt political censorship. When the censors suppressed the publication of his lithograph of *The Execution of the Emperor Maximilian* early in 1869, he issued a statement describing it as 'une oeuvre absolument artistique'. However, his plea went unheeded, and his large painting of the *Execution* was likewise excluded from the Salon of 1869.[93]

As Dianne Pitman has recently stressed, the idea that a certain type of painting should be regarded as being only interesting *as* painting belongs to a critical viewpoint that was firmly established by the 1860s; but at the same time this cannot be seen as a presage of modernist notions of subject-less painting. The nineteenth-century view did not exclude the possibility that the subject treated might be significant; rather, it focused on the means by which the subject was conveyed, insisting that the painting should achieve its effects by its formal language alone, without invoking extraneous literary references or making sentimental appeals to the viewer's emotions.[94]

The attempts of Mantz and Castagnary to aestheticise Manet were both accompanied by anxieties about the ways that he treated his subjects. As we have seen, Castagnary was concerned in *The Balcony* and *Luncheon* by the apparently inappropriate behaviour of the figures – the women looking out into the street and the boy with his back to the table. Mantz, too, argued in 1868 that Manet's treatment of his subjects reflected a problematic world view:

> . . . he is little interested in nature, and life's spectacles do not move him. This indifference will be his undoing. M. Manet seems to us to have less enthusiasm than dilettantism. If he had even a little passion, he would impassion someone, for there are still twenty or so people in France who have a taste for innovations and boldness.[95]

Mantz's comment about indifference can be related to Thoré's discussion of Manet's 'pantheism' in his review of the same Salon.[96] The implications of these two terms, pantheism and indifference, will lead us to broader conclusions about the nature of Manet's acts of opposition and the ways in which they were understood.

The closest analogy for his stance is the idea of the *flâneur*, the observer of the byplay of Parisian life, as enshrined in Baudelaire's essay 'Le Peintre de la vie moderne', published in 1863 and based on the work of the graphic artist Constantin Guys. A key notion in Baudelaire's text is fundamental to Manet's art: *curiosité*. The genius of Baudelaire's artist derived from 'childhood recovered at will' – the pursuit of the 'innocent eye'. It is *curiosité* that drives this born-again child to focus on all the sense-data around him with the 'fixed and animally ecstatic gaze of children face to face with the *new*, whatever it is' (I say 'him' because in these texts the *flâneur* unequivocally represents a male viewpoint).[97]

Yet there were two very different ways of characterising the relationship of the *flâneur* to his surroundings. In one, propounded by Victor Fournel in 1858 in *Ce que l'on voit dans les rues de Paris*, the *flâneur* is analogous to the detective, able to classify and read everything that he sees through decoding the visual clues offered him.[98] Baudelaire seems to share this view in 'Le Peintre de la vie moderne'; for him, in Guys's work 'differences of class and breed are made immediately obvious to the spectator's eye, in whatever luxurious trappings the subjects may be decked'.[99] The same can be argued for Manet's work up to 1865, including *Olympia*. Whatever Zola might say, critics of *Olympia* had no difficulty in determining what type of woman was depicted here.[100] This represented a type of *curiosité* that was fascinated by subjects that were considered inappropriate for such scrutiny, but never lost view of what they were and what they stood for.

More subversive was the type of *curiosité* that seemingly scrutinised everything indiscriminately, refusing to register questions of value, and recognising that ultimately the signs might not add up, and that the modern might be fundamentally unknowable. Here, the most significant text is one cited by Baudelaire, but not followed by him in all its implications: Edgar Allen Poe's 'The Man of the Crowd', in which the *flâneur*/viewer pursues a figure whom he finds fascinating, without ever managing to establish his identity.[101]

This type of *curiosité* is closer to the position adopted by Manet from the mid-1860s, as he moved away from his identifiable 'types' of the early 1860s to figures like *A Young Lady in 1866* (*Woman with a Parrot*), and came to weave into the fabric of his most ambitious subject pictures the deep-seated uncertainties about social identity that we have examined in *A Young Lady in 1866* and *The Balcony*. This approach was at the core of the 'pantheism' for which Thoré criticised Manet; his refusal to attribute relative values to what is seen was profoundly subversive of society and its ordering structures.

These two different forms of *curiosité* correspond to two distinct notions of modernity, both of which were current in these years. Recent historical accounts have emphasised illegibility and uncertainty – the elision of clear markers of identity within the modern city – as the keynote of a distinctively modern way of viewing the world.[102] However, Michael Fried has reminded us that the alternative view was also strongly expressed, the view that saw the modern in terms of types – in terms of the viewer's ability to identify and classify the multifarious elements that characterised the modern metropolis.[103] Here, Fournel's detective is the model viewer. Of these two views, one demonstrated its mastery over the city; it is no coincidence that Napoleon III's government, very concerned about the potential threats posed by the modern city, sponsored ambitious social surveys designed to set up criteria for the classification (and hence control) of the working population[104] – to say nothing of the opening out of the city itself through Baron Haussmann's network of new boulevards. From the other point of view, by contrast, the essence of urban experience lay (tantalisingly, but thrillingly) beyond such decoding and control.

But in what wider context can we locate Manet's rejection of social and moral legibility? We cannot answer this simply by looking at the personal politics of the artist and his friends.[105] His devices, by their very illegibility, resist appropriation by any clear-cut social or political ideology, such as the moralistic republican opposition to the excesses of the last years of the Second Empire. Indeed, it was their lack of any clear-cut standpoint that made them so disconcerting; this links them to a central area of concern about the state of contemporary society in the 1860s – the increasing difficulty that was perceived in classifying the men and women seen in the street. The scenario of Poe's 'The Man of the Crowd' was a lived, daily experience for many Parisians.

In part the reasons for this difficulty were material, with the new availability of inexpensive machine-made imitations of high fashion, which were betrayed only by small details of finish.[106] But the uncertainties were also symptoms of moral fear – that society was becoming infected by a tide of economic and sexual corruption. The licence of the imperial court and the social triumph of the *lorette* were often blamed, but the most disconcerting symptom was the widely perceived impossibility of distinguishing confidently and unequivocally, on the basis of dress, appearance and manner, between *vrai monde* and *demi monde*.[107]

Conventional modern life genre painting might treat risqué subjects, like the hints of sexual intrigue in fashionable circles depicted by painters such as Charles-Edouard Boutibonne, Baugniet and Toulmouche (e.g. pl. 24). But the uncertainties they presented were playful ambiguities within the reassuring certainties of an unequivocally delineated milieu and set of stock social roles, paraded in clearly legible form for the viewer. By contrast, uncertainty runs right through pictures such as *The Balcony*. Manet's blatant challenges to classification were also a challenge to the authorities who sanctioned these

24 Charles Baugniet, *First Trouble of the Heart* (*Premier trouble du Coeur*), c.1865, size and present whereabouts unknown (reproduced from photograph published by Goupil and Co.; Witt Library, Courtauld Institute of Art, London)

classifications; his paintings insisted that the tidy compartmentalisation of conventional representations – ranging from those of social theorists to those of genre painters – were a myth in the face of an unprecedentedly mobile and complex society.

Manet's *The Execution of the Emperor Maximilian* (final version Städtische Kunsthalle, Mannheim), his one major painting with an overtly political subject, dates from these years. It was conceived soon after news of the emperor's execution reached Paris in June 1867, but he did not complete the picture in time for the Salon of 1868. As we have seen, early in 1869 his 'purely artistic' lithograph of the subject was banned, and he was told that the painting would be rejected at the Salon; in the event he did not submit it. Although its subject is so different from the works that we have been examining, it acquires its charge in a similar way. It is not a dramatised indictment of human folly or bad faith, but a disconcertingly deadpan and inexpressive presentation of a loaded subject, which in a sense leaves its viewers to draw their own conclusions. But in the political context of 1867–9, Napoleon's abandonment of Maximilian, whom he had imposed as emperor on an unwilling Mexico, was a subject that would have left few viewers neutral, and Manet's cool anti-heroic image of Maximilian's fate shows him as victim of events way beyond his control – and events for which responsibility lay firmly at home, in Paris.[108]

In his other paintings, like *The Balcony* and *Luncheon*, Manet's challenge cannot be tied to any precise political position or programme, but this vision belonged to a particular sector of Parisian artistic culture, which cultivated a distance and detachment from dominant social and political values, and yet set itself up as anatomist of contemporary society. Opponents such as Mantz characterised this as 'indifference'. In part this stance developed from a rejection of the stereotypes and hierarchies that underpinned current social norms, but it was also crucially bound up with the question of censorship: an assumed and ironic distance was a cogent mode of opposition, even if this repudiation of bourgeois moral and social values was less tangible than overt confrontation.[109]

As we have seen, both supporters and opponents of Manet's art could argue that its merits – and demerits – were primarily 'artistic'; and many reviewers noted that a taste for his art and that of his friends was the province of 'the artistic' – of an elite of taste.[110] In 1870 Burty argued that this elite taste was alone able to appreciate 'the abstractions of form and colour', while popular taste was preoccupied by subject matter.[111] But, as we have seen, this appeal to the 'artistic' was also a strategic position that attempted to divert the all-pervasive attentions of the censor – as in Zola's essay on Manet of 1867, so insistent on his lack of concern for his subject matter, and Manet's own insistence on the 'purely artistic' qualities of his Maximilian lithograph.

Monet can less readily be analysed in these terms. The forms and format of *Women in the Garden* and his *Luncheon* were evidently experimental and unconventional, but, as we have seen, their themes, unlike Manet's, do not raise significant social and moral issues or engage with questions about the nature and structure of society. Yet it was they, not the Manets, that were rejected by the Salon jury. In part this may have been because Monet was younger and less well known, and in part because, in *Women in the Garden* at least, the attack on conventions of composition and technique was so blatant.

But a further factor may have contributed to Monet's reputation before 1870: his cultivation of a vividly bohemian life style. His activities in the 1860s – his sex life, his debts, his battles with his parents and so on – were, almost point for point, a re-living of the descriptions of bohemian life, or rather prescriptions for it, in a manual such as *Paris-Bohème* of 1854.[112] Monet's private life does not help us to explain his paintings, but his paraded lifestyle clearly contributed to his public image and very possibly also to the jury's response to him.

Strictly speaking, bohemianism cannot be directly compared to avant-gardism, since the term refers to lifestyles, while 'avant-garde' relates to practices. Moreover, taken at face value, the image of the bohemian – by analogy with the term's origin, the gypsy – is of someone who lives outside society, whether by force of circumstances or voluntarily. However, just as the notion of cultivating the 'innocent eye' necessarily involved a repudiation of norms of educated vision, so the deliberate adoption of a bohemian lifestyle can be understood only in terms of its 'Other', bourgeois life. In its various forms, bohemian life must be viewed as a repudiation of, or an exclusion from, bourgeois social and cultural norms.[113]

In 1854 *Paris-Bohème* emphasised that the bohemian lifestyle of the Second Empire had no specific political commitment, seemingly picking up on the tone and tenor of Henri Mürger's celebrated *Scènes de la vie de bohème* and transferring them from the realm of semi-autobiographical fiction into the ostensibly neutral medium of the *Physiologie*, the anatomy of a particular social type and lifestyle.[114] However, the disavowal in *Paris-Bohème* of any political dimension to bohemianism needs to be seen in the context of the rigorous censorship of the period, which sought to control and suppress the possible forums for subversive political debate and activity.[115] Issues of class played a crucial role in the thinking behind the censorship regulations; these were directed primarily against the lower classes, since it was felt that they posed the main threat to social and political order. In this context, the notion of groups who had voluntarily rejected bourgeois values, or who felt themselves systematically excluded from them, would have aroused special anxieties.

In these years, Courbet represented an alternative, politicised form of bohemianism, both in his art and in the image that he propagated of his lifestyle. In 1850 he wrote to Francis Wey (a writer and journalist who would, we can be sure, have disseminated his words): 'In your so-civilised society, it is necessary for me to lead the life of a savage. I must even emancipate myself from governments. The people enjoy my sympathies. I must address myself to them directly and draw my knowledge and my livelihood from them. For this reason, I have just embarked on the great vagabond and independent life of the *bohémien*.'[116] The visual manifesto of this politicised bohemianism appeared at the Salon of 1850–51 in the form of Courbet's portrait of the Fourierist philosopher Jean Journet, depicted in the guise of the Wandering Jew, and submitted to the Salon with the provocative title *The Apostle Jean Journet*, accompanied by a quotation from Journet: 'Departing for the Conquest of Universal Harmony'; Courbet anticipated that the picture would need a gendarme placed alongside it at the Salon.[117] However, after censorship, the title appeared in the Salon catalogue as *Portrait of M. Jean Journet*, and there is no record of the painting causing a disturbance.[118]

Another associate of the *école des Batignolles*, Paul Cézanne,[119] combined a blatant bohemianism with flagrant artistic iconoclasm, seeking, it seems, to outdo both Courbet and Manet in terms of controversy and provocation. Like Manet before 1865, Cézanne in the mid- to late 1860s set out to rework all the major genres of painting and at the same time to explore the implications of many aspects of the art of the past. The compositions of the resulting paintings and the gestures of the figures in them are dramatic and exaggerated, the handling of paint crude and extravagant.[120] By submitting them to the Salon – confident, we must assume, that they would be rejected – and by parading his unorthodox behaviour, Cézanne presented himself as the ultimate outsider artist of the late 1860s. His notoriety was assured at the time of the Salon of 1870, when the *Album Stock* published a caricature of the artist holding the two paintings that the jury had rejected, accompanied by a short 'interview' in which Cézanne insisted that he alone had the courage of his convictions: 'Yes, my dear M. Stock, I paint as I see, as I feel – and I have very strong sensations. They too, they feel and see like me, but they don't dare . . . they make Salon pictures . . . But me, I dare, M. Stock, I dare . . . I have the courage of my opinions . . . and he laughs best who laughs last.'[121] The accompanying text made it clear that it was artists such as Courbet, Manet and Monet whom he was accusing of compromising their vision and producing 'Salon pictures'.

In this context, bohemian lifestyles and bohemian subject matter could prove a cogent weapon in the emergence of artistic groupings and practices that challenged dominant cultural values, and could assume a distinctively political guise. However, we cannot make any easy equation between bohemianism and political radicalism or republicanism. Although some of the Batignolles circle in the 1860s were committed republicans, the bohemianism of Monet's and Cézanne's lifestyles and the anti-authoritarianism of their art had no overtly political dimension, whereas Manet, the most committed republican of the group, presented himself externally as an impeccable bourgeois man

25 Henri Fantin-Latour,
Portrait of M. M. [Edouard
Manet] (*Portrait de M. M.*),
1867, 117.5 × 90, The Art
Institute of Chicago,
The Stickney Fund, 1905.207

about town, to the surprise of many hostile commentators.[122] This image was strongly
endorsed by Fantin-Latour's portrait of him, in the immaculate guise of the fashionable
boulevardier, shown at the Salon of 1867 (pl. 25).

*   *   *

No single, definitive reading can be given of either Manet's or Monet's pictures. We have
explored the spaces in which artistic radicalism operated in the late 1860s: these were
artistic spaces, but also social and ideological spaces. Within the quite close-knit context
of the *école des Batignolles*, we can draw clear distinctions about the form that the
painters' acts of opposition took and the spaces with which they engaged. In these contexts, Monet appears as an *enfant terrible* who made no clearly articulated link between
artistic defiance and social critique; and Manet, perhaps, as a child too, but the infi-
nitely reflective, wise born-again child of Baudelaire's essay, whose studied disengage-
ment from society's hierarchies could be seen to question the bases upon which those
hierarchies were constructed.

It is difficult to pin down the position that Manet took as explicitly avant-garde. His
publicly declared aesthetic of 'sincerity', and the *curiosité* with which he viewed the
world, do not carry with them any implications of a defined goal in view towards which
his art was leading. Like Zola and Baudelaire, he was seeking the fullest immersion in
'modernity' and the fullest expression of the ways in which he experienced it. The notion

of progress does not seem to be implied either by his aesthetic position or by his paintings. Indeed, Manet himself talked about his art in ways that seemingly preclude the possibility of reading the sequence of his own paintings in linear terms:

> Each time he begins a picture, says he, he plunges headlong into it, and feels like a man who knows that his surest plan to learn to swim safely, is, dangerous as it may seem, to throw himself into the water . . . Each work should be a new creation of the mind . . . The eye should forget all else it has seen, and learn anew from the lesson before it. It should abstract itself from memory, seeing only that which it looks upon, and that as for the first time . . .[123]

Yet in many ways the stance assumed by the *école des Batignolles* does qualify as an avant-garde position. Fantin-Latour's painting (pl. 1) stands as a visual declaration

26 Bertall, *'Jesus among his Disciples'* or *'The Divine School of Manet'*, *Religious Picture by Fantin-Latour* (*Jésus peignant au milieu de ses disciples, ou La divine école de Manet, tableau religieux par Fantin-Latour*), published in *Le Journal amusant*, 21 May 1870

of independence – even as a form of manifesto. The younger painters and the critics who acted as the group's mouthpiece stand around the master painter – the leader. The picture's title, too, *A Studio in the Batignolles*, hinted at the group's distinctive public image, and the responses to the picture in caricatures in the press endorse this: Bertall transformed Manet into Christ, and titled his sketch *'Jesus among his Disciples'*; or, *'The Divine School of Manet'*, *Religious Picture by Fantin-Latour* (pl. 26).[124] The persona created for Manet by critics in the late 1860s is of central importance here. Despite Zola's disavowals of being a prophet of 'the painting of the future', the group's activities were clearly viewed as an oppositional practice, seeking to redirect the mainstream of current French painting.

But we must not view the position of the *école des Batignolles* as homogeneous. The contrast between Fantin's picture and Bazille's *Studio* of 1870 (pl. 2) is significant. The public rhetoric that surrounded them might be of an 'avant-garde', but their private world could be presented in a very different way. Bazille's painting presents an archetypal image of the easy private camaraderie of artists, both in the relaxed sociability it portrays and in its scattered, informal composition. Yet Bazille's picture was not intended for exhibition, although he, too, did exhibit at the Salon of 1870. At that Salon, it was Fantin's canvas, with its measured technique and centred composition and its overt reminiscences of Dutch seventeenth-century group portraits, that staked out the group's vanguard position and public image: a marginal group given the pictorial status of worthy burghers.

2   Sketch and Finished Painting

THE CENTRAL FOUR CHAPTERS OF THE BOOK will explore the Impressionists' art of the 1870s from different perspectives: first, by examining the implications of the distinctions that they drew between sketches and finished paintings; then, by exploring in turn the imagery of their landscapes of the environs of Paris and their treatment of the figure within the urban environment; and finally by analysing the Impressionist 'mark' – the visible brushstroke that was the physical bearer of the meanings of their paintings.

* * *

In his review of the Salon exhibition of 1880, Emile Zola wrote:

> ...M. Monet has given in too much to his facility of production. Many *ébauches* [beginnings of paintings] have emerged from his studio in difficult times, and this is worth nothing; it pushes a painter down the slippery slope. When one is too easily satisfied, when one delivers an *esquisse* [sketch] that is scarcely dry, one loses the taste for paintings studied at length; it is sustained effort which produces solid works, M. Monet is today suffering for his haste, for his need to sell... He must resolutely devote himself to important canvases, worked at over a period of time.[1]

The general message of these comments has usually been associated with the type of criticism that the Impressionists had been receiving, even from their supporters, since they first appeared before the public as a group, in the first 'Impressionist' exhibition of 1874, for instance in Castagnary's generally very supportive and understanding review:

> The stronger of these artists, those with real class, will come to recognise that, while there are some subjects which are well suited to being treated by *impressions* or by summary *ébauches*, there are others, and very many more, that demand a crisp expression and a precise execution; that the superiority of a painter consists precisely in treating each subject in the manner that best suits it... Those artists who make progress and perfect their drawing will leave Impressionism behind, which will become for them far too superficial a form of art.[2]

Comments such as these can in turn be directly related back to criticisms of the technique of the previous generation of landscapists, and notably of Charles-François Daubigny. In 1861 Théophile Gautier wrote:

> It is a great pity that [Daubigny], who has such a faithful and truthful feeling for nature, should content himself with an *impression* and neglect to such a degree the

details. His canvases are only *ébauches*, and *ébauches* that are not far advanced. It is not that he has been short of time, for he has exhibited no fewer than five quite significant pictures. One must attribute this loose manner to a system . . . It would have taken only a few days to make excellent paintings out of these insufficient preparations.[3]

Criticisms of this sort were certainly typical of early responses to Impressionism. But Zola's critique in 1880 was not just an elaboration of the same general pattern of argument. Some of his comments are far more precise and specific in their reference to Monet's habits: 'Many *ébauches* have emerged from his studio in difficult times . . . [W]hen one delivers an *esquisse* that is scarcely dry . . . M. Monet is today suffering for his haste . . .'.

The proof that Zola was speaking from detailed knowledge of Monet's personal habits emerges from the notebooks that Monet kept from 1872 onwards, in which he listed all his sales.[4] We have long had a picture of Monet between 1876 and 1879, chronically short of money, hawking his latest work around to every possible buyer and often selling pictures extremely cheaply. The notebooks add an essential detail to this: during these years, many of the pictures he sold most cheaply are characterised in his lists as sketches (*esquisses* or *pochades*), and he used these terms in such a way that a clear distinction is made between these and his finished paintings.

So it is not enough simply to say that the typical Impressionist painting seemed sketch-like to outsiders; Monet himself drew the distinction between sketch and finished painting within his own *oeuvre*. One example will show what this meant in visual and financial terms: in March 1878 he sold to Gustave Caillebotte three of his paintings of the Gare Saint-Lazare, one, listed as *Gare Saint-Lazare*, for 685 francs (pl. 27), and two, listed as 2 *esquisses* (*chemin de fer*), for 300 francs the pair; by comparison these are both rapidly and loosely executed – especially the remarkable *The Signal* (pl. 28).[5]

This distinction forces us to rethink our understanding of the Impressionists' paintings of the 1870s – not only of Monet's work, but also that of his colleagues. It helps to explain the extreme diversity of the paintings they produced, and raises broader questions about the markets and audiences that they were seeking for their art and the notions of artistic creativity and genius that this art enshrined.

In order to make sense of these distinctions, we need a brief outline of the vocabulary used by artists and critics to describe these paintings and the ways in which they used it.[6] All the paintings in question are painted in oil on canvas. The term *tableau* was always used to describe fully finished canvases. *Ebauche* was used, by artists, to characterise the lay-in, the first stages of work on a particular canvas; critics also used *ébauche* to describe exhibited pictures that to them looked unfinished, like mere lay-ins (as Gautier did in writing about Daubigny in 1861, and Zola about Monet in 1880), but the artists never described as *ébauches* paintings that they themselves considered to be in any sense complete.[7]

As we have seen, Monet used the terms *esquisse* and *pochade* to describe quickly worked canvases that he considered to be complete in their own terms, but not brought to a degree of finish that would qualify them as *tableaux*. They are the happy sketches that would be spoiled by reworking. A quick notation of an atmospheric effect was already widely described as an *impression*.[8] The most complex term was *étude*. Monet generally used it to characterise paintings that he did not consider complete, but very occasionally he did exhibit a work that he called an *étude*.[9] However, as we shall see,

27   Claude Monet, *The Gare Saint-Lazare (La Gare Saint-Lazare)*, 1877, 75.5 × 104, Musée d'Orsay, Paris

28   Claude Monet, *The Gare Saint-Lazare: The Signal (La Gare Saint-Lazare: Le Signal)*, 1877, 65.5 × 81.5, Niedersächsisches Landesmuseum, Hanover

both Renoir and Cézanne more often exhibited paintings as *études*, and Renoir, in particular, seems to have used the term to mean what Monet meant by *esquisse* – a resolved, successful sketch.

The history of these terms is a long one. Originally, *esquisse* and *étude* referred to two different types of preparatory studies for larger finished paintings: the *esquisse* was a rapid notation of the whole composition, the *étude* a closer study of a part of it. However, well before the Impressionists began to use them, they had both come, on occasion, to designate independent sketches, complete in their own terms and not preparatory for something else.

Titles labelling pictures as *études* were unusual at the Salon, but a number of examples from the 1850s and 1860s enable us to see in what ways they differed from pictures with no such subtitles. On occasion, Corot exhibited smaller, informal landscapes with *étude* as subtitle, to differentiate them from the more elaborated studio works that he included in the same show; but academic artists might show as an *étude* a canvas that was just as highly finished as a *tableau*, but differentiated by the status of its subject – lacking any literary or historical content or clear narrative, but focused rather on a single figure, without significant setting or context.[10]

The Impressionists-to-be began to use this vocabulary early in their careers. The complexities of *étude* emerge in two letters from Monet in 1864: he had painted some outdoor *études* of seascapes at Sainte-Adresse, designed as raw material for *tableaux* that he planned to execute in the studio, but he then decided that he preferred these *études* and sought to sell them as works in their own right.[11] In 1866 Renoir submitted two pictures to the Salon, one of which he characterised as a *pochade*, apparently executed in a fortnight. His other submission, a landscape with two figures, was rejected by the jury, and in the end he exhibited nothing in the Salon of that year; we can only assume that he withdrew the *pochade*, thinking that it could not stand on its own – unfortunately it cannot be identified.[12]

Renoir's Salon exhibit in 1869 was titled in the catalogue *En été; étude* (*In Summer; Study*) (pl. 29). The significance of this title emerges from comparison with his exhibit at the previous Salon, entitled *Lise* (pl. 21). In contrast to this near-life-size figure, with elaborate costume and quite fully defined woodland setting, *En été; étude* is smaller and more informal. Although the figure is quite highly finished, the background is particularly broadly handled, in bold coloured slashes that suggest sunlit trees or bushes.

In the late summer of 1869 Monet and Renoir were painting together at La Grenouillère, on the Seine to the west of Paris. Monet reported on their plans in a letter to Bazille: 'I have a dream, a *tableau*, the bathing place of La Grenouillère, for which I've done several bad *pochades*, but it's only a dream. Renoir . . . also wants to paint the same subject.'[13] The only paintings that can be identified as these 'bad *pochades*' are Monet's now-celebrated canvases of La Grenouillère (pls 32, 54), both quite substantial in scale, and one smaller painting of boats. To early twenty-first-century eyes, habituated to such sketches, the two larger canvases seem dazzlingly achieved, but in 1869 Monet seemingly could not consider them in a fit state to be presented as completed works.[14]

We cannot, though, be sure what sort of picture of La Grenouillère Monet would in 1869 have regarded as fully complete. He did paint another substantial picture of the subject, showing a more panoramic view of the site in a longer, narrower format, but scarcely larger that the surviving pictures; photographs of this now-lost canvas suggest

29 Pierre-Auguste Renoir, *In Summer; Study* (*En été; étude*) [now known as *Lise* or *The Gypsy Girl*], 1868, 85 × 59, Staatliche Museen zu Berlin– Preußischer Kulturbesitz, Nationalgalerie

that it was rather more highly worked than the other versions, but in it, too, the reflections in the foreground are treated in bold dashes of paint.[15] It has been suggested that this was the landscape by Monet that the Salon jury rejected in 1870 together with *Luncheon* (pl. 6), but this seems unlikely, since Astruc described the rejected canvas as a *marine*.[16] The lost painting may, though, have been the La Grenouillère canvas for which the dealer Durand-Ruel paid Monet the surprisingly large sum of 2,000 francs in February 1873;[17] but this identification cannot be securely made.

31   Pierre-Auguste Renoir, *La Grenouillère*, 1869, 66.5 × 81, Nationalmuseum, Stockholm

30 (*left*)   Pierre-Auguste Renoir, *Bathing Woman* (*Baigneuse*) [now known as *Bather with a Griffon*], 1870, 184 × 115, Museu de Arte de São Paulo, Assis Chateaubriand

Like Monet, Renoir did *pochade*-type paintings of La Grenouillère in 1869 (e.g. pl. 31), but he finally executed for the Salon of 1870 not a larger picture of the bathing place, but a riverside subject of a quite different order, *Bather with a Griffon* (pl. 30), a near-life-size canvas like his *Lise* of 1868, presenting a modern-life nude in the mould of Courbet and Manet. The pose of the figure invokes the classical image of Venus Pudica, but the Seine riverbank setting, the discarded fashionable clothes and the inclusion of the clothed female companion and the little dog clearly associate it with the imagery of contemporary prostitution.[18]

However, the contrast between ambitious paintings for the Salon and *esquisse*-type pictures was not the whole story. In the later 1860s the Impressionists-to-be were increasingly focusing their attention on a third sort of canvas: comparatively highly finished medium-sized or small paintings intended for sale through art dealers. Since the 1840s such paintings had become an increasingly significant element in the French art market, as dealers came to play the part of intermediary between painters and collectors, catering in particular for potential buyers who had no personal entrée into the art world, and were seeking pictures for the modest-scaled walls of urban apartments.[19] Paintings such as these were too small to attract attention on the huge and crowded walls of the Salon, as the painter François Bonvin indicated in 1861, writing to Louis Martinet, director of an alternative exhibition space in Paris: 'Yet another good mark for your idea of holding a permanent exhibition! The picture that I brought you a week ago has just brought me to the attention of the Ministry. Placed in the big exhibition,

32   Claude Monet, *The Bathing-Place at La Grenouillère (Les Bains de la Grenouillère)*, 1869, 73 × 92, National Gallery, London

this canvas would not, perhaps, have been noticed. Intimate painting, large or small, needs a setting like yours: larger is too large.'[20] Dealers at the time did not generally have substantial exhibition spaces, but rather operated from quite small shops, displaying their latest merchandise in their windows, to attract the attention of passers-by.[21]

The distinction between Salon paintings and dealer pictures is clear even in the work of painters such as Jean-François Millet, whose Salon exhibits, such as *Gleaners* (Musée d'Orsay, Paris), exhibited in 1857, were by contemporary standards not large. The canvases designed for dealers were smaller again, less heavily modelled and less densely painted; the *Angelus* of 1857–9 (Musée d'Orsay, Paris), later to become a famous icon of the French peasantry, was one of these.[22] Likewise the paintings that Manet sold to dealers and exhibited in venues other than the Salon were generally more informal and less insistently frontal in composition than his Salon pictures.[23] Yet for the Impressionists-to-be, the prime examples of painters who were seeking to make their reputa-

33 (*above left*) Johan Barthold Jongkind, *The Faubourg Saint-Jacques (Le Faubourg Saint-Jacques)*, 1867, 32 × 42, present whereabouts unknown (sold Menasce Sale, Petit, Paris, 7 May 1894)

34 (*above right*) Camille Pissarro, *The Versailles Road at Louveciennes [Snow] (La Route de Versailles à Louveciennes [neige])*, 1869, 38.4 × 46.3, Baltimore Museum of Art

35 (*right*) Claude Monet, *Lilacs, Sunlight (Lilas, soleil)*, 1873, 50 × 73, Pushkin Museum, Moscow

tions with such smaller paintings were Johan Barthold Jongkind and Boudin, both of whom sold extensively through dealers during the 1860s.[24] Jongkind's dealer pictures, in particular, with their brushwork, fluent, varied and subtle nuances of colour (e.g. pl. 33), were an important example for the Impressionists-to-be as they embarked on this type of painting. Indeed, the two small paintings of the Canal Saint-Martin in Paris that Sisley exhibited at the Salon of 1870 are particularly close to Jongkind in their handling.[25]

A few fragments of evidence survive that reveal their attempts to find a market through dealers during the 1860s. In 1867 Monet sold two pictures to dealers – a small *marine* to Cadart and one of his Paris views of that spring (probably pl. 90) to Louis Latouche;[26] in 1869 Renoir was trying to sell paintings through Carpentier;[27] and in winter 1869–70 Camille Pissarro sold a snow-scene to the backstreet dealer *père* Martin, who in turn sold it to the American art agent George A. Lucas. This small and simple yet crisply defined painting, *The Versailles Road at Louveciennes (Snow)* (pl. 34), is

36   Claude Monet, *The Seine at Bougival* (*La Seine à Bougival*), 1869, 63.5 × 91.4, Currier Museum of Art, Manchester, N.H., Museum Purchase: Mabel Putney Folsom Fund, 1949.1

quite unlike Pissarro's ambitious Salon landscapes of the previous few years.[28] The distinction between sketch and dealer picture in Monet's work emerges particularly vividly from comparison between his La Grenouillère *pochades* and *The Seine at Bougival* (pl. 36), which was bought from him by Martin – apparently for 50 francs plus a small painting by Cézanne.[29] *The Seine at Bougival* is exactly the same size as *The Bathing-Place at La Grenouillère* (pl. 32), but more delicate in handling and precise in finish, and more conventional in composition and coloration.

In 1872 and 1873 Monet, Pissarro and Sisley found a regular market for such small-scale paintings with the dealer Paul Durand-Ruel, whom Monet and Pissarro had met while they and the dealer were taking refuge in London during the Franco-Prussian War. The titles of Durand-Ruel's purchases are recorded in the firm's stock books, although not all the paintings can be identified. Most of these purchases were from among their more highly finished paintings; in addition, he bought the few still lifes that they painted at the time – still life seems to have been more readily marketable than landscape. Monet did, though, sell him two pictures that he himself entitled *pochades*;[30] and the other purchases that can be identified include a few more boldly executed canvases, such as the remarkable *Lilacs, Grey Weather* (Musée d'Orsay, Paris) and *Lilacs, Sunlight* (pl. 35), where the trees and figures are translated into a virtual mosaic of coloured dabs that absorb the figures into their surroundings.

However, during the same years Monet executed a number of even more informal, rapidly painted canvases which he did not sell to the dealer. One of these, *Regatta at*

37 Claude Monet, *Impression, Sunrise (Impression, soleil levant)*, 1872, 48 × 63, Musée Marmottan–Claude Monet, Paris

Argenteuil (pl. 40), executed in broad slabs of bright colour, he sold to the painter Gustave Caillebotte in April 1876 as *Pochade, Argenteuil*. Another, a particularly summary, thinly brushed port scene, was exhibited in the first group exhibition in spring 1874 with the title *Impression, Sunrise* (pl. 37).

Because its title led to the group being called the 'Impressionists', *Impression, Sunrise* has come to be seen as the archetypal Impressionist painting. In its original context, though, it would have appeared exceptional. Later in his life, Monet explained why he had given it this title: 'I had sent a thing done at Le Havre, from my window, of the sun in the fog, with some ships' masts . . . They asked me for a title for the catalogue; it really couldn't pass for a view of Le Havre, so I replied, "Put *Impression*."'[31] As we have seen, the term *impression* was already in use to refer to such rapid sketches of fleeting atmospheric effects. These reminiscences make more sense because in the same show Monet exhibited another Le Havre port scene, entitled *Le Havre, Fishing Boats Leaving the Port* (pl. 38); presumably this canvas, larger and far more specific in its subject and the details within it, could pass as a view of Le Havre. Indeed, a contemporary photograph of the site (pl. 39) confirms its specificity.

With its exceptional sketchiness and rapidity of execution,[32] *Impression, Sunrise* must be viewed as some sort of travesty of two familiar themes in the landscape painting of the period – the sunrise and the port scene. Standard images of sunrise presented it in elemental terms, as part of a seemingly natural order, while the ports of France (a theme with a long history) were depicted as busy scenes of productive communal activity – very much as 'views'.[33] Moreover, at this date images of the 'natural' and the 'modern' were considered to belong to two very different spheres of significance, as we shall see in Chapter Three; Monet's combination of the two was itself provocative. The immaterial, transitory world of his *Impression* is at the opposite end of the conceptual spectrum from the stock, reassuring images of both themes.[34]

Monet's other exhibits at the first group exhibition were very diverse. They included a view of the Boulevard des Capucines (pl. 89), the more elaborate of his two canvases of the scene, which was characterised by one critic, Ernest Chesneau, but not by Monet himself, as an *ébauche*,[35] and his huge *Luncheon* (pl. 6), rejected at the Salon of 1870. The works shown by many of the other exhibitors were similarly varied; Renoir, for instance, juxtaposed quite highly finished figure pieces such as *The Theatre Box* (pl. 121) and *Parisienne* (National Museums and Galleries of Wales, Cardiff) with a very loosely brushed landscape, *Harvesters* (pl. 71).

38 Claude Monet, *Le Havre, Fishing Boats Leaving the Port (Le Havre: Bateaux de pêche sortant du port)*, 1874, 60 × 101, Los Angeles County Museum of Art, Anonymous

39 *View of the Avant-Port, Le Havre*, carte-de-visite photograph, early 1870s, private collection, London

40   Claude Monet, *Regatta at Argenteuil* (*Régates à Argenteuil*), 1872, 48 × 75, Musée d'Orsay, Paris

Renoir did not distinguish *Harvesters* from his other pictures in the show by giving it the subtitle *esquisse* or *étude*, but Cézanne used the titles of his three exhibits to make complex distinctions between their status: *La Maison du pendu, à Auvers-sur-Oise, Une Moderne Olympia: Esquisse* and *Etude: Paysage à Auvers*. *Une Moderne Olympia* (Musée d'Orsay, Paris) conforms to traditional notions of the *esquisse* by being a rapid notation of an imaginative figure composition, although there is no evidence that he planned to execute a large version of the subject.[36] *The Hanged Man's House* (pl. 41), with its densely worked, granular surface, presumably qualified as a fully finished *tableau*. *Etude: Paysage à Auvers* cannot be securely identified, but it may well have been the painting now known as *The House of Père Lacroix* (pl. 42); unusually for Cézanne at this date, this is signed and dated, but it is conspicuously broader and bolder in technique than *The Hanged Man's House*.[37]

Similar distinctions were occasionally made in the titles of the paintings shown in the later Impressionist group exhibitions. In 1876 Renoir's *Nude in Sunlight* (pl. 43) was shown with the simple title *Etude*; its broad, rapid execution is in marked contrast to the finesse of the painting titled *Woman at the Piano* (pl. 44) in the same show. In 1877 Monet exhibited two views of the same panorama over the Tuileries Gardens, one a rapidly worked sketch, as *Les Tuileries, esquisse* (pl. 92), the other a far more highly finished canvas, as *Le Jardin des Tuileries* (private collection). In his review of the exhibition, Georges Rivière described one as the *esquisse* for the other,[38] but they show quite

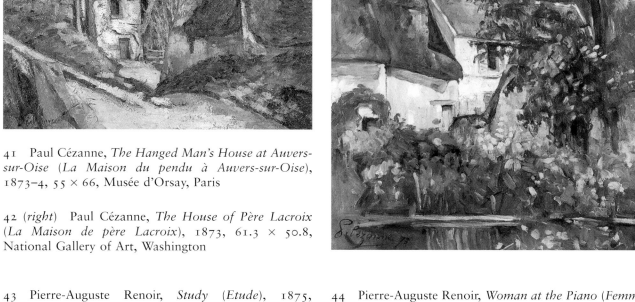

41   Paul Cézanne, *The Hanged Man's House at Auvers-sur-Oise* (*La Maison du pendu à Auvers-sur-Oise*), 1873–4, 55 × 66, Musée d'Orsay, Paris

42 (*right*)   Paul Cézanne, *The House of Père Lacroix* (*La Maison de père Lacroix*), 1873, 61.3 × 50.8, National Gallery of Art, Washington

43   Pierre-Auguste Renoir, *Study* (*Etude*), 1875, 81 × 65, Musée d'Orsay, Paris [also known as *Nude in Sunlight*]

44   Pierre-Auguste Renoir, *Woman at the Piano* (*Femme au piano*), c.1875, 93 × 74, The Art Institute of Chicago, Mr. and Mrs. Martin A. Ryerson Collection

45 Paul Cézanne, *The Sea at L'Estaque (La Mer à l'Estaque)*, 1876, 42 × 59, RAU Collection–Foundation UNICEF, Cologne

different light effects, and the *esquisse* must have been an independent sketch; Monet listed it as *Tuileries esquisse* when he sold it to Caillebotte in May 1877. In the same exhibition he exhibited one of the large decorative canvases that he had painted for Ernest Hoschedé, *The Turkeys* (Musée d'Orsay, Paris), with the subtitle *décoration non terminée*. It has been argued that Monet must have reworked this after exhibiting it,[39] but the brushwork is far looser and less rhythmic in *The Turkeys* than in the other three decorations that he painted for Hoschedé,[40] and the forms less clearly defined. Of the eight paintings of the Gare Saint-Lazare that he showed in 1877, none was subtitled *esquisse* in the catalogue, perhaps because he only decided at the last moment which to include. However, those that were exhibited differed vastly in finish: both *The Gare Saint-Lazare* (pl. 27) and also, it seems, *The Signal* (pl. 28), the more summary of the *esquisses* that Caillebotte purchased with it in 1878, were put on view.[41] Their diversity, in treatment as well as viewpoint, shows how misleading it is to regard the Gare Saint-Lazare paintings as prototypes of Monet's highly integrated later series.[42]

In 1877 it was again Cézanne who made the most complex distinctions in his titles. His four landscapes were all listed as *Paysage; étude d'après nature*, although they included the richly and elaborately worked *The Sea at L'Estaque* (pl. 45).[43] The two flower-pieces he showed were listed as *Etude de fleurs*,[44] but by contrast three fruit still lifes were listed as *Nature morte*,[45] perhaps implying that he saw them as more resolved than the flowers and landscapes. One figure painting was catalogued as *Figure de femme; Etude d'après nature* (unidentified) and another as *Tête d'homme; Etude* (a portrait head of Victor Chocquet[46]), and two watercolours were titled *Aquarelle, Impression d'après nature*.[47] Beyond this, he exhibited a composition of male bathers as *Les Baigneurs; Etude, projet de tableau*. This title has been taken to imply that he exhibited the small, informal version of this composition; but it seems likely that the exhibited picture was in fact the larger, elaborately worked version (pl. 46), perhaps substituted for the smaller one at the last moment.[48]

The other members of the group did on occasion use these terms as subtitles to indicate the status of the work being shown. In 1876 Degas described two of his exhibits as *ébauches* and one as an *esquisse*; in 1879 he called one an *esquisse* and one an *étude*. Pissarro showed an *esquisse* in 1879 and two *études* in 1882, and Morisot an *étude* and two *esquisses* in 1881. In some cases, as with Cézanne's watercolours in 1877, these

46   Paul Cézanne, *Bathers Resting (Baigneurs au repos)*, 1876, 79 × 97, Barnes Foundation, Merion, Pa.

were works in a medium other than oil, and thus perhaps considered lower in status; but all three of these artists also used one or more of these terms to describe oil paintings in the catalogues of the group exhibitions.[49]

*　　*　　*

So far, we have viewed the Impressionists' exhibiting practices in isolation. However, they were far from alone in seeking forums where they could exhibit informal paintings and sketches. In these years, it was a regular practice for artists to organise auction sales of their own works, in which they could display their works in far larger numbers than was possible elsewhere, and could try to sell paintings of types that were unsuitable for the Salon.[50] When in February 1874 Duret sought to discourage Pissarro from joining the planned group exhibition, it was the auctions at the Hôtel Drouot that he saw as the only viable alternative to the Salon, as a means of putting Pissarro's work before 'a mixed and numerous public'.[51] In April 1875 Philippe Burty explained the reasons for organising such sales in the preface to the catalogue of an auction mounted by the genre and still-life painter Amand Gautier:

> Unfortunately, no discreet, convenient location yet exists in Paris where one can, without pretension but also without reticence, display a few hundred studies or drawings – or even paintings – each of which is completed and explained by the others. The Hôtel Drouot alone has the advantage of attracting the mass public every day and thoroughly provoking the critics as a result.[52]

Just a week before the Gautier sale, another sale had taken place at the Hôtel Drouot, with another preface by Burty: the auction of paintings by Monet, Morisot, Renoir and Sisley that has played a prominent part in histories of Impressionism.[53] Far from being an unusual experiment, such sales were much more frequent than independent exhibitions of the type that were organised by the group. Although the artists seem not to have given subtitles indicating their status to any of the works at the sale, it did include some of their more informal canvases, among them Renoir's *High Wind* (pl. 75);[54] in the second auction, organised by Caillebotte, Pissarro, Renoir and Sisley in May 1877, Pissarro subtitled two of his canvases *esquisse* and Renoir one as an *étude*.[55]

A further outlet for artists' more informal paintings in these years were the exhibitions of *cercles*, the French equivalent of gentlemen's clubs, elite, semi-private venues very different from the auction house, and in some ways, as Martha Ward has suggested, more comparable to the Impressionists' group exhibitions, which also attracted primarily an 'insider' audience.[56] For Victor Champier, the exhibitions of the *cercles* offered the ideal alternative to the Salon: 'Amateurs, disheartened by the exhaustion of the Salon … prefer these intimate exhibitions that seem improvised … Artists freely send to them the piece that they have to hand: a successful sketch, a curious *pochade*, an indication of landscape, as well as a painting pushed to perfection.'[57] Others, though, felt that the *cercles* offered only second-choice works by the artists who showed at the Salon: 'At the Salon, they show the paintings that create their reputation, their most resolved and lasting works; at the *cercles*, portraits painted on commission or out of obligation, paintings quickly executed, successful sketches …'.[58]

The patterns of Manet's exhibiting in these years are also revealing. He was convinced that the Salon was the true field of battle, and that the Impressionists' group exhibitions

47 Edouard Manet, *The Swallows* (*Les Hirondelles*), 1873, 65 × 81, Foundation E. G. Bührle Collection, Zürich

were a major tactical error. Indeed, as if to reinforce his opposition to their plans, two of his three submissions to the Salon of 1874 were small, informal canvases, *Masked Ball at the Opera* (National Gallery of Art, Washington) and *The Swallows* (pl. 47) – canvases of just the sort that might have seemed more appropriate for the first group show; both, in the event, were rejected. A further rejection by the Salon jury in 1876 led him to adopt another mode of displaying a range of his work, by opening his studio, where visitors could see not only the rejected canvases but also a selection of previous paintings. Finally, in April 1880, simultaneously with that year's Salon, he mounted a show of smaller, more informal works, ten oils and fifteen pastels, at the offices of Georges Charpentier's fashionable magazine *La Vie moderne*; many of these were evidently sketch-like in treatment, among them *Before the Mirror* (pl. 142), though none of them was exhibited with a subtitle that indicated its status.[59] Renoir, in 1879, and Monet, in June 1880, also held one-artist shows at *La Vie moderne*, at the moment that each of them withdrew from the group exhibitions.

Yet for Manet these alternative outlets were always supplementary to the Salon. Historical hindsight may suggest that his decision not to join the group exhibitions was an opportunity missed. But he remained committed throughout his career, as the central element in his production, to making striking and substantial individual works of art that gained their visibility on the crowded walls of the Salon; the minority audience and more intimate viewing conditions of the group exhibitions were not an appropriate setting for them.[60] Beyond this, Manet clearly felt that it was only in the big forum that his canvases would attract the attention he sought for them, among the half million visitors who visited the Salon. He would have agreed with every word of Duret's arguments against the group exhibitions in his letter to Pissarro of February 1874:

You have one more step to take, that is to be known by the public and to be accepted by all the dealers and collectors. That can only be done through the sales at the Hôtel Drouot and the big exhibition at the Palais de l'Industrie [the Salon]. You now have a group of patrons and collectors who have bought your work and who support you. Your name is known among artists and critics – a special public. But you must take a further step and gain great notoriety. You will never achieve this by exhibitions of private societies. The public does not go to such exhibitions, there is only the same little group of artists and collectors who know you already . . .

At the Salon, you will be seen, among the 40000 [sic] people who, I suppose, visit the exhibition, by fifty dealers, collectors and critics who would never seek you out and find you anywhere else . . . I urge you to exhibit; you must make a noise, brave it, attract criticism, set yourself before the general public. You can only achieve this at the Palais de l'Industrie.[61]

Yet Duret was also clear that Pissarro would need to modify his manner of painting if he returned to the Salon: 'I urge you to choose pictures that have a subject and something resembling a composition, pictures that are not too freshly painted and have aged a little.'[62] Any decision about where to exhibit also necessarily involved decisions about what type of picture and treatment was appropriate for the particular exhibition forum and context.

∗   ∗   ∗

Monet's notebooks show that it was in the years 1876–8 that he most often sold pictures that he listed as *esquisses* or *pochades*. At times his financial problems led him to accept very low prices, most notably on one occasion in December 1877 when he sold five *pochades* to the pastrycook Eugène Murer for 125 francs in all; one of these was probably the very sketchy *The Basin at Argenteuil, Sunset* (pl. 48). His notebooks also show that sometimes his friends responded to his importuning by loaning him as little as five francs, and on one occasion, in September 1877, Astruc lent him one franc, a sum so trivial as to be insulting.

48 Claude Monet, *The Basin at Argenteuil, Sunset* (*Bassin d'Argenteuil, soleil couchant*), *c.*1875, 54 × 73, Sotheby's, 28 June 1978, lot 16

Zola's account of 1880 argued that Monet had destroyed his reputation as a serious artist by selling pictures such as *The Basin at Argenteuil, Sunset*, and doubtless Zola was right to associate the flood of such sketches that left Monet's studio, particularly between 1876 and 1878, with his financial problems. It would, though, be wrong to assume that such paintings only saw the light of day when he could sell nothing else. The fact that he included some in the group exhibitions proves otherwise, though they were always accompanied by far more elaborated canvases that showed his work at its most fully realised. Presumably he felt that the *esquisses* revealed one crucial facet of his art.

However, by the time that Zola issued his broadside in 1880, Monet had already realised that the rapid sale of *esquisses* was getting him nowhere. He had submitted two pictures to the Salon of 1880, of which one was accepted – *Lavacourt* (pl. 168), a measured, quite carefully finished five-foot-wide canvas which Monet described as 'sage' and 'bourgeois'.[63] He had also once again begun to find a market with dealers, which meant an end to his activities as a peddler of his own work, as he explained in January 1880 in a letter to Georges de Bellio, one of his most loyal supporters over the past five years:

> Good news: I've sold to M. Petit [the dealer Georges Petit] for 500 francs the still life you saw, and two snow effects for 300 francs each, with the promise of further sales; this is a good thing, since M. Petit much liked my paintings. I must warn you, though, that he recommended me no longer to sell my work cheap; it's on this condition that he'll do business with me.[64]

Monet's notebooks show that in 1879–80 he found a readier market for still lifes, and at higher prices, than for his landscapes.[65] When Durand-Ruel, after a fresh injection of capital, began again to buy his landscapes early in 1881, Monet soon stopped painting still lifes regularly. At the same time the landscapes that he sold became consistently more richly and elaborately finished (e.g. pls 146, 147; see Chapter Five, pp. 162–4).

The changes in his art were saluted in very much the same terms by two critics who knew much about him. Joris-Karl Huysmans wrote in 1882:

> M. Monet has for a long time been messing around, parting with slight improvisations, half-finishing scraps of landscape . . . It was too obvious that there was a carelessness and a lack of serious study about his work. Despite the talent that some of his *esquisses* demonstrated, I admit that I was becoming less and less interested in this rough and hasty painting . . . M. Monet is certainly the man who has contributed most to persuading the public that the word 'impressionism' meant a type of painting that had remained in a rudimentary and confused state, merely a vague *ébauche*. Happily, there has been a transformation: this artist seems now to have decided not to dabble away haphazardly at a heap of canvases . . . This time he has presented us with very fine and very complete landscapes.[66]

The next year, reviewing Monet's one-artist show at Durand-Ruel's gallery, Philippe Burty commented:

> M. Claude Monet has made incontrovertible progress. He is no longer slave to a hasty production provoked by the necessity of selling day in, day out . . . By selling at higher prices, he can work for longer on a canvas, can realise his intentions more precisely, and can even rest from working on days when reverie and exhaustion take over.[67]

49   Pierre-Auguste Renoir, *Woman Reading (La Liseuse)*, *c.*1875, 46.5 × 38.5, Musée d'Orsay, Paris

50   Pierre-Auguste Renoir, *Portrait of Madame A. D.* [*Alphonse Daudet*] (*Portrait de Madame A. D.*), 1876, 46 × 38, Musée d'Orsay, Paris

These two critics' conversion to Monet's art was not the result of changes in their critical position; rather, they were responding to a crucial shift in his art, away from selling cheap *esquisses* to a new conception of the finished picture as both artefact and commodity. These changes and their implications will be further explored in Chapters Five and Six.

With Renoir, the formless immediacy of *Woman Reading* (pl. 49), purchased by Caillebotte, must be set alongside his virtually contemporary *Portrait of Madame A. D.* (pl. 50), in which the artist felt his way towards a fuller characterisation of the sitter with a delicate, almost fussy touch. This dilemma had two sides for Renoir. In part, it reflected the rival claims of finish and drawing, on one side, and formless colour painting on the other; but it also reflected the pressures of patronage, between the freely sketched image of a 'type' and the demand that a commissioned portrait should be seen to resemble its sitter; as he wryly put it, 'it's necessary for a mother to recognise her daughter'.[68] From these conflicting pressures grew Renoir's so-called crisis of the 1880s when for a time he wholly abandoned the fluency of his sketches, only to rediscover the values of an apparent spontaneity of touch around 1890 when, in a new sense, he had learned to draw in coloured paint.

Until about 1877 Pissarro on occasion signed and dated works that were quite informally and sketchily handled. But thereafter he became more self-conscious, or self-critical, about the values that he was seeking in his finished paintings, and few, if any, of his signed canvases between around 1877 and 1892 were left in a sketch-like state. Only in his last decade did he once again on occasion sign pictures that were less elaborated.

Monet's later work, too, grew out of his rival concerns of the 1870s. On his travels of the 1880s the occasional successful *pochade* could refuel his interest in the far more elaborated canvases that were his normal practice. On the island of Belle-Isle in 1886, he wrote with excitement of his efforts to capture the effects of a violent storm in a group of *pochades*. These were not simply standard pictures that the bad weather did not allow him to finish more fully; rather, during the storms, he began a number of canvases explicitly as *pochades*. He wrote to Alice Hoschedé: 'I am carrying on working, not at the *études* [by this date his standard term for an unfinished *tableau*] that I began some time ago, but at some attempts at *pochades* . . .'.[69]

At the same time as his fully finished paintings were becoming more elaborate and more densely reworked, Monet began to construct a personal myth around one of his most delicate earlier sketches, *Vétheuil in the Fog* of 1879 (pl. 51). Soon after painting it, he offered it to one of his principal patrons, the singer Jean-Baptiste Faure, but Faure rejected it because 'there was not enough paint on it', whereupon Monet, according to

51   Claude Monet, *Vétheuil in the Fog (Vétheuil dans le brouillard)*, 1879, 60 × 71, Musée Marmottan-Claude Monet, Paris

his own many later accounts of the incident, vowed never to sell the picture.[70] He did not, it seems, exhibit it at the time he painted it, but he did several times in the later 1880s; on the first occasion, at Georges Petit's fashionable gallery in 1887, it was shown (alongside the Belle-Isle paintings) with the title *Vétheuil dans le brouillard (impression)*, to indicate that it was a rapid sketch of a transitory effect.[71] When he showed it again two years later, he explained its significance at length to an interviewer. He described how he had lain in wait in his boat on the river for the church to emerge from the morning mist, and said that he was exhibiting the picture, although it was unfinished, to inform people about his methods of work and his 'vision'.[72]

*　　*　　*

The distinction between *esquisse* and *tableau* was not just a matter of working practices and markets. Wider issues are involved, which enable us to place this particular historical moment in a longer history of changing ideas about the nature of the work of art and of creativity.

The positive value that the Impressionists saw in their *esquisses* was spelt out forcefully by Duranty in *La nouvelle peinture* in 1876:

> The public . . . only understands correctness, and demands finish above all. The artist, charmed by the delicacy or boldness of a colour effect, by the character of a gesture or a grouping, of a gesture, of a group, is much less concerned about finish and correctness that are the only qualities appreciated by the inartistic . . . It matters little that the public does not understand. It matters that artists understand, and in front of them one can exhibit *esquisses*, preparations, underpaintings [*dessous*] where the thought, the intention and the draughtsmanship of the artist are often expressed with more rapidity, more concentration.[73]

Esquisses, thus, could best be appreciated by artists, a point that Monet reiterated much later, in 1891, telling Durand-Ruel: 'I sometimes sell *esquisses* a bit more cheaply, but this is only to artists or to my friends.'[74] In 1886 he wrote of a group of not fully finished paintings being 'too incomplete for the private collector'.[75]

The particular suitability of *esquisses* for fellow artists belonged to a long tradition; it was spelt out in 1777 in Paillet's introduction to the sale catalogue of the Varanchan de Saint-Geniès collection, which included some of Fragonard's most ebullient sketches:

> This collection would appear to be that of a rich artist with good taste rather than of a collector . . . Though finished paintings are more generally popular, a certain class of collector rejoices particularly in a simple sketch; he looks for the soul and thoughts of the man of genius whom he can see and recognise.[76]

It is in this context that Caillebotte's collection must be viewed. Although it included a few of the Impressionists' most elaborate and ambitious canvases, notably Renoir's *Ball at the Moulin de la Galette* (pl. 110), it was for the most part very much an artist's collection, including a high proportion of *esquisses*, among them Monet's two Gare Saint-Lazare *pochades*, and Renoir's *Woman Reading* (pl. 49). Caillebotte bequeathed the collection to the French nation, and the government's reluctance to accept it in its entirety after his death in 1894 has been the subject of much debate.[77] The *esquisses* in the collection may well have added to the difficulties; they would have seemed particu-

facing page　Claude Monet, *Regatta at Argenteuil* (*Régates à Argenteuil*) (detail of pl. 40)

larly inappropriate for the national collection of modern art in the 1890s, since these were virtually the first Impressionist canvases to be acquired by the State. The modern art represented in the Musée du Luxembourg, where Caillebotte's pictures were destined to hang, was dominated by the elaborate and ambitious canvases purchased by the State at recent Salon exhibitions.

The Impressionists' paintings of the 1870s cannot be viewed as a single, coherent group: the artists themselves made clear distinctions between different types of painting within their own work, and regarded some as more suitable for some outlets, some for others. To understand these distinctions, we have to view them in relation to the artists' exhibition policy and the various types of market they were seeking – through fellow artists, friends and 'men of taste' on one side, through dealers and *amateurs* on the other. The two distinct types of work demand separate analysis, not only for the outlets and markets they looked to, but also for the artistic conventions they adopted and the past artistic examples they invoked.

The *esquisse* cannot be treated as the archetypal Impressionist painting. As we have seen, Monet's *esquisses* were not simply the result of financial pressures, for he and his colleagues made a point of exhibiting them alongside the other facets of his work. But equally we cannot argue that the 'dealer pictures' were simply a response to market pressures, and that, left to themselves, they would have produced nothing but *esquisses*. Even Cézanne, who never had to earn his living, was endlessly preoccupied by the problems of *réalisation* – of finding a fully realised material form for his paintings; and Monet became increasingly concerned with the problem of how to go beyond the simple sketch, seeing this not as a response to commercial pressures, but as a way of giving his work what in 1892 he called 'more serious qualities'.[78]

It is in the relationship between the sketches and the finished paintings that our understanding of the Impressionists' art must be based. In the mid-1870s they kept these two types of painting in a sort of equilibrium, parading the virtuosity of their *esquisses* alongside their more elaborated canvases. But by the end of the decade all of them in their different ways were, like Monet, seeking to develop and emphasise the more resolved and premeditated facets of their art. The material changes in their technique will be further discussed in Chapter Five.

The Impressionists were cultivating their individual, personal *sensations* of nature. But, as Richard Shiff has shown, there was a central dichotomy in this ambition – between notions of truth to nature, or 'realism', on one side, and an insistence on the essential subjectivity of the painter's vision on the other.[79] The *tableau* privileged the former, the sketch the latter. It was thus that Paillet could write, in 1777, that in a sketch the viewer 'looks for the soul and thoughts of the man of genius whom he can see and recognise'. In literal terms, of course, this is a nonsense: it is a drastic metaphorical leap to see crisp strokes of oil colour on canvas as revealing the human soul. But it becomes a potent metaphor for a particular mode of viewing and a particular notion of artistic creativity: the picture as an artefact is effaced and becomes an open window between viewer and artist, inviting the elite viewer's empathetic engagement with the artist's personal, private experience.

For those who accepted this notion, the rapid, informal notations of the sketch came to signify the artist's originality and the uniqueness of his personal vision; Monet seems to have cultivated this quite deliberately, particularly in exhibiting *Vétheuil in the Fog* as a talisman in the later 1880s. For those who rejected the idea, though, the sketch remained an incoherent and meaningless set of dabs or slabs of colour. Alongside it, the *tableau*, the resolved 'dealer picture', remained primarily concerned with its physical subject, and the 'effect' that it recorded was primarily viewed in terms of the external world. Hence the juxtaposition of *Impression, Sunrise* with *Le Havre, Fishing Boats Leaving the Port* at the first group exhibition in 1874 – of the personal *impression* with the painting that could pass as a 'view' of Le Havre; this dichotomy was presented as part of the Impressionist programme from the start.

However, the extreme opposition was between the sketch and the traditional notion of the major public painting – the Salon picture, whose appeal was to shared public values in the public forum of the large, impersonal exhibition halls of the Palais de l'Industrie, and whose primary commercial appeal was to the French State, in the hope that the government would buy the picture at the Salon for a museum or public building. In this opposition between the private and the public, the *tableau* occupied the middle ground, as the archetypal commodity of the commercial art dealer, marketed in the public sphere, but presented to potential buyers in ways that evoked the intimacy of the private spaces in which the paintings were intended to hang.[80]

The Impressionists rejected the imposed canons of public taste – the comparatively rigid expectations of academic values. Their Salon paintings of the 1860s sought to update, and on occasions subvert, the conventions of the exhibition picture; in their sketches, they cultivated the personal, the individual; and in their *tableaux* they found a form of expression that allowed them to strike a balance between private and public, in the individual entrepreneurial world of the dealer/collector market. Their distinction between sketch and finished painting brings out particularly clearly their position in the development of the modern art world.

3 Modernising the Landscape: The Environs of Paris

To twenty-first-century eyes, the landscape subjects chosen by the Impressionists during the 1870s do not at first sight seem problematic. There are a number of reasons for this. We no longer share the associational values that the subjects had for their first viewers, and indeed may simply not recognise them for what they were. Second, the all-pervasive Impressionist publicity machine of recent years has tended to focus on their images of sunny rivers, rather than backstreets in dirty snow. And thirdly, the world that their landscapes depict tallies closely with the mundane imagery now so widespread in all visual media, whereas in the nineteenth century the sphere of fine art was generally expected to transcend the everyday.

Much of the recent scholarship on the subject matter of Impressionist landscape painting has been primarily enumerative – devoted to the identification of sites and motifs.[1] This emphasis on *what* is represented distracts attention from *how* these subjects appeared – what they meant to their original viewers when seen in the context of a fine art exhibition in Paris during the 1870s. Some sense of this may be gleaned from Charles Bigot's comments on the third group exhibition in 1877:

> In the final analysis, it is not true nature that they have looked at and strive to render, but rather the nature that one glimpses on escapades in the great city or its surroundings, where the harsh notes of the houses, with their white, red or yellow walls and their green shutters, get mixed up with the vegetation of the trees and form violent contrasts with it. How much better have the Dutch painters, and our modern landscapists, the Rousseaus, the Corots and the Daubignys, understood how to express not only the poetry but also the truth of nature! How much better have they represented the countryside, with its waters, its woods, its fields and its meadows, with its distant and calm horizons![2]

Bigot clearly viewed subject matter as generic, not topographically specific. For him, the subjects that the Impressionists favoured were typical of Paris or its surroundings, and, significantly, characteristic of the experience of a particular type of viewer – the city-dweller making an excursion in or from the city. The stumbling block, for Bigot, was the intrusion of overtly contemporary elements into the 'natural' scene – not ruins and cottages, but modern villas that clashed with their 'natural' surroundings. Sisley's *The Bridge at Argenteuil* of 1872 (pl. 52), lent by Manet to the exhibition of 1877, was presumably one of the pictures that Bigot had in his mind's eye. In canvases such as this, the problems were twofold: the physical landscape around Paris was becoming defiled by the irruption of new building; and the inclusion of such buildings in a picture was a betrayal of the values that fine art landscape painting represented.

facing page Alfred Sisley, *Louveciennes, Footpath on the Hillside (Louveciennes, sentier de la mi-côte)* (detail of pl. 58)

52   Alfred Sisley, *The Bridge at Argenteuil* (*Le Pont d'Argenteuil*), 1872, 38.5 × 60.9, Memphis Brooks Museum of Art, Memphis

Behind Bigot's ostensibly aesthetic distaste for the 'harsh notes' of the houses, there was also a moral dimension, a viewpoint that saw the edges of Paris as in a sense epitomising the problems of the capital itself – its physical and moral unhealthiness, and its loss of a fundamental set of values. This emerges particularly clearly in the preface to the 1877 edition of Adolphe Joanne's popular guide to the environs of Paris. Joanne urged Parisians to explore the surroundings of the city – the landscape, and the castles, churches, abbeys and palaces – for their beauties and their historical associations. But at the same time he lamented how little Parisians knew of these:

> Parisians do not know how to go on excursions in a profitable way. If they escape for a few hours from the appalling prisons of stone or plaster in which they purchase at too great expense the right to be shut up without air, space or light, they rush in bands to particular places in which their naïve curiosity is attracted by shameful publicity; they crowd together promiscuously in public establishments that are even more unhealthy and unappealing than their homes, in order to seek out trivial diversions that have nothing to do with the countryside and which they could have procured more cheaply within the great city.[3]

Landscape painting could counter the tainted viewpoint of the excursionist by seeking out the purifying influence of unspoiled 'nature', as Frédéric Henriet, a close associate of Daubigny, spelt out in 1867:

The landscapist . . . passionately loves cottages eaten away by moss, muddy ponds, rough tracks and narrow paths with crumbling banks. With crayon in hand, he ferociously pursues his love of the picturesque; but he sadly admits that all the savage and grandiose aspects of nature are being erased, as science exploits every richness in the soil, and civilisation . . . makes everything uniform: customs, costumes, social practices and habitations! Every conquest of industry and every material improvement involves some sacrifice of the poetry of memories or of picturesque beauties . . . Poetry! it is in the heart of the artist . . . We would say to the devotees of pure art . . . : Immerse yourselves again ceaselessly in life-enhancing contact with nature, eternal sources of truth, beauty and strength. Sing once again the woods and valleys, the naïve incidents of rural life, the beautiful golden harvests and the slow-moving waters that encourage reverie. There still exist remote footpaths and forgotten corners where your inspiration will not risk breaking its wings against the factory chimney, the telegraph pole or the black funnel of the locomotive.[4]

There is a further crucial dimension to Bigot's and Henriet's texts. Their notion of 'truth' is evidently grounded in an idealist world view. This was based not on the individual's everyday sensory experience – on the *sensation* – but rather on a universalising notion of 'nature' that encompassed not only the ideal ingredients of the countryside – waters, woods, fields and meadows – but also its moods and its aesthetic properties: 'calm horizons' and harmonies of green vegetation. Any taint from the city was categorically excluded. For Bigot, this 'nature', enshrining both 'truth' and 'poetry', was expressed by Théodore Rousseau, Corot and Daubigny, and negated by the Impressionists. This idealist position was philosophical and theological as well as aesthetic, and formed a central ingredient in the criteria of judgement that were dominant in the art-critical writing of the period. The Impressionists' repudiation of it, in favour of a vision dependent on subjective sense experience alone, was more than an aesthetic gesture. It represented a rejection of a whole world view that saw 'nature' in terms of divine providence, in favour of an explicitly secularised vision, committed to the specifics of the experience of the here-and-now. This fundamental challenge to frameworks of belief was especially provocative in the repressive years of the mid-1870s, in the aftermath of the Franco-Prussian War and the Commune.

In traditional landscape theory, the painter was urged to seek a *motif*. This term was not simply a synonym for the subject chosen; rather, the depicted scene was meant to transcend the mundane through the choice and combination of the ingredients in it. As Edmond About put it:

Forests, rocks, shorelines, valleys, flocks, palaces, ruins, cottages, costumes, types, these were the ingredients from which one composed a landscape. Rightly or wrongly, artists thought that the first corner of nature that they came on was not the material for a *tableau*, and that before taking up their brush they needed to have at their disposal a good choice of interesting objects. When by chance one encountered a combination of beautiful things well grouped in nature, one said: 'That's a picturesque site', that is to say a site worthy of being painted, comparable to those that true artists represent.[5]

In the 1860s Daubigny had been widely criticised for ignoring these criteria and focusing instead on mere *effets* – on fleeting effects of atmosphere (see pl. 65); in 1865 he was described as the leader of 'the school of the *impression*'.[6] The fact that Bigot felt

53   Charles Busson, *The Village of Lavardin [Loir-et-Cher]* (*Le Village de Lavardin [Loir-et-Cher]*), 1877, 175 × 220, Musée des Beaux-Arts, Angers

able to include him in 1877 among the painters of 'true nature' shows how far, by the later 1870s, these concerns had been assimilated into the dominant view of the acceptable face of landscape. But for Bigot the explicit contemporaneity of the Impressionists' landscapes set them beyond the pale.

Landscape painting at the Salon, particularly during the 'moral order' regime of the mid-1870s, closely followed Henriet's exhortations. It focused on images of an unspoiled deep countryside in which all the elements coexisted in seamless harmony, whether in old villages, as in Charles Busson's *The Village of Lavardin* (pl. 53), open farmland (e.g. pl. 72) or deep forests. Untouched by modernisation or industrialisation, untainted by urban influences, unscarred by the recent passage of the Prussian armies through rural France,[7] this vision of *la France profonde* presented the French countryside as a stable repository of seemingly timeless values – in every way the antithesis of the insecurities of the city.

Viewed in this context, the Impressionists' choice of subjects marked an unequivocal repudiation of conventional notions of landscape and the values for which it stood. Beyond this, the small scale and informal handling of the paintings emphasised that they should not be viewed as weighty pronouncements about 'poetry' and 'nature'. Their compositions, too, were usually open, with multiple small focuses of attention and no central pivotal point to which special significance was given. In scale, execution and composition, they seemed to reject any predetermined hierarchy of values. By contemporary standards, these little, informal, sketchy scenes of everyday life were an overt rejection of the picturesque, of beauty in landscape, and indeed of 'true nature' itself.

*   *   *

We must now look more closely at the imagery of these landscapes and the ways in which their subjects are presented. The scenes depicted by the Impressionists gained their meanings for the viewer in relative terms – when viewed from a particular viewpoint, that of the centre observing the periphery. In this context, the pictures took their place amid a range of other commentaries, both verbal and visual, on the transformation of the countryside around Paris – comic, sentimental, sociological, statistical or whatever. This dimension of the Impressionists' landscape subjects of the 1870s has been richly explored by T. J. Clark.[8] A number of key themes emerge from contemporary writings, as commentators scrutinised the visible effects of change in the countryside around Paris and sought to anatomise their causes and implications. The issues raised are central to the landscape subjects chosen by the members of the Impressionist group in the later 1860s and the 1870s. The first of these was agriculture, and the relationship between traditional practices and new types of production for new outlets, notably the growth of market gardening for the ever-growing appetites of Paris. Secondly, there was much discussion of the relationship between old villages and towns and new villas and developments – their gradual suburbanisation. These areas were also rapidly becoming centres for urban leisure, ranging from the semi-professional sailing of the Argenteuil regattas to the social and moral ambivalence of the hostelries on the river banks, for which Bougival was particularly notorious. At the same time, the area was becoming increasingly industrialised. And finally, amid these landscapes of change, the surroundings of Paris contained many remnants of the historical past – or rather, of the various epochs that had left their traces in the region.

There was also a more immediate sense in which the pictures need to be viewed within a Parisian context – the physical context of their display and sale. The Impressionists' paintings were not intended to be viewed where they were painted; Monet did not exhibit in Argenteuil or Pissarro in Pontoise. Their viewers in Paris might have little or no local knowledge about the sites depicted. Few, if any, of them would have known what was done in a particular factory, still less what building stood just outside the painter's field of vision in a particular canvas. Guidebooks had little to say about most of the sites they chose in these places. The viewer's understanding of a picture would have been based on what could be seen in the picture itself, combined with its title. These titles were mostly very unspecific, generally naming only the place and the most obvious element in the picture. It is misleading for the modern scholar to retitle a canvas on the basis of detailed local knowledge;[9] the picture's original title, however inexplicit, was an integral part of the image for its first viewers, and played a central role in generating the meanings that they found in it.

In a few exceptional cases the subject would have been well known to the Parisian viewer. Most obviously among the sites around the edges of Paris, La Grenouillère, the bathing place and restaurant on an island in the Seine opposite Bougival, ten miles west of Paris, had a vivid public reputation. This was delicately described by Berthe Morisot's mother around 1868: 'It is said to be a very rustic meeting-place for a very frivolous society, and that if one goes there alone, one returns in the company of at least one other person.'[10] A revealing glimpse of the place of La Grenouillère in the cultural mythology of the period emerges from a story told by Paul Lenoir, who accompanied Jean-Léon Gérôme on an expedition across the Sinaï desert in 1868. As they left the monastery on Mount Sinaï, the abbot promised them that on their next visit he would offer them some of his home-brewed liquor: ' "When you come through Bougival", we

54 Claude Monet, *La Grenouillère*, 1869, 74.6 × 99.7, The Metropolitan Museum of Art, New York, H.O. Havemeyer Collection, Bequest of Mrs. H. O. Havemeyer, 1929. (29.100.112)

replied, we will take you boating and we will present you *à la Grenouillère*." Convinced that this was a person of high birth, the good Father expressed his gratitude for a favour of which he believed himself unworthy.'[11]

As we have seen, both Monet and Renoir planned to make ambitious Salon paintings of the place (see pp. 48–50). Their surviving sketches are in many ways very similar – views across the river and along the bank, showing the floating restaurant, walkways and islet with a tree on it (the so-called camembert) peopled with lively groups of figures. Yet there is a significant difference between the two men's treatment of the place. In Renoir's canvases (e.g. pl. 31), the figures blend together quite seamlessly, whereas in each of Monet's there is a single grouping that evokes more clearly the equivocal reputation of the place – the clothed man and the two women in bathing costumes on the walkway at the right of plate 32, and the women in bathing costumes to the left of the 'camembert' in plate 54, who are being addressed by a male bather in the river. The presence of women in bathing costumes out of the water, together with the implied interchange between them and the men, hints at the encounters evoked in Madame Morisot's letter; but in neither picture is the nature of the interchange made clear. Many and varied interpretations are possible of the gestures of the man and the responses of the women in each canvas; the viewer is invited to construct his or her own narrative from their deftly indicated silhouettes.

facing page   Claude Monet, *The Bathing-Place at La Grenouillère* (*Les Bains de la Grenouil-lère*) (detail of pl. 32)

55 Claude Monet, *The Promenade at Argenteuil* (*La Promenade à Argenteuil*), 1872, 50.4 × 65.2, National Gallery of Art, Washington, Ailsa Mellon Bruce Collection

By contrast with La Grenouillère, the reputation of the other sites in the surroundings of Paris would have been far less specific. Of these, only Argenteuil, ten miles north-west of Paris, where Monet lived from 1871 to 1878, had any distinctive current reputation – as a centre for sailing, both competitive regattas and recreational boating. But, apart from this, the place had no particularly notable features or associations. The pictures that the Impressionists painted there are conspicuous for their diversity, both in their specific subjects and the range of light and weather depicted. Sailing boats frequently put in an appearance; but, apart from this, there is little in the pictures of Argenteuil to distinguish it from other sites in the region. Both at Argenteuil and at the other sites around Paris that the Impressionists painted, we find factories on river banks, modern villas slotted into old villages or punctuating open countryside, figures in bourgeois dress in the meadows or by the river, fields and plots that juxtapose different crops and types of agricultural production. Indeed, there are often close similarities between the sites chosen by different painters at different places. Monet's views of the Prome-

56 Camille Pissarro, *The Banks of the Oise at Pontoise (Les Bords de l'Oise à Pontoise)*, 1872, 55 × 91, private collection

nade at Argenteuil, showing a riverside walk peopled by bourgeois figures and framed by an alternating pattern of trees, houses and factory chimneys (e.g. pl. 55), are comparable to a Pissarro view of Pontoise (pl. 56). Pissarro's oblique perspective onto the roofs of Pontoise (pl. 57) is very similar to Sisley's view of Louveciennes (pl. 58); in both, the chosen viewpoint is seemingly casual and the motif trivial, and there are brusque contrasts between foreground and background.

Much attention has been paid to the occasions when a single subject was painted by more than one painter.[12] Certainly, if the two paintings were painted at the same time, these enable us to focus on similarities and differences of style and interpretation. But an over-emphasis on these moments of collective activity privileges biographical detail over a broader understanding of the painters' artistic projects. In this context, similarities between pictures made at different sites are far more telling than comparisons of works executed side by side.

Moreover, there may be startling differences between two painters' renderings of a single site. A vivid example of this is the pair of canvases by Pissarro and Renoir of about 1869–70 (pls 59 and 60), showing a road at Louveciennes, the village just to the south of Bougival and the Seine where both men were living at the time. Pissarro's shows the road in early spring, peopled only by a few quiet peasant figures, whereas Renoir depicts the view in summer, with the road invaded by a lively bourgeois family group. Pissarro's canvas belongs to the traditional genre of rural village scenes, whereas Renoir's is emphatically about modern leisure. Contemporary commentators were keen to define where Paris ended and the country began, and to tell their readers how far from the city they now had to go to reach the 'real' countryside. Pissarro's view can comfortably be set alongside a passage from 1867, cited by T. J. Clark, in which Victorien Sardou wrote of Louveciennes: 'This is the real village! You can enter, take off your coat, if you are hot, sing, if you are happy! Here you won't offend anyone! Chatou is far away; and those little white flurries which the wind stirs up round you on the road, they are not rice powder . . . they are real dust.'[13] However, Renoir's canvas shows how fluid these boundaries were: the day trippers from Bougival and La Grenouillère, below Louveciennes on the river, could readily bring their 'rice powder' into Louveciennes's dusty rural spaces. The two pictures might be discussed in terms of the interests, or temperaments, of the two painters, opposing Pissarro's feeling for peasant life to Renoir's celebratory

57   Camille Pissarro, *Pontoise*, 1872, 40.5 × 54.5, Musée d'Orsay, Paris

58   Alfred Sisley, *Louveciennes, Footpath on the Hillside* (*Louveciennes, sentier de la mi-côte*), *c.*1873, 38 × 46.5, Musée d'Orsay, Paris

59   Camille Pissarro, *Springtime at Louveciennes (Printemps à Louveciennes)*, c.1869, 52.7 × 81.9, National Gallery, London

60   Pierre-Auguste Renoir,
Road at Louveciennes
(*Chemin à Louveciennes*),
c.1870, 38.1 × 46.4,
The Metropolitan Museum of
Art, New York, The Lesley
and Emma Sheafer Collection,
Bequest of Emma A. Sheafer,
1973. (1974.356.32)

61 Claude Monet, *Autumn Effect at Argenteuil (Effet d'automne à Argenteuil)*, 1873, 55 × 74.5, Courtauld Institute Gallery, London

vision of the recreations on the edges of Paris. But to reduce this contrast to matters of personal preference ignores two crucial points: the canvases are pictures of different types, of different genres; and the difference between them is an expression of a wider set of debates, about modernity and its representation. The site of these debates was Paris.

Likewise, the same site might provide a single artist with the material for very varied pictures, depending on the angle of vision and viewpoint chosen, and on the season and weather effect. Monet's canvases of the backwater of the Seine opposite Argenteuil are a particularly clear example of this. Looking towards the town, the place may be seen serenely framed on both sides by autumnal trees (pl. 61), or set against two bright new villas on the river bank, stressing the changes overtaking the region (pl. 62).[14] Yet even the tree-framed view is equivocal. Topographical knowledge tells us that the light-toned central vertical accent is a church spire, but in the autumn scene, unlike plate 62, it is treated so summarily that, without local knowledge, this form may readily be interpreted as a factory chimney, which radically changes the experience of the picture.

62   Claude Monet, *The Seine at Argenteuil (La Seine à Argenteuil)*, 50 × 61, Musée d'Orsay, Paris

Looking in the other direction, away from the town, the same backwater could be treated as an untouched country scene, as when viewed in springtime in plate 63. However, seen from the opposite bank in late autumn in plate 64, the effect is very different. The general outlines of the scene follow the conventions established by painters such as Daubigny (see pl. 65), with an open river flanked by trees on one side, and a hazy distance beyond. But behind the – evidently planted – trees on the right we see the unmistakable silhouette of a modern villa, while in the foreground the river bank has been dug up for some reason, and two crisply defined little figures appear at the water's edge; they might be fishing or surveying the land for future building, but their gestures are not specific enough for us to be sure.[15] As with the La Grenouillère pictures, viewers are left to make their own readings.

63   Claude Monet, *Spring at Argenteuil (Printemps à Argenteuil)*, 1872, 51 × 65, Portland Museum of Art, Maine

64   Claude Monet, *The Petit Bras of the Seine at Argenteuil (Le petit bras de la Seine à Argenteuil)*, 1872, 52.6 × 71.8, National Gallery, London

65 Charles-François Daubigny, *River Scene (Scène de rivière)*, 1860, 28 × 58, Courtauld Institute Gallery, London

Over a period of two years, in 1872–3, this backwater provided Monet with a wide-ranging repertoire of potential subjects. These occasionally evoked unspoiled country-side, but in the main showed clear signs of the processes of change and modernisation. The very diversity of these pictures – in their ingredients, compositions, brushwork and colour schemes – shows that they cannot be read as transparent expressions of Monet's personal responses to the place. Rather, they belong to the larger project that Monet shared with his colleagues in these years, of exploring the many facets of the rapidly changing landscape around Paris.

Another group of paintings will bring the issue of the painters' attitudes to the subjects they chose into clearer focus. In 1873 Pissarro painted a sequence of pictures of the banks of the river Oise in which factories on the river bank play a prominent role, as physical intruders in the landscape.[16] This intrusion of contemporaneity is an overt rejection of the conventional imagery of the banks of the Oise, as popularised by Daubigny, which present the misty rural river bank as an unspoiled retreat (e.g. pl. 65).

66 Camille Pissarro, *Factory near Pontoise (Usine près de Pontoise)*, 1873, 45.7 × 54.6, Museum of Fine Arts, Springfield, Mass., James Philip Gray Collection

67 Camille Pissarro, *The Oise on the Outskirts of Pontoise (L'Oise aux environs de Pontoise)*, 1873, 45.3 × 55, Sterling and Francine Clark Art Institute, Williamstown, Mass.

68 Camille Pissarro, *Banks of the Oise, Pontoise (Bords de l'Oise, Pontoise)*, 1873, 38.1 × 55.2, Indianapolis Museum of Art, James E. Roberts Fund

But should we use Pissarro's pictures as evidence for his personal attitude to this invasive presence in the rural scene? He could of course have avoided painting the factories, and chosen a different view, or he could have simply omitted them. But can his choice to paint this view be interpreted as a commentary on the industrialisation of the landscape? The answer to this question is complicated by the very different ways in which he presented the factories in different pictures. In *Banks of the Oise, Pontoise* (pl. 68), the building is relegated to the background, though it is still a significant element in this humdrum panorama of everyday life on the banks of an unpicturesque stretch of the river, viewed in grey weather. In *Factory near Pontoise* (pl. 66), by contrast, the large factory is the central feature, its sheds and smoking chimneys dominating the scruffy remnants of 'nature' around it; here, an ecological reading, in terms of its destruction of the landscape, might seem appropriate. Yet in a third canvas, *The Oise on the Outskirts of Pontoise* (pl. 67), the same buildings are seen from further away, and framed by trees, bushes and flowers, now seemingly a benign presence in the landscape, and bathed in sunshine, with the smoke from the factory blending into the clouds.

This group of paintings, all painted in the same year, 1873, is a salutary reminder that we cannot seek to read off personal feelings or social attitudes from fine art images such as these; the differences between the effect and mood of the paintings are the result

69   Camille Pissarro, *The Red House* (*La Maison rouge*), 1873, 59 × 73, Portland Art Museum, Oreg.

of Pissarro's choices – of weather and viewpoint; and these are part of his artistic project, not an expression of a view about the landscape itself. Taken as a whole, his project, like Monet's, suggests that the presence of the modern could assume many faces in the landscape, when viewed in different conditions and from different viewpoints – both physical and ideological. He was insisting that a truly modern type of painting should bring together just those contrasting elements that traditional landscape imagery had kept categorically separate.

In many other canvases of 1872 and 1873, whether painted at Louveciennes or Pontoise, Pissarro chose particularly mundane sites, often punctuating them with recently constructed houses and villas – incongruous intruders in the rural scene – as if to insist that the imagery of *la France profonde* no longer had any credible currency in the surroundings of Paris. Instead, a scene like *The Red House* (pl. 69) is fragmented and disparate, presenting a world made up of small, separate pockets of activity, both human and pictorial. Many of Monet's Argenteuil scenes of the same years can readily be viewed in the same terms (see pls 70, 144); the motif of the modern villa intruding into village or fields recurs at Louveciennes, Chatou, Marly, Argenteuil and Pontoise.

Evidently, these themes can be closely linked to the key issues about the surroundings of Paris that we have noted – issues that dominated contemporary debates about the

70　Claude Monet, *Houses
at Argenteuil (Maisons à
Argenteuil)*, c.1873, 54 × 73,
Nationalgalerie, Berlin

effects and implications of urbanisation. Yet the very diversity of the pictures makes it impossible to tie them to any particular position or viewpoint within these debates. Rather, the distinctive character of these images, appearing in fine art paintings, emerges from a different context – from their consistent rejection of the stock conventions of contemporary landscape painting as it appeared at the Salon, and at times from their explicit travesties of them. This was a two-pronged attack on dominant values, both aesthetic and political; the imagery of rural harmony and integration that proliferated on the walls of the Salon in these years underpinned the myth of the French countryside as source of the nation's well-being. In the pictures' original context, in the immediate aftermath of the Franco-Prussian war, when that countryside had been so easily overrun by the invader, the Impressionists' challenge to this myth was all the more pointed.

Renoir's *Harvesters* (pl. 71), shown at the first Impressionist group exhibition in 1874, presents one of the most hackneyed themes in the imagery of the countryside at the period. However, he does not show the harvest as a seemingly timeless ritual framed by the beauties of nature, as Léon Lhermitte did, for example, in *The Harvest*, bought by the State at the Salon of 1874 (pl. 72). Instead, Renoir's harvesters are relegated to the right side of the picture, and juxtaposed with a cabbage patch on the left, a modern villa on the horizon, and an unexplained pair of figures approaching down the central path. The extremely summary, sketch-like technique, too, denies the harvesters the dignity conventionally given to field workers in the art of the period.

The stock image of the country road was also taken in new directions by the Impressionists. In a canvas such as Camille Bernier's huge *Road near Bannalec*, shown at the Salon of 1870 (pl. 73), the crumbling old stone walls, mature trees and figures in local costume present us with a remote, unchanging world. Impressionist road scenes are often bordered by irregular, heterogeneous houses and other buildings (e.g. pl. 144). In Monet's *The Sheltered Path* (pl. 143), the serried rank of trees shows that they have been planted, rather than being an organic part of the landscape; apart from this, the rest of the scene gives no clue to what sort of place this is or what the figure is doing there, rather than presenting the viewer with a seemingly natural world in which everyone knows their place.

71 Pierre-Auguste Renoir, *Harvesters (Moissonneurs)*, 1873, 60 × 74, private collection

The traditional theme of the seasons was conventionally associated with the cyclical patterns of agriculture and village life, or treated in terms of the impact of natural forces – of the elements – on the open countryside. The Impressionists, by contrast, no longer treated the seasons as an immutable part of a natural order. Winter might be viewed at a railway station, or in the ugly backstreets of a town, with the snow churned up by passers-by (pl. 144); spring might be the occasion for a visit to the outdoor places of entertainment on an island in the Seine (pl. 82); summer was more often seen as a time for leisure than for work (pl. 40); and autumn might be viewed in terms of colour and optical effect alone; there is no sense in Monet's *Autumn Effect at Argenteuil* (pl. 61) of the traditional association of autumn with *tristesse*. Certainly, explicitly seasonal subjects appear in a great variety of guises, but common to the vast majority of these is a refusal to engage with the stock imagery of the annual cycle of work in the countryside.

Likewise, elemental forces are treated in a calculatedly mundane way. A high wind may be seen in terms of a wind-swept regatta day on the river at Argenteuil, with the

72 Léon Lhermitte, *The Harvest (La Moisson)*, 1874, 122 × 205, Musée des Beaux-Arts, Carcassonne

73 Camille Bernier, *A Road near Bannalec (Un Chemin près de Bannalec)*, 1870, 200 × 302, Musée des Beaux-Arts, Nantes

race umpire's little boat perilously tossed on the choppy water (pl. 74). Renoir's *High Wind* of about 1872 (pl. 75) treats the theme in terms of pure visual effect, with a cascade of improvisatory brushwork evoking the rush of air across a screen of foliage; a single tiny villa, quickly notated on the horizon to the right, suggests that this site – otherwise unidentifiable – was within the orbit of urban impact. Likewise in *The Plain of Epluches (Rainbow)* of 1876–7 (pl. 76) Pissarro included one of the most traditional emblems in the history of landscape painting and highlighted its presence in the title he gave the painting when he exhibited it in 1877; but in the picture itself the rainbow is just one element in a conspicuously scattered and diverse composition. The image may invoke reminiscences of Rubens,[17] but the composition's multiple points of emphasis are a far cry from Rubens's cosmic vision. In Pissarro's landscape the elemental phenomenon is just another element in an essentially modern conception of 'nature', alongside the factory and the anonymous peasant figures in the foreground.

Although they represent specific, and generally identifiable, sites, all of these examples are of generic themes – of subjects that might be presented in a wide range of physical settings, and where the specifics of the particular location were less significant than the conjunction of disparate elements within the scene. There is, though, one group of pictures in which the specifics play a different role – the canvases that include the remnants of *ancien régime* architecture that punctuated the landscapes around Louveciennes and Marly. Pissarro's and Renoir's Louveciennes views of 1869–70 (pls 59, 60) show

74 Claude Monet, *The Boats, Regatta at Argenteuil (Les Barques, Régates à Argenteuil)*, c.1874, 60 × 100, Musée d'Orsay, Paris

an ordinary rural road, but on the horizon we see the end of a celebrated structure, the Marly aqueduct, monumental remnant of the system by which Louis xiv drew Seine water up the steep riverside hills to pipe it to Versailles. The presence of this very recognisable feature complicates the social networks that each picture constructs. In one of Sisley's paintings (Toledo Museum of Art, Ohio) the end of the aqueduct is the prime focus of the painting, though ignored by the casual little figure of a passing rider; and in other canvases Sisley depicted the *Machine de Marly*, the pumping system at the bottom of the hill, recently rebuilt by Napoleon iii.

Such vestiges of the architecture of the *ancien régime* recur in other images of this part of the Seine valley, notably Sisley's views of the Watering Place at Marly-le-Roi, sole remnant of the huge palace of Marly, one of Louis xiv's most ambitious projects. Several of these pictures, such as plate 77, include the massive, ornamental wall that marked the bottom of the park, and through which water was passed from the palace above into the public pond below, for reuse by the local population; but Sisley's pictures refuse to attribute to it any special significance. Likewise, his *Chemin de la Machine, Louveciennes* (Musée d'Orsay, Paris) includes on the right the frontage of the villa where Louis xv's mistress Madame du Barry had lived, but treats it as just another incidental part of the scene.

Yet these were sites that many viewers would have recognised. Contemporary accounts, including Sardou's essay, stressed the contrast between the grandiose Watering Place and the humble village around it,[18] and guidebooks devoted many pages to

75   Pierre-Auguste Renoir, *High Wind* (*Grand vent*) [now known as *The Gust of Wind*], *c.*1872, 52 × 82.5, Fitzwilliam Museum, University of Cambridge

vivid evocations of the lavish life led by the court at the now-destroyed palace. One account imagined a narrative of the history of the area, as viewed from a passing boat on the Seine:

> Row slowly, and listen to the conductor on the tramway on the riverbank, as he names these radiant landscapes: Louveciennes – and you will think of Dubarry, of Louis XV, of the negro dwarf Zamore who looked after the rich and discreet château from which, one day, much against her will, the favourite drew a fatal number in the lottery of Saint Guillotine; and Marly – and you will be tempted to go and seek amid the riotous foliage, in the confused paths of the park, the almost untraceable remnants of the splendid palace . . . Of these much vaunted splendours, . . . scarcely anything remains except the site, a few rotting gates, and the melancholy watering place where Coustou's horses used to rear.[19]

Sisley himself lived in a house that overlooked the Watering Place, and certainly we can see his pictures of the site as part of a world view that treated all visual data, all *sensations*, alike. But a biographical explanation is not enough, since he chose to paint it so frequently, from among the myriad possible subjects in the vicinity, and chose to present it as he did. Viewed within a fine art context, these pictures can be seen as a subversion of the traditional notion of the *motif*. Traditionally, the artist was expected to stress the special status of the key elements in a scene, through both the composition and the execution of the painting, as for instance in Henri Harpignies's *Ruins of the*

76　Camille Pissarro, *The Plain of Epluches [Rainbow] (La Plaine des Epluches [Arc-en-ciel])*, 1877, 53 × 81, Kröller-Müller Museum, Otterlo

Château of Hérisson, shown at the Salon of 1872 (pl. 78), with the castle ruins silhouetted on the central hilltop, and the humdrum life of the contemporary peasantry continuing around them. By contrast, Sisley systematically demoted the structure of the Marly Watering Place, often, as in plate 77, playing down its architecture to such an extent that only prior knowledge would enable one to identify it for what it was. Beyond this, though, we might see a further significance in his choice of *ancien régime* references, in the specific context of the early to mid-1870s; for it was in just these years that there was, for the final time, a real possibility of the re-establishment of the French monarchy.[20] We have no evidence that either Sisley or his initial audience viewed these paintings in these terms, but the loaded associations of these structures at this particular moment cannot be ignored.

The Impressionists faced one central problem in their project to create a modern form of landscape. They needed to find markets for their work, through their exhibitions and, wherever possible, through dealers and other intermediaries. Little evidence survives of a direct linkage between their choice of subjects and the pressures of the market in these years, but we have a clear indication that commercial factors played a central role in the changes in Pissarro's subject matter in the years 1873–5.

Late in 1873, at Pontoise, Pissarro shifted his focus from explicitly contemporary subjects to seemingly timeless themes – old cottages, peasant figures and animals.[21] This did

77 Alfred Sisley, *Watering Place at Marly* (*L'Abreuvoir de Marly*), 1875, 49.5 × 65.5, National Gallery, London

78 Henri Harpignies, *Ruins of the Château of Hérisson* (*Ruines du château d'Hérisson*), 1871, 71 × 103, Musée Fabre, Montpellier

coincide, roughly, with his move to a house at L'Hermitage, on the more rural side of Pontoise, to the north-east, in October 1873,[22] but it also coincided with a direct, documented intervention from Paris, in the form of a letter from Duret, encouraging him to focus on 'rustic, rural nature with animals' since this was what best suited his talent.[23] Pissarro replied welcoming this advice.[24] *Hoar-Frost* (pl. 79), painted late in 1873, is indeed a Pontoise subject,[25] but vastly different from its predecessors, including no markers of a precise site and no signs of modernisation.

A monographic model of art history would here emphasise Pissarro's biography – his move of house. However, pictures of both types, both the 'modern' and the 'timeless', were interventions in larger debates sited in Paris. Pissarro's switch to 'rustic, rural' subjects, from the evidence of his interchange with Duret, was clearly a market strategy, in turning to a particularly lucrative genre, with clear references to the example of the now-celebrated Millet. *Hoar-Frost* was exhibited at the first group exhibition in 1874 with this title, but no topographical subtitle, and it belongs to a type of subject that could have been practised almost anywhere in rural northern France.

79 Camille Pissarro, *Hoar-Frost* (*Gelée blanche*), 1873, 65 × 93, Musée d'Orsay, Paris

80 Camille Pissarro, *Farm at Montfou-cault* (*Ferme à Montfoucault*), 1874, 60 × 73, Musée d'Art et d'Histoire, Geneva

Moreover, Pissarro's rustic subjects of the mid-1870s alternate quite without contrast or disjunction between Pontoise and Montfoucault, the farm in a remote corner of eastern Brittany owned by his friend Ludovic Piette. In paintings from both places, we find just the same un-individualised peasant figures placed within a seemingly timeless, enfolding agricultural landscape (see pls 80 and 151). No one, then or now, among the wider audience of these pictures would have known anything about Montfoucault or would have known where it was; the name of the nearest village is never given, although when Pissarro first exhibited a Montfoucault painting, in 1876, he indicated in the title that it was in the *département* of the Mayenne – a very uncelebrated region, in contrast to the famous sites of western Brittany.

In 1876–7 Pissarro turned again to Pontoise's modernised landscape, painting further pictures of the factory beside the river and also including factories in broader pano-

81   Claude Monet, *Argenteuil, the Bank in Flower*, 1877, 54 × 65, private collection, Japan

82   Claude Monet, *Spring on the Ile de la Grande-Jatte* (*Printemps à l'Ile de la Grande-Jatte*), 1878, 50 × 61, Nasjonalgalleriet, Oslo

ramas of the landscape around Pontoise (e.g. pl. 76); in 1877 Monet painted further pictures of the Promenade at Argenteuil, backed by factory chimneys (e.g. pl. 81). Again, there are clear parallels between the two groups of pictures; both show a rather different approach to these subjects, blending the factories into their surroundings, rather than crisply noting their distinctive forms. In the case of Monet, it has been argued that this, followed by his decision to move away from Argenteuil later in 1877, reflects the painter's disillusion with the place itself, as a result of the increasing pollution of the area.[26] Yet when in 1878 he painted again on the Seine banks, he chose a site still more polluted and more evidently transformed by industrialisation than Argenteuil, the Ile de la Grande Jatte, on the western fringes of Paris (pl. 82).

As will be argued below, in Chapter Five, the changes in both Monet's and Pissarro's treatment of their subjects in these years need to be viewed in terms of their changing technique and aesthetic aims, and not primarily in relation to their attitudes towards their physical environment. Likewise, their final abandonment of explicitly contemporary landscape subjects, at the end of the decade, was part of a broader shift in their position within the Paris art world – a shift that involved commercial and political factors, and cannot be explained in biographical terms; this will be explored in Chapter Six.

*　　*　　*

The argument in this chapter has been that, between around 1872 and 1877, the Impressionists were seeking to forge a distinctively modern form of landscape, rejecting traditional notions of the picturesque and the mythic image of *la France profonde*, in an attempt to create a landscape imagery that expressed the complexities of the changes that were transforming the environs of Paris. Precedents for this imagery appear, certainly, in the steel engravings that appeared in travel guides from the 1850s onwards, and notably in the series of *Guides Joanne* whose paths followed the newly laid arterial railway lines, and often focused on the engineering feats that these lines represented (e.g. pl. 83). Indeed, paintings such as Monet's *The Railway Bridge at Argenteuil* (pl. 84) are clearly in tune with the recurrent imagery in these guides, where figures are depicted seemingly admiring the achievements of technology.[27]

However, the assumptions behind such engravings and the interests that informed them were very specific: the promotion and celebration of rail travel. By contrast, many of the paintings that we have been examining treat subjects with no such clear-cut connotations. If we are seeking comparisons for the seemingly casual yet calculatedly anti-picturesque scenes that the Impressionists favoured in the early to mid-1870s, the closest parallels may be found in stereoscopic photographs. Some of these, like the engravings in the guidebooks, present the achievements of technology in the landscapes around Paris, for instance a view of the bridge at Auteuil (pl. 85), which adopts a form and format particularly close to Monet's Argenteuil railway bridge canvas. However, there

83　*Viaduc de Barentin*, from Eugène Chapus, *De Paris à Rouen et au Havre*, 1862 edition

84 Claude Monet, *The Railway Bridge at Argenteuil (Le Pont du chemin de fer à Argenteuil)*, c.1873, 60 × 99, Helly Nahmad Gallery, London

are other photographs with no such clear-cut points of interest, which show scenes of no obvious significance in either aesthetic or associational terms, with conjunctions of disparate elements comparable to the deliberately fragmented and mundane scenes that we have been examining. A photograph of the town of Versailles from the 1850s (pl. 86), for instance, with a newly built villa behind a blank wall in the foreground dominating the view over the town, incorporates jarring contrasts of space and ingredients very comparable to paintings such as Pissarro's *Pontoise* and Sisley's *Louveciennes, Footpath on the Hillside* (pls 57 and 58), with an abrupt leap from foreground to background, and no apparent links between the different zones of the image.

85 *The Pont d'Auteuil*, single frame from a stereoscopic photograph, c.1870, private collection, London

86 *Versailles*, stereoscopic photograph, late 1850s, private collection, London

Comparisons such as these do not seek to reintroduce the 'influence of photography' into the history of Impressionism.[28] Occasional images produced in a medium that was physically on a very small scale, mass-reproduced and considered to be merely mechanical, were a far cry from the expectations that viewers in the 1870s held about the purposes of fine art landscape painting and the interests for which it stood. Indeed, the three-dimensional effects that stereoscopic photographs created when seen through a viewer, with their scientific associations, were utterly unlike the visible mark-making on the canvas surface that was one of the defining characteristics of an Impressionist painting. Yet the very existence of such images, in a medium evidently considered modern, if not aesthetic, raises the possibility that they acted as some sort of catalyst that allowed the Impressionists to see the possibility of radically anti-picturesque forms of landscape imagery.

But the crucial decision was to harness such forms and imagery to fine art, and to present these canvases as a viable form of 'modern' landscape painting. It is in the fine art context that we must view both the Impressionists' choice of mundane, contemporary subjects and their deliberately informal compositions and technique. The distinctiveness of their secularised vision emerges when set against Bigot's definition of 'true nature', quoted at the start of this chapter, and the conventional treatment of themes of *la France profonde* at the Salon, in the aftermath of the Franco-Prussian War and the Commune: they offered a sustained critique of the idealist vision of landscape and 'nature' that underpinned the intense cultural and political conservatism of MacMahon's 'moral order' regime.

Yet, beyond this, we must ask further questions about the viewpoint of the paintings. What attitudes to the sites themselves do they express? Do they suggest any judgement – social, moral or aesthetic – of the transformations that were overtaking the surroundings of Paris? By this date, an ecological perspective on these changes was certainly possible. This emerges particularly clearly from an essay by the geographer Elisée Reclus, 'Du sentiment de la nature dans les sociétés modernes', published in 1866. Discussing the French taste for the 'humanised' landscape, he insists that the countryside can be truly valued only by those with education and *délicatesse*, whereas peasants and bourgeois 'exploiters of the soil' measure it only for its utility.[29] He warns of the vast damage currently being inflicted on the countryside. Here, the villains are fourfold: tourists and visitors, who leave their debris everywhere; speculators, who divide up beautiful areas of the landscape into small plots for their own benefit; industrialisation, which pollutes the air with factory smoke; and engineers, who impose ugly bridges and viaducts onto the natural scenery.[30] Yet at the end Reclus is able to bypass these pressing threats, and to praise man's desire to find solace and regeneration in unspoiled nature, in contrast to the decadence of urban society.[31]

Throughout, we have stressed the diverse ways in which the Impressionists approached these contemporary subjects. The sites that they chose were often precisely those that Reclus highlights as examples of the damage caused by modernisation, but they seem to pass no judgement on this. For every picture that seems to spotlight the spoiling of nature, there are others in which very similar elements are treated in a far more positive way – with an air of celebration, not regret. Taken together, the pictures that we have been examining demonstrate a fascination with a whole range of subjects and effects that had previously been considered quite outside the sphere of fine art. Many of these were by traditional standards unpicturesque – indeed, many pictures seem purposefully to combine elements in ways that make a mockery of traditional landscape aesthetics. But in all these cases the painters' visual engagement – their *curiosité* – teases out the pictorial potential of even the most unprepossessing raw material.

In the pictures that resulted, these subjects were transformed by the way in which they were treated – by the network of coloured touches that made up the physical fabric of the painting (on this, see Chapter Five). But this is not to play down the painters' engagement with the scenes around them and with the changes that were transforming them. For the pictorial language they evolved – the endlessly flexible shorthand of coloured *taches* – was itself an expression of the complex mixing of diverse and often seemingly incongruous elements that characterised the landscapes of the environs of Paris.

This was seen very clearly by one critic in the spring of 1877, Frédéric Chevalier, who was able to bring subject and technique together, and to argue that these small, informal landscapes could be viewed as an expression of the uncertainties and insecurities of that historical moment:

> The characteristics that distinguish the Intransigents – the brutal handling of paint, their liking for down to earth subjects, the appearance of spontaneity that they seek above all else, the deliberate incoherence, the bold colouring, the contempt for form, the childish *naïveté* that they mix casually with exquisite refinements – this disconcerting mixture of contradictory qualities and defects is not without analogy to the chaos of opposing forces that trouble our era. An art whose ideal is vague and execution rudimentary reflects most faithfully our current uncertainties and vulgarity.[32]

4 The Viewer of Modern Life

PREVIOUS DISCUSSIONS OF THE IMPRESSIONISTS' MODERN LIFE figure scenes have focused primarily on the subject matter they chose – on the worlds of theatres and cafés, boulevards and brothels, that they represented.[1] However, the distinctive qualities of these paintings, and of the vision of the modern world that they propose, emerge most clearly from an exploration of the ways in which their subjects were formulated and presented to the viewer. This may better be discussed in terms of the positions, both physical and social, that the paintings construct for the viewer.

At the same time, many of their paintings depict acts of looking and viewing. Whereas in conventional genre paintings, as we have seen in Chapter One, the interplay of attention between the figures was used as a means to direct the viewer towards a ready reading of the image, the Impressionists' figure scenes often make the business of viewing problematic, obscuring the object that is being looked at or the nature of the figure's attention. These uncertainties, in turn, offer us a key to the modes of viewing that the paintings demand of their viewers.

The viewer's relationship to any painting is determined by the organisation of the picture. This may sometimes involve positing a precise physical location for the spectator, as with a Renaissance altarpiece whose perspective reads correctly from a single point in the chapel for which it was designed. More often, though, the position that the picture determines for the viewer is less literal, less explicit. Yet this does not mean that the viewing position is undetermined; a whole set of means may be deployed in order to direct the processes of reading and interpretation. In part, this involves an implicit physical viewpoint; but, crucially, face to face with a modern life subject picture, the viewer is also implicated as an historical subject, whose scrutiny of the painting inevitably involves issues of class, gender and ideology.

As we have seen, Castagnary's prescription for a successful genre painting posited an ideal relationship between viewer and image:

> Like characters in a comedy, so in a painting each figure must be in its place, play its part, and so contribute to the expression of the general idea. Nothing arbitrary and nothing superfluous, such is the law of every artistic composition.[2]

As the comparison with the theatre shows, the viewer's position here is analogous to the theatre audience, before whom, and towards whom, the comedy is enacted. From a viewpoint in the stalls, the action is visible, intelligible, coherent – laid out before the viewer so that each figure can be seen to be 'in its place', and the 'general idea' is made clear. Yet it was not only the viewer's physical position that was at stake. Comprehension of the 'general idea' depended, too, on a shared set of interpretative procedures, protocols, and these depended, in turn, on shared frameworks of assumption about the shape of the social universe – about issues of gender, class and race.

facing page   Pierre-Auguste Renoir, *Ball at the Moulin de la Galette (Bal du Moulin de la Galette)* (detail of pl. 110)

Nineteenth-century viewers approached the business of interpretation rather differently from the ways in which we do today. The impact of modernist aesthetics has led us first to look at the overall effect of a work of art, and only later, if at all, to scrutinise its details. By contrast, this close scrutiny, this search for cues – or clues – to interpretation, was fundamental in the nineteenth century. We, now, tend to look at a picture from the outside in; they viewed it from the inside out, as the detailed readings of pictures in nineteenth-century art criticism show so clearly. In this process, they were constantly alert to a range of signs and clues in the image – the physiognomies, gestures and expressions of the figures, together with the attributes and details that surrounded them.

As we have seen, it was Manet's *The Balcony* (pl. 7) and *Luncheon* (pl. 4) that spurred Castagnary to formulate his prescriptions for the ideal genre painting. His specific criticisms of them demonstrate nineteenth-century viewing procedures in practice. He found the viewer's position in them indeterminate; there was no coherent interaction between the figures, and their focuses of attention were unclear; and some of the details in the pictures appeared puzzling or inconsistent. Beyond this, as we have argued in Chapter One, these uncertainties can be seen as posing a wider challenge to the systems of classification upon which the standard codes were based; Manet's universe was not only illegible, it was also disruptive.

The ideal notion of total visibility of the theatre audience was a one-way relationship. The action on the stage was placed at the disposal of the viewer, who in turn remained anonymous, invisible to the protagonists, protected by the barrier of the proscenium arch – the barrier that, as we have seen, Castagnary felt was threatened by the position of the boy in Manet's *Luncheon*. Michael Fried's celebrated distinction between absorption and theatricality helps to clarify the issues here.[3] In an absorptive composition or stage scenario, the action is self-contained, exclusively directed towards the other protagonists in the scene, or contained within a single figure. The theatrical mode, by contrast, turns towards the audience, seeking to engage its attention and emotions by addressing it directly. Yet in its classic forms – whether in a Renaissance altarpiece or a decorative canvas by François Boucher – the theatrical mode treats the audience as an anonymous unit, whether it be at prayer before the altar in the chapel or at leisure in a Rococo palace. Neither the absorptive nor the theatrical picture implicates the viewer as an individual, as a potentially active participant in the scene. In both modes, there remains an impermeable barrier that tells the viewer that the action on the stage, or in the picture, belongs in a categorically different realm from the viewer's own space.

The characteristic viewpoints adopted by the Impressionists, in their different ways, break down the barriers between the worlds of the picture and the viewer. They place the viewer in a closer, more engaged relationship with the scene, rejecting the all-commanding position that allowed the whole scene to be immediately taken in and comprehended, as if from the theatre stalls. Scenes are sometimes viewed from above, sometimes in a casual or fragmentary way, while in other pictures the viewer seems directly implicated by one figure within the scene, thus denying the habitual distance that enables the all-over view.

To borrow a phrase from Ross Chambers, the Impressionists' modern life subjects are a 'first-person genre':[4] their scenarios are constructed in such a way that they invoke the painter's presence as an active viewer of a real-life scene, and invite the viewer of the painting to visualise himself or herself in a similar position. Renoir's brother Edmond expressed this explicitly in 1879: 'What [Renoir] has painted, we see every day; it is our own existence that he has registered in pages that will for sure remain among the most alive and the most harmonious of the epoch.'[5]

The viewer's presence may be invoked in a number of distinct ways. The engagement is at its most immediate when a figure looks directly out of the canvas at the viewer, as so often in Manet. As Fried has argued, this marks a return to a form of theatricality, but one that is very different from the classic forms of theatricality, because the address of these figures is so direct. This is a crucial element in the type of relationship with the viewer that Fried has characterised as 'facing' – a term that he uses to encompass both the positioning of the figures and the shallow, frontally orientated picture space.[6] Yet a focus on 'facing' ignores the other ways in which the scene may actively engage the viewer. The argument in this chapter is that the other types of characteristic viewpoint in the Impressionists' modern life scenes also involved, and implicated, the viewer in unfamiliar ways, by collapsing the barrier between the viewer's space and the action within the picture.

Broadly, we can distinguish three different ways in which this engagement was envisaged. The presence of a frontal figure within the picture invites the viewer to imagine himself or herself as a bodily participant in the scene, with whose physical presence the figure in the picture is engaging. This contact is immediate and seemingly personalised: it is as if this figure is engaging with each viewer individually, as a personal contact, and that the viewer is directly implicated in the implied narrative of the picture. By contrast, especially in Degas's work, the viewer's participation may be more spatial than bodily; he or she may be located in a specific, identifiable viewpoint, able to survey the scene, but remaining invisible – seeing without being seen. The third position can be described as optical; here the viewing does not seek to penetrate the viewed space, but rather focuses on the play of visual *sensations*, viewing the ebb and flow of modern life in terms of patches of colour. This position is what has conventionally been characterised as an 'Impressionist' vision; in the present context, it is most relevant to the work of Monet and Renoir, although, as we shall insist in this and the next chapter, its claims to optical neutrality cannot be taken at face value.

However, the viewers' active involvement with the world depicted in the picture was not only a matter of their implied physical presence; nineteenth-century viewers were also, crucially, implicated as historical subjects.[7] Very often, the sites and activities depicted were scenarios with which they would have been personally familiar, or at least would have known well by reputation. Beyond this, these particular places were not neutral during the 1870s; they were loaded with associations that would inevitably have involved the viewer as a social, political and moral agent. More specifically, these experiments occurred in a very distinctive historical and political situation – during the repressive 'moral order' regime that followed the disasters of 1870–71, the French defeat in the Franco–Prussian War and the civil strife of the Paris Commune; the conclusion of the chapter will explore the implications of this historical conjunction.

These issues offer a revealing framework for a discussion of the Impressionists' figure subjects of the 1870s. The argument that follows will focus on the principal means by which the organisation of the picture might guide – or thwart – interpretation. First of these is the question of the physical viewpoint that the paintings propose, and the implications of the viewer's positioning. We shall then explore the interrelationships between figures within the picture and the relationships established between them and the viewer, and the uses of details and attributes as aids – or obstacles – to reading. The final issue is characterisation – the relationship between individualisation and typecasting in the treatment of the figures.

The title of this chapter seeks to embrace all of these issues. Among the 'viewers of modern life' were of course the painters; but we shall also be centrally concerned with the viewers of the pictures, in their original contexts, and with depictions of acts of viewing. Nor can we avoid our own position as historical viewers, scrutinising both the pictures and the complex literature that has grown up around them, literature to which this chapter adds and with which it seeks to engage. We are dealing with active relationships – between viewers and pictures, and between figures within pictures; a social history of art is richer and more productive if it conceives its project in these dynamic terms, rather than primarily in the enumeration of contextual information about the artists' subject matter.

What emerges from the paintings is not a consistent pattern. As we shall see, at times standard markers of social classification, especially of class and gender, remain in play, though these may be complicated by the proximity of the viewer – by the ways in which the pictures invite the viewer to imagine himself or herself as a witness of the scene, or even an active participant. Elsewhere, such markers are blurred or actively subverted. This reiterates the distinction made in Chapter One, between the two contrasting notions of the viewpoint of the *flâneur* – the detective and the *curieux*. The detective seeks out the clues that will enable him to identify and locate everything he sees, and ultimately to make sense of the whole complex organism of the city. By contrast, the other type of viewer recognises that, in the flux of the modern city, the quintessential experience is of *curiosité* – he is constantly open to the experiences around him, but aware that the city is ultimately unknowable.

A further central issue will help us to unravel the complex networks of relationships that the paintings create – the question of work and leisure. Images of work abounded in the exhibition paintings of the 1860s and 1870s. However, the work depicted was generally remote from the world of the viewer, set in the fields of rural France; and the workers shown were usually women (e.g. pl. 72), though what we know of French agricultural practices at the period tells us that most field workers were in fact men.[8] In these pictures, the corollary of work was rest, often depicted in images of figures resting in the fields after labour, presenting rest as a seemingly natural reward for work. Leisure belonged to a rather different sphere – to the world of the privileged, who did not need to work, or to the professional, who earned leisure through work. In fine art, the theme of leisure generally belonged in the private spaces of the bourgeois home (e.g. pl. 3); in these feminine spaces, work appeared on occasion in the person of the domestic servant (e.g. pl. 5).

The experience of the city challenged the normative view of the relationship between work and rest that the rural images express so clearly. In them, rest was the reward for committed work. In the city, the position was less clear. For some – for the wealthy – leisure might be the norm, not a privilege; for the successful bourgeois professional, leisure was a right, earned through his skills and success; for workers further down the economic scale, it was a privilege that they were seeking to turn into a right, through legislation to limit the hours of the working week. However, for the unemployed it was work that was the privilege, and leisure the all-too-permanent state of having nothing to do and no money to enjoy the leisure activities that Paris so abundantly offered.[9] The painter's position was still more complex. Generally, in urban themes the viewpoint presented was implicitly that of a person – generally a man – of leisure; yet the painter was a worker, and the painting the product of work, though designed for sale as a leisure item, a form of high-class luxury goods. In the relationships that we are exploring, these were issues of immediate relevance.

*   *   *

A key passage in Duranty's essay of 1876, *La nouvelle peinture*, insists on the central importance of the physical viewpoint in the 'new painting'; for him, novel viewpoints are one of the defining characteristics of the modern experience of the world. Insisting that 'in real life the appearance of things and people are unexpected in a thousand different ways', he lists some of the most characteristic experiences: figures seen off-centre, objects viewed from above or below, scenes observed out of windows, and forms seen only partially, cut off by a frame or some other intruding object.[10] All of these viewing positions, of course, also contravene standard artistic conventions; when they were presented in fine art, their unexpectedness was at one and the same time a marker of the modernity of the experience itself and of the 'newness' of the painting. Yet in practice the effects they created were complex, as an exploration of some of the most recurrent patterns will show.

At first sight, the high viewpoint may seem to be a means of maximising visibility and knowledge, and hence control over the scene; the quintessential visual form for this in the nineteenth century was the panorama, presenting a 360-degree view of a place, as seen from a real or imaginary viewpoint.[11] This vision appeared, too, in rectangular paintings, for instance in the views of Paris by Victor Navlet from the early 1850s; these culminated in his gigantic *General View of Paris, taken from the Observatoire* (pl. 87),

87   Victor Navlet, *General View of Paris, taken from the Observatoire* (*Vue générale de Paris, prise de l'Observatoire*), 1855, 390 × 708, Musée d'Orsay, Paris

88   J. J. Grandville, illustration from
Le Diable à Paris, 1845–6

shown in the architecture section of the Exposition Universelle of 1855, and purchased
there by Napoleon III for the nation. From the imagined viewpoint of a balloon high
over the southern edges of the city, we look down on Paris bathed in sunshine, its streets
(pre-Haussmannisation) laid out beneath us, with the newly built Palais de l'Industrie,
site of the Exposition Universelle, nestling in the distance alongside the Champs Elysées.
The same idea of the omniscient view from above was used with satirical intent in *Le
Diable à Paris*, a widely circulated volume of sketches of modern Parisian life, first published in 1845–6, which begins with the conceit of the devil's emissary deciding that
it was 'sensible to *flâner* a little above the vast Parisian ant-hill in order to get a sense
of its overall shape' (see pl. 88).[12] Yet, used in other ways, the raised viewpoint might
equally serve to distance the viewer, or indeed to obscure the scene itself: the veil of mist
was one of the leitmotivs of the imagery of the nineteenth-century city.[13]

89   Claude Monet, *The Boulevard des
Capucines* (*Le Boulevard des Capucines*),
1873, 61 × 80, Pushkin Museum, Moscow

90 Claude Monet, *The Quai du Louvre* (*Le Quai du Louvre*), 1867, 65 × 92, Gemeentemuseum, The Hague

Four groups of pictures by Monet will introduce the issues – his views from the Louvre of 1867, the canvases of the Boulevard des Capucines of 1873, the Tuileries Gardens views of 1876, and the street scenes of the Fête Nationale of 1878. The canvases of 1867 show the daily life of modern Paris – the comings and goings of diverse types in the street and on the newly refurbished *quai*, against the backdrop of the buildings of old Paris. The novelty lies in the personnel, and in the distinctive street furniture; in *The Quai du Louvre* (pl. 90) the form of the dome of the Panthéon on the horizon is wittily played off against the kiosk down on the *quai* where the action is, and the equestrian statue of Henri IV on the Ile de la Cité in the background against the horses on the roadway. The informal compositions with their multiple focuses enhance the sense of immediacy. Yet there was another way in which the viewpoint of these paintings marked Monet's rejection of artifice and convention. In order to paint on the Louvre balcony, Monet had to write to the authorities for permission – as did any young artist wishing to copy from the old masters in the museum.[14] Yet Monet's project was literally to turn his back on the masters, and to explore the living world that lay outside the museum windows; it was a marvellously apt viewpoint from which to launch himself as a painter of modern Paris.

The Boulevard des Capucines views of 1873 (e.g. pl. 89) have been seen as reflecting a 'meretricious delight in the modern' and nothing more than 'touristic entertainment'.[15]

91 Claude Monet, *The Tuileries (Les Tuileries)*, 1876, 53 × 72, Musée Marmottan–Claude Monet, Paris

Certainly the figures in them are scarcely differentiated and little is made of the specific topographical elements in the scene depicted. Yet the presence of the figures at the right margin, surveying the scene from a balcony adjacent to our own, alerts us to the act of viewing and to the relativeness of our own viewing position – a central ingredient in the experience of the modern city. In the more highly worked version of the scene (pl. 89) – presumably the one exhibited in 1874 – these figures are crisply and clearly defined. Moreover, the dehumanisation of the figures below can be read as a comment on the experience of strolling on the crowded boulevard. It was, perhaps, not wholly in jest that Louis Leroy, in his satirical review of the first group exhibition, had his imaginary academic painter M. Vincent ask what these 'innumerable black tongue-lickings' represented, and expostulate: 'So I look like that when I stroll along the boulevard des Capucines? . . . Are you making fun of me at last?'[16]

Monet's views of the Tuileries Gardens of 1876 (pls 91, 92) are one instance where we can legitimately discuss what lay beyond the margins at which Monet chose to frame his pictures, since the site would have been so well known to his viewers. Overlooking the radiant, sunlit gardens stood the ruins of the Tuileries Palace, burnt out by the Communards in 1871, and left standing until 1883. In *The Tuileries* (pl. 91), the

92 Claude Monet, *The Tuileries*, *Sketch* (*Les Tuileries, esquisse*), 1876, 50 × 75, Musée d'Orsay, Paris

reminders are explicit: in front of the Pavillon de Flore, the end pavilion of the Louvre that frames the canvas on the left, can be seen the foundations of the south end of the Tuileries Palace, demolished before the remainder of the palace (see pl. 93); and the shadowed block in the far right background of the picture, though not treated in any detail, represents the ruined façade of the Cour des Comptes (on the site of the present Musée d'Orsay), another of the public buildings fired by the Communards, and left standing as a mute witness.[17] In the other three of Monet's views, including plate 92, the shadowy form of the Cour des Comptes can be seen to the left, across the river.[18]

93 *The Tuileries Palace in Ruins*, carte-de-visite photograph, *c.*1871, private collection, London

94 (*right*) Giuseppe de Nittis, *Place des Pyramides*, 1875, 92 × 74, Musée d'Orsay, Paris

95 Claude Monet, *Rue Saint-Denis, 30 June 1878 (La Rue Saint-Denis, le 30 juin 1878)*, 1878, 76 × 52, Musée des Beaux-Arts, Rouen

96 (*facing page*) Edouard Manet, *The Rue Mosnier with Flags (La Rue Mosnier pavoisée)*, 1878, 65.5 × 81, The J. Paul Getty Museum, Los Angeles

It was, certainly, possible to address the ruins of the Tuileries and their implications far more directly, as Giuseppe de Nittis did in *Place des Pyramides* (pl. 94), exhibited at the Salon of 1876, in which we, and Emmanuel Frémiet's newly installed equestrian statue of Joan of Arc, watch over the reconstruction of the Pavillon de Marsan, with the ruins of the Tuileries and the Pavillon de Flore beyond.[19] However, Monet's canvases, and especially *The Tuileries* (pl. 91), seem pointed in their juxtaposition between casual leisure and the lessons of history, rather than simply seeking to anaesthetise recent history by focusing exclusively on visual *sensations*.

Much the same issues are raised by Monet's street scenes of the Fête Nationale held on 30 June 1878 (e.g. pl. 95). The effect of the sea of flags and the crowds below – all sketched with seemingly effortless virtuosity – is immediately festive. Yet, as Jane Roos has pointed out, Manet's street scenes painted at the same time (e.g. pl. 96) seem to register far more pointedly the equivocal politics of this festival. It was invented to celebrate France's recovery after the Franco-Prussian War and the opening of the Exposition Universelle, and yet at the same time the government was determined to avoid any troubling political associations (as we shall see, the institution of the Republican festival of 14 July in 1880 allowed a far more overt declaration of political values).[20] Manet, looking out of the window of his studio, peopled his street with pointed juxtapositions of figures. On the left, a one-legged man on crutches (presumably a war veteran, unable to work) appears alongside a ladder, implicitly carried by an able-bodied worker, while

on the right a top-hatted man and two women are placed on the pavement alongside a small fashionable carriage, perhaps hinting at the very different type of work–leisure relationship represented by prostitution, for which this area of the new Paris was already renowned.[21] Alongside this, Monet's scenes seem distanced and merely spectacular. Whereas Manet gives us an overview of the street and its passing occupants, though leaving the relationships among them and with the viewer undetermined, the distancing effect of Monet's viewpoint prevents any scrutiny of the individuals who make up the crowd. However, in *The Rue Saint-Denis* (pl. 95), the flag on the right is, virtually illegibly, inscribed 'vive la répub[lique]', and, amid the play of coloured touches, it is easy to miss the banner hanging across the street that reads 'vive la France'. Should these be seen merely as uncritical transcriptions of the slogans of the Fête Nationale, or can their absorption into the overall spectacle be viewed, rather, as a comment of sorts on the evasion of politics and history that the festival itself represented? Monet's art of the 1870s leaves us with many questions such as these.

As has often been noted, the Impressionists' views of Paris from high viewpoints invite comparison with the stereoscopic views of the city that had been produced in huge quantities over the previous two decades.[22] In the face of arguments that these photographs played a formative part in the Impressionists' street scenes, Kirk Varnedoe asked: 'what did photographic pictures show painters that other pictures had not shown?' and concluded: 'little of any significance'.[23] Certainly, Monet's views of 1867 from the Louvre

97   *The Boulevard Saint-Martin, Paris*, stereoscopic photograph, late 1850s, private collection, London

are fully in line with a whole range of previous topographical imagery, in the form of paintings and prints as well as photographs, and, as Varnedoe has shown, the radical disjunctions of space and scale in Degas's *Place de la Concorde* of 1875 (currently Hermitage, Saint Petersburg) have no parallels in photography at that date.[24] In more general terms, too, as I have insisted (see pp. 96–8), an Impressionist painting was quite unlike a photograph in several crucial ways: in scale and colour, in its ostentatiously handmade quality, in the premeditation involved in its composition and in the arrangement – however apparently random – of figures, and in being presented in a fine art context.

Yet there are qualities in many of these photographs, as in some of the surroundings of Paris (see pl. 86), that cannot be found in any other contemporary or previous imagery – specifically, an informality and impromptu appearance that bypassed the conventions of the topographical print. This might appear in the oblique angle of vision, in the casual placing of figures, in abrupt contrasts of scale between foreground and background, or in the seemingly casual intrusion of forms at the edges of the composition (see pls 97–101).[25] It is clearly inappropriate and anachronistic to discuss these in terms of a specifically photographic aesthetic; yet stereoscopic photographs were a very widely circulated form of visual imagery that presented the urban scene with an unparalleled immediacy. It is in such photographs, too, that we can find the closest parallels to Monet's figures on a balcony overlooking the boulevard des Capucines (pl. 97, compare pl. 89), and to Manet's backstreet framed by a building site (pl. 98, compare pl. 96), as well as to the plunging viewpoints in some of Caillebotte's street scenes (cf. e.g. pls 99, 101) and the stark juxtaposition of foreground bridge and distant vista in some of Monet's river scenes (cf. pl. 100).

98 *Chaussée d'Antin, Paris: Streets Under Construction*, single frame from a stereoscopic photograph, early/mid-1860s, private collection, London

99 *Boulevard des Capucines, Paris*, single frame from a stereoscopic photograph, early/mid-1860s, private collection, London

100 *The Pont du Carrousel, Paris*, single frame from a stereoscopic photograph, late 1850s, private collection, London

101 *Quai Voltaire and the Pont Royal, Paris*, single frame from a stereoscopic photograph, early/mid-1860s, private collection, London

102   Gustave Caillebotte, *Young Man at his Window (Jeune homme à sa fenêtre)*, 1875, 117 × 82, private collection

The viewer's position is especially complex in Caillebotte's *Young Man at his Window* of 1875 (pl. 102). Although the model has been identified as Caillebotte's brother René, his face is unseen and the original title of the picture establishes only the young man's proprietorial position at his own window. Nor can we see what he is looking at, or indeed whether he is focusing on anything at all. We, the viewers of the picture, see a carriage on the far side of the street, a single female figure, placed pivotally from our standpoint, and a horse just to the left of her, perhaps attached to another carriage. But the young man's angle of vision is different from ours, and we do not know what he can see that is hidden from us. The picture poses alternative points of view, spatially and socially. The young man may be waiting for someone, or he may have the leisure habitually to survey the street; we may imagine ourselves as either an insider or an outsider in the room, and may visualise ourselves either watching the young man or looking past him onto the street.[26]

In Degas's art, the high viewpoint appears primarily in theatre interiors. Here he systematically undercuts the imaginary ideal view from the stalls that Castagnary had posited. Characteristically, his views from theatre boxes scan the stage diagonally, their line of vision cutting across the ideal frontal view. Where an actual performance is depicted, the figure of one of the performers may be cut off by the margin of the picture, or else we may see dancers or male onlookers waiting in the wings who would be invisible from the stalls (e.g. pl. 103). In rehearsal scenes (e.g. pl. 104), the dancers who are actually performing are often subordinated to the clusters of waiting figures – distracted, fidgeting, scratching themselves – who divert our attention from what we would expect to be the primary action.

Yet the viewer is rarely left in any doubt about the status of the figures in Degas's compositions and their reasons for being where they are. The dancers are identifiable by their clothes, and the dancing masters clearly differentiated. We are placed in a world with which the original viewers of the pictures would have been very familiar and which they would have been well able to interpret. The unexpected viewpoints and the inclusion of the peripheral figures and incidental gestures place the viewer in the position of insider – familiar with the inside workings of the ballet world, not just with the view from the stalls. This viewer is a man of leisure and with privileged access,[27] watching figures at work or resting after tiring work.

Even when Degas did represent the stage as seen from the stalls, he ensured that we are not given a straightforward view. Seated in the front row as we are in *The*

103   Edgar Degas, *L'Etoile*, 1876–7, 58 × 42, pastel on monotype, Musée d'Orsay, Paris

104 (*below*)   Edgar Degas, *Rehearsal on the Stage* (*La Répétition sur la scène*), *c.*1874, 53.3 × 72.3, The Metropolitan Museum of Art, New York, H. O. Havemeyer Collection, Bequest of Mrs H. O. Havemeyer, 1929. (29.100.39)

105 Edgar Degas, *The Orchestra of the Opera* (*L'Orchestre de l'Opéra*), c.1870, 56.5 × 46.2, Musée d'Orsay, Paris

106 Edgar Degas, *Ballet of Robert le Diable* (*Ballet de Robert le Diable*), 1876, 76.6 × 81.3, Victoria and Albert Museum, London

Orchestra of the Opera (pl. 105), we focus on the players, not the dancers on the stage, who are beheaded by the framing of the scene. Seated further back, as in *The Ballet of Robert le Diable* (pl. 106), our attention is diverted from the action on the stage by the man in the audience who gazes through his binoculars at a box out of sight to our left; this is evidently of far more interest to him – and implicitly perhaps to us, denied the knowledge of what he is looking at – than the celebrated ballet of nuns in the third act of Giacomo Meyerbeer's opera that is unfolding on the stage before us.[28]

This introduces the second type of viewpoint that is characteristic of the Impressionists' Parisian scenes, the position at ground level that allows us to see a scene in a seemingly casual or partial way. Four paintings shown at the third group exhibition in 1877 tackled this approach in a particularly ambitious way – Caillebotte's street scenes and Renoir's *Ball at the Moulin de la Galette*.

Caillebotte's canvases place us on the pavement. In *Paris Street: Rainy Weather* (pl. 107) the umbrellas make this a constricted space. The male figure cut off by the right margin has to duck to the side to avoid the seemingly impervious couple coming towards us, and we are invited to imagine ourselves repeating this manoeuvre: no privileged viewpoint, this. Beyond the complexities of negotiating this foreground space, the star-shaped road intersection offers the viewer a range of options, of where to turn; it is up to us to chart our imaginative path through the rectilinear streets of the new Paris. *The Pont de l'Europe* (pl. 109) offers a wider space, but one that represents an equally casual intersection of different lives and different agendas. Only the dog, it seems, is headed in the same direction as we are; but at the same time the two male figures in working-class dress who lean on the railing offer us the alternative of pausing to look out over the tracks leading into the Gare Saint-Lazare. Class is still more central to our position in *House-Painters* (pl. 108), since the working-class figure standing on the pavement blocks our path; he forces us to imagine ourselves repeating the detour into the roadway that we assume the top-hatted figure further down the pavement has made before us, as he, and we, pursue a path down the relentless straightness of the new street.[29] The status of this standing worker, though, is uncertain; nothing in the picture tells us whether he is part of the painting team or a passer-by who has stopped to watch (he is dressed very similarly to the foreground worker in *The Pont de l'Europe*): he might represent work, or privileged leisure, or forced leisure.

As in these pictures by Caillebotte, we are not placed in a direct relationship to any of the protagonists in Renoir's *Ball at the Moulin de la Galette* (pl. 110). Our eye plays across the casually grouped figures – those dancing and conversing in the background, the woman and child at lower left – and rests on the cluster of young men and women in the right foreground. Yet here, by contrast with the Caillebottes, there is no disjunction between our viewpoint and the scene in front of us; we can readily imagine making our way to the dance floor or joining the group on the right. Even the backs of the benches and the chair in the foreground pose no barrier to our engagement with the scene; indeed, the elbows of the woman in the striped dress and the nearest man cross, and seemingly defuse, this apparent barrier.

The relationships established between the viewer and the scene in these canvases cannot be separated from the relationships that are set up between the figures within the scene. Here the contrasts between Caillebotte and Renoir are particularly striking. Although some of the figures in *Paris Street: Rainy Weather* are in pairs,[30] there is no trace of communication between any of these pairs or the many isolated figures; the

107 Gustave Caillebotte, *Paris Street: Rainy Weather (Rue de Paris: temps de pluie)*, 1877, 212.2 × 276.2, The Art Institute of Chicago, Charles H. and Mary F. S. Worcester Collection

108 Gustave Caillebotte, *House-Painters (Peintres en bâtiments)*, 1877, 87 × 116, private collection

109   Gustave Caillebotte, *The Pont de l'Europe* (*Le Pont de l'Europe*), 1876, 124.7 × 180.6, Musée du Petit Palais, Geneva

dominant effect of the picture is of an atomised society in which everyone goes about their own business or pleasure. The relationships between figures are much more problematic in *The Pont de l'Europe*. Here, recent commentators have proffered wholly different readings of the bourgeois man and woman who walk towards us – of the relationship (if any) between them and of what they are looking at. For one, the man's 'rapid pace has carried him beyond the woman, in whom, none the less, he shows an interest (as she does in him)';[31] for another, they are 'uninhibitedly engaging in a flirtatious exchange';[32] whereas for a third recent viewer the man is looking at the view across the rail tracks, beyond the picture frame to the right, while the woman appears to look beyond the man to the left.[33]

The very fact of such a stark disagreement should alert us to the fundamental ambiguity of the relationships that the picture presents. To nineteenth-century viewers and to Caillebotte himself, these uncertainties would have been all the more evident, habituated as they were to reading the relationships in genre paintings that followed the convention that 'each figure must be in its place, play its part, and so contribute to the expression of the general idea'. The two commentators in 1877 who described this group in any detail agreed that there was some relationship between the two, but seem to differ on the nuances of the interchange. Gaston Vassy wrote, no doubt with a touch of irony:

'The principal figure is the painter himself, chatting from close to with a very pretty woman – doubtless another portrait. Our compliments, M. Caillebotte . . . That day, you must have had *des impressions gaies*![34] For Jacques, there was a hint of prostitution; they were 'a young man of leisure, walking ahead of *une élégante*, exquisite beneath her speckled transparent veil: a common little comedy, that we have all observed, with a discreet and benevolent smile'.[35] Certainly the juxtaposition of these two figures and the seeming reciprocity of their gestures invite us to imagine a relationship between them. But close examination of the picture confirms that the male figure is looking out to his left, and not directly at the woman; thus it remains possible that their proximity is just one of the meaningless momentary conjunctions characteristic of city life. And, even if we do pursue the idea of a relationship between them, we have no means of telling whether they are a couple on a joint promenade who are momentarily out of step,[36] or whether the man is about to proposition a *passante* – a woman whom he has spotted in passing in the street.[37]

The relationships work very differently in Renoir's *Ball at the Moulin de la Galette*. In the main, people are in pairs or small clusters. These many groupings are generally

110   Pierre-Auguste Renoir, *Ball at the Moulin de la Galette (Bal du Moulin de la Galette)*, 1876, 131 × 175, Musée d'Orsay, Paris

111　Federico
Zandomeneghi,
*The Moulin de la
Galette* (*Le Moulin de
la Galette*), 1878,
80 × 120, private
collection, Milan

relaxed and harmonious, and are woven into an overall composition that has none of
the gaps and disjunctions that are so evident in Caillebotte's canvases. Only at three
points in the background are there hints of disaccord: on a bench at back left, a woman
turns away from the attentions of a top-hatted man; in the centre, the female in a dancing
couple seems to pull away from her over-ardent partner; and on the right a woman leans
against a tree-trunk, her back turned to the man who seeks to engage her attention.

Most interesting is the larger group in the right foreground – three men and three
women. The men are seated around a table, the women all on the other side of a bench,
and thus not part of the same party. Yet the nearer seated woman and her standing companion engage with the nearest man, whose companions look on; the third woman –
not emphasised, and recognisable only by her ear and the contour of her hat – turns
her back on the other two, yet sits so close to them that we sense no psychological
distance. Certainly, by the standards of decorum expected of the nineteenth-century
genre painting, this is a questionable group; we are witnessing some sort of meeting in
a place of public entertainment, across the divide suggested by the bench-back. Yet
Renoir moulds this potentially disorderly subject into a gentle and seamless interplay
that defuses its disruptive associations. However, like Caillebotte, he does avoid the
clearly signposted scenarios of conventional genre painting. The harmonious interplay
of figures generates an overall mood, but consistently his groups defy precise interpretation, denying the viewer the possibility of reading any specific sentimental narrative
into them.

This seamlessness is integral to the vision of class relationships that Renoir's picture
presents. Most of the male figures are informally dressed, but among them there are a
number of top-hatted figures – some seemingly *haut bourgeois*, some more bohemian
in appearance; the women are smartly and prettily dressed, but clearly not figures of
high fashion or high class. Subsequent accounts of the picture – mostly based on the
testimony of Renoir's friend Georges Rivière – have 'emphasised the working-class
origins of the women who posed' for the picture, and have identified the male figures
as friends of Renoir's.[38] Yet, outside the painter's immediate circle, the picture's original
viewers would have had no idea of the identity of Renoir's models. Their point of reference would have been the contemporary reputation of the Moulin de la Galette itself,

112 Edouard Manet, *Café-Concert*,
1878, 47.5 × 30.2, The Walters Art
Gallery, Baltimore, Acquired by Henry
Walters, 1909. 37.893

and of Montmartre as a centre of political dissent and – recently – of the activities of
the Commune. It is in this context that Renoir's image of harmonious coexistence would
have seemed so striking.[39] Striking too is the contrast between Renoir's picture and
another painting of *The Moulin de la Galette* by an associate of the Impressionist group,
Federico Zandomeneghi, of 1878 (pl. 111); here, we see the outside of the place, with
figures furtively yet eagerly entering through a door in a blank wall which excludes the
viewer from the imagined activities within.

Renoir's domestication of markers of class in places of urban entertainment is in
marked contrast with Manet's treatment of similar themes. In Manet's café scenes of
the later 1870s, such as *The Café-Concert* (pl. 112), class difference is paraded, and the
effect of these contrasts is heightened by the stark disjunctions between figures – often
looking in opposite directions, often cut by the picture frame. City life, as depicted here,
is fragmented, incoherent; the individuals in the scene live in separate worlds, seemingly
without the possibility of shared experience. The effect of dislocation is heightened by
the figure of the waitress, herself pausing to drink: a moment of leisure for the worker
in the scene, and one that would have been especially disturbing for nineteenth-century
viewers, for whom these so-called *femmes de brasserie* were emblems of the moral degradation of the city.[40]

This sense of non-communication is carried over into Manet's canvases of a man and
a woman together. In *Argenteuil* (pl. 113) the woman looks impassively at the viewer,
seemingly impervious to the man, all of whose gestures invade her space. At first sight,
the relationship in *In the Conservatory* (pl. 114) can be more easily read, as the man
leans towards the woman across the back of the bench, and their hands, with their
wedding rings, almost meet; but her gaze is distant, and we notice that his hand is placed

113 Edouard Manet, *Argenteuil*, 1874, 149 × 115, Musée des Beaux-Arts, Tournai

114 (*below*) Edouard Manet, *In the Conservatory* (*Dans la serre*), 1879, 115 × 150, Nationalgalerie, Berlin

115 Edgar Degas, *In a Café* (*Dans un café*) (known as *L'Absinthe*), 1875–6, 92 × 68, Musée d'Orsay, Paris

where it is in order to hold a large cigar. In both pictures, we are denied access to the couple's relationship. Yet there is nothing in their treatment – in their facial expressions or their body language – that gives any explicit indication of trouble or disturbance between them, and Manet makes nothing of the hothouse associations of the conservatory, which play so central a role in the erotic drama of Zola's novel *La Curée* of 1872. The seemingly casual moments that Manet has chosen to present yield no clues and deny the viewer any imagined access to the figures' interiority.[41] Even where some form of flirtation is clearly taking place, in *Chez le Père Lathuille* (Musée des Beaux-Arts, Tournai), the oddity of the man's position (seemingly crouching without a chair[42]) and the total inscrutability of the woman's expression prevent any clear reading of their relationship. The titles of the canvases, indicating only the location of the scene, are equally uninformative.

In some ways the same is true of Degas's *In a Café* (pl. 115), where again a man and a woman are shown side by side but not communicating. Yet here the blank expression of the female figure invites empathy in a way that the figures in Manet's paintings do not; reviewing the canvas at the third group exhibition in 1877, Frédéric Chevalier described her as 'une dame troublante'. When the picture was given the title *L'Absinthe* at an exhibition in London in 1893, responses to its imagery became far more outspoken.[43] In its original context, and with its original neutral title, the hints of misery and degradation would have been more oblique – for Chevalier, she was 'disturbing' (*troublante*), not 'disturbed' (*troublée*). Chevalier's phrase highlights the viewer's response to the figure; a sense of the viewer's presence is also activated by the arrange-

116 Edgar Degas, *Interior (Intérieur)*, *c.*1868–9, 81.3 × 114.3, Philadelphia Museum of Art: The Henry P. McIlhenny Collection in memory of Frances P. McIlhenny

117 (*below*) Edgar Degas, *Sulking (Bouderie)*, *c.*1870, 32.4 × 46.4, The Metropolitan Museum of Art, New York, H. O. Havemeyer Collection, Bequest of Mrs. H. O. Havemeyer, 1929. (29.100.43)

ment of tables in the foreground, and by the newspapers and even Degas's signature: he places himself – and implicitly us – in the café as mute witnesses of these mute figures, watching them obliquely across the angle of the room, but categorically separated from them.

Two earlier canvases by Degas use the languages of gesture and expression more strongly to create the possibilities for psychological narrative. Although *Interior* (pl. 116) has been associated with passages from various novels, notably one from Zola's *Thérèse Raquin* of 1867, it does not correspond to any of these texts.[44] Yet it is rich in details that a nineteenth-century viewer would have sought to interpret: the gestures and expressions of the figures; the discarded corset on the floor and the sewing box on the table; the man by the door and the top hat on the chest at back left; the couple in the room, in contrast to the single bed. Taken together, these thwart the viewer's search for a coherent narrative in the picture. Likewise *Bouderie* (pl. 117; the title can inadequately be translated as *Sulking*[45]) frustrates attempts at interpretation. Its background details, the window-counter at top left, the racing print and the ledgers, can all be associated

with banking and gambling – not inconsistent with each other. But we are given no clue to the relationship between these insistent details and the figures; and the relationship between the figures themselves is ambiguous – the woman turned towards us, the man turned away. Like Manet's canvases of the late 1860s that we explored in Chapter One, these pictures seem deliberately to invite narrative interpretation and then obstruct – or indeed defy – the interpretative process. But,

118 Claude Monet, *The Bench*
(*Le banc*), c.1873, 60 × 80,
The Metropolitan Museum of Art,
New York, The Walter H. and Leonore
Annenberg collection, Gift of Walter H.
Annenberg, 2002. (2002.62.1)

even more than Manet, Degas emphasises bodily gesture and attributive details, forcing
the viewer to seek to interpret them and yet denying the possibility of a 'right reading';
as with Manet, this can only have been a deliberate strategy on Degas's part. However,
as we shall see, Degas's characteristic modern life scenarios of the 1870s do not pose
the same problems. In them, as in the ballet and theatre scenes that we have already
examined, figures are once again 'in their place' and 'play their part'.

Closest to the psychological tensions evoked by *Bouderie* and *Interior* is, perhaps surprisingly, a canvas by Monet, *The Bench* (pl. 118). Although the model for the female
figure was clearly Monet's wife Camille, the picture must be seen as a genre painting,
not a portrait; this carefully staged pictorial scenario should certainly not be seen as evidence of strains in Monet's marriage.[46] We are invited to interpret the relationship
between the two figures, but cannot tell whether the woman is turning away from a
problematic approach, or simply because her attention has been distracted. Interpretation is further hindered by the ambiguity of the object that she holds in her left hand,
which could be either a fan or a sheet of paper, such as a letter.

Monet also painted a sequence of pictures of Camille with their son Jean, sometimes
set in the semi-privacy of their Argenteuil garden, sometimes in the open fields or by
the river. Although varied in their forms and formats, all of these canvases reject the
standard formulae for the depiction of mother–child relationships, which stress the
mother as both protector and admirer of the child (e.g. pls 3, 5). By contrast, Monet's
female figure is never attentive to the child and often looks towards the viewer, while
the boy is sometimes shown playing alone, more often simply standing and facing us.
In the most ambitious of these pictures (pl. 119),[47] Camille stands facing us amid a sea
of flowers and plants, her hands to her head and seemingly parading herself before us,
while Jean sprawls across the grass on his back. Both the mother's seeming self-
absorption and the abandon of the boy's pose (by nineteenth-century standards, surely
both undisciplined and unhealthy) are a travesty of stock parent–child roles. Again, as
with *The Bench*, we should not see these as a commentary on the Monets' family life

119   Claude Monet, *Camille and Jean in the Garden at Argenteuil* (*Camille et Jean au jardin d'Argenteuil*), *c.*1873, 131 × 97, private collection

120 Edouard Manet, *The Railway* (*Le Chemin de fer*), 1873, 93.3 × 114.5, National Gallery of Art, Washington, Gift of Horace Havemeyer in memory of his mother, Louise H. Havemeyer

or Camille's failings as a mother. They can, rather, be viewed in two ways: as a critique of the artifice of the stock representational formulae, and at the same time as a visual evocation of the rival claims placed on the modern bourgeois woman by the worlds of fashion and motherhood. In a more playful mode, Manet explored similar questions in *The Railway* (pl. 120), shown at the Salon of 1874, in which there is no visible contact between the woman – perhaps too young to be the mother – and the young girl, while on the woman's lap a puppy occupies the space usually reserved for a protected child.

Among all these genre scenes of pairs of figures, only Degas's *Interior* is sited in an unequivocally private space, and in this picture alone is the composition wholly absorptive, in Michael Fried's terms. The other canvases all activate the viewer's position in two ways, by showing the figures in settings to which the viewer, in the person of a passer-by or visitor or friend or family member, might have access, and by turning one of the figures to look out of the picture, and often directly at the viewer.

Another such painting, Renoir's *The Theatre Box* (pl. 121), plays on a number of standard contemporary ideas about viewing. The woman looks straight out from the picture, but her gaze seems distanced, abstracted, as if she is looking past or through the viewer, and she makes no use of the instruments of vision – the opera glasses – that she holds in her hand, while her companion looks out through his binoculars – upwards, and thus not towards the stage. Related themes were a stock-in-trade of mid-nineteenth-century engraving. Grandville's *It is Venus in Person* (pl. 122) presents an iconic image of a beautiful young woman in a theatre box, admired by serried ranks of men in the stalls whose heads have been transformed into gigantic staring eyes, while Gavarni's *A Lioness in her Box* (pl. 123) gives an ironic twist to the contrast between the male actively gazing and the female as the passive object of the male gaze; here, the woman is clearly past her prime and perhaps less of an object of admiration than she would like to think, while her male companion, in a swirl of agitated lines, looks eagerly through his binoculars – presumably at another woman. In a sense Renoir's canvas synthesises these two images. He retains Gavarni's joke of the man who, unseen by the woman, looks at someone else, but defuses it by representing the female figure – like Grandville's – as young and desirable. Contemporary critics, though, strongly disagreed about the implied moral status of the woman. Marc de Montifaud (Marie-Amélie Chartroule de Montifaud) saw her as 'borrowed from the elegant world', while both F. de Gantès and Jean Prouvaire viewed her as an archetype of vulgarity and moral corruption, and as an object lesson to the viewer.[48]

By turning the female figure towards us, Renoir places us at the centre of the picture. It is we who – like Grandville's eyes – are looking at the woman and it is our gaze that she receives, but our position is indeterminate, disembodied even, seemingly floating in front of her, quite close to her, yet outside the box she occupies – perhaps suggesting that we, too, are looking through binoculars. The viewer, here, stands for the generic male – the roving eye – in the theatre audience, but the figure's distanced expression and our unspecific spatial location exclude us from an active involvement in the scenario depicted.

In this context, we might note the generic similarity between *The Theatre Box* and Titian's *Woman at her Toilet* in the Louvre (pl. 124). In format, the pictures are closely comparable, and Renoir's canvas may be viewed as a modernisation of the Vanitas theme that is made explicit in the Titian by the play of mirrors: we can imagine Renoir's model as viewing her own reflection in the mirror of our gaze. Of all the Impressionists, it was Renoir alone who continued throughout the 1870s to engage in a close creative dialogue with the art of the past (see also pp. 165–6 and 202–3 below); the developments in his art in the early to mid-1880s were a less radical change of direction than he later liked to make out.

Direct frontal eye contact was the most immediate device used by the Impressionist painters to engage the viewer as a potentially active protagonist in the scene. In the art of the past, there was only a restricted range of situations in which eye contact between a figure in a multi-figure scene and the viewer was permitted. Both the iconography and – often – the physical environment for which the picture was designed ensured that the figure in the picture was seen as belonging to a different sphere of reality from the spectator. Images of the Virgin Mary often make such contact, and figures of saints, and, on occasion, artists' self-portraits may also do so, acting as mediators between the scene and the viewer, whether in a sacred subject such as Botticelli's Lami *Adoration of the*

121 Pierre-Auguste Renoir,
The Theatre Box (La Loge), 1874,
80 × 63, Courtauld Institute Gallery,
London

Magi (Galleria degli Uffizi, Florence) or in a secular situation, as in Velázquez's *Las Meninas* (Prado, Madrid). By contrast, the Impressionists' scenes of modern life belong to the viewer's own world. In recent French art, such contact was extremely unusual; the only subject in which it was regularly deployed was in images of begging, in which a figure made direct appeal to the viewer's charity, as in Adolphe-William Bouguereau's *Indigent Family* (pl. 125).

Yet, even when directly addressed by a figure within the picture, the viewer can assume a wide range of roles. Sometimes few clues are offered. In Manet's *The Railway* or *Argenteuil* (pls 120, 113), where the scene is set in a public space, we may imagine ourselves either as an acquaintance of the figure or as a wholly casual passer-by, the object of a mere passing glance. In the semi-private settings of Monet's garden pictures the male viewer can see himself as the husband/father before whom the tableau of family relationships is being enacted, but we may equally imagine ourselves as a friend or visitor, male or female. Likewise in Degas's *Bouderie* (pl. 117) we cannot tell whether our presence is a factor in the seeming distance between the figures – whether we are implicated in the scene.

122 (*top left*) J. J. Grandville, *It is Venus in Person* (*C'est Vénus en personne*), illustration from *Un autre monde*, XVI, 1843

123 (*top right*) Gavarni, *A Lioness in her Box* (*Une Lionne dans la loge*), illustration from *Le Diable à Paris*, 1845–6

124 (*bottom left*) Titian, *Portrait of a Woman at her Toilet* (*Portrait d'une femme à sa toilette*), c.1514–15, 93 × 76, Musée du Louvre, Paris

125 (*bottom right*) Adolphe-William Bouguereau, *The Indigent Family* (*Famille indigente*) [now known as *Charity*], 1865, 121.9 × 152.4, City Museum and Art Gallery, Birmingham

In Manet's *A Bar at the Folies-Bergère* (pl. 126) such uncertainties become the central theme of the picture, and, as x-rays of the canvas have shown, were deliberately accentuated by Manet during the execution of the canvas.[49] We are immediately invited to imagine ourselves as a client at the bar, but everything else in the picture makes this position problematic. The barmaid's expression is opaque; contemporaries could not agree on how to read it, one describing her as 'full of character', another writing of the 'brightness of her gaze', while a third described her as 'paralysed'.[50] The notorious discrepancies between image and reflection complicate our perception of the viewer's 'real' position; we are invited to imagine ourselves in the position of the top-hatted male figure in the reflection, yet his apparent close engagement with the barmaid is a far cry from the sense of distance that we feel as we face the central figure. Further uncertainties arise from the ambivalent social and moral status of the barmaids in establishments such as the Folies-Bergère – not, it seems, professional prostitutes, but women able to choose their sexual partners.[51]

In *Le Déjeuner sur l'herbe* and *Olympia*, by contrast, the viewer is more unequivocally implicated: in *Le Déjeuner sur l'herbe* by the expression of casual acceptance with which the naked female figure views us, and in *Olympia* by the self-presentation of the figure's pose as well as the directness of her gaze.[52] In *Nana* (pl. 127) our position is still more troubling. A male viewer is faced with a rival, in the person of the top-hatted man seated in a seemingly proprietorial position watching the woman as she applies her make-up; a female viewer, accepted so readily by Nana's gaze, can presumably see herself only as a woman of the same status as Nana. In all three of these canvases, the gaze of

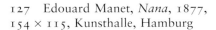

126 (*facing page*)   Edouard Manet,
A Bar at the Folies-Bergère (*Un Bar
aux Folies-Bergère*), 1881–2,
96 × 130, Courtauld Institute
Gallery, London

127   Edouard Manet, *Nana*, 1877,
154 × 115, Kunsthalle, Hamburg

128   Edgar Degas, *Woman
Looking through Field-Glasses*
(*Femme regardant avec une
lorgnette*), *c.*1868, pencil and
essence on paper, 31.4 × 18,
Burrell Collection, Glasgow

the female figures is active and seemingly in control of the situation, denying the male viewer a confident standpoint; yet in broader terms all of them present facets of the world of illicit sex and prostitution, a world in which the male consumer – and viewer – was firmly in control.

In one group of studies by Degas the theme of the woman actively looking at the viewer is treated in a way that leaves its moral connotations more open-ended – in the small canvas *At the Racetrack* (private collection), in which a woman at bottom centre stares directly at us through binoculars; the many related studies of this single figure (pl. 128) testify to the fascination that it held for Degas. This figure, who is accompanied by a fashionably dressed man in *At the Racetrack*, cannot readily be classified in social or moral terms, though her *curiosité* would inevitably have been viewed as problematic in the public space of the racecourse. However, Degas exhibited none of these works and later obliterated this figure, alone, from *At the Racetrack*.[53]

In all the canvases that make such eye contact, the directness of the encounter with the figure in the painting forces the viewer to seek to articulate the nature of that encounter. Our implied bodily presence is one factor, but far more than this is involved in the ways in which these paintings implicate the viewer – and, specifically, implicated their original viewers. For they present a set of signs that would have engaged those who saw them in the 1870s and early 1880s on many levels. In one sense, the compositions of the pictures positioned the viewer spatially; but they also invite us to position ourselves in other ways in relation to what we see – socially, politically, morally, emotionally. And, as we shall see, this positioning involved a whole range of contextual factors, especially during the mid-1870s, that would have conditioned and complicated the viewer's experience of the image.

In this context, the work of Berthe Morisot presents a clear exception, since it conspicuously fails to engage with, or rather actively defuses, the thematics of looking and being looked at that we have been examining. It would be easy to attribute this to Morisot's position as a bourgeois woman, excluded from the public spaces where this male game took place. Yet there is something more calculating, more paradoxical about her treatment of the theme of modern woman that suggests that she was deliberately adopting an anti-flâneurial position, systematically undercutting and repudiating the play of gazes and glances that constituted modernity for the male viewer. When female figures are presented in open spaces, they consistently turn their backs on any wider vistas, absorbed in their own thoughts or solitary activities (e.g. pl. 129);[54] even when, in *Young Woman at her Window* (pl. 130), exhibited at the Salon of 1870, a woman is seated before an open window with a balcony and a view beyond, she remains self-absorbed, looking downwards, not, as we might expect, at a book, but merely at the fan that she holds. The picture's title foreshadows Caillebotte's *Young Man at his Window* (pl. 102), but the figure's relationship to the window could not be more different: Caillebotte's is proprietorial of the space and the view, Morisot's withdrawn and inward-looking.[55]

In her genre paintings of single bourgeois women of the mid- to late 1870s, too, Morisot generally avoided placing the figure in explicitly public spaces, and tended to depict the model's eyes as averted, denying the viewer any imagined interaction with the subject; the eyes, too, are generally downcast and abstracted, not engaged with anything outside the picture space. Even when, as in *At the Ball* (pl. 131), one of the first of this sequence, shown with this title at the group exhibition of 1876, the picture's title spec-

129　Berthe Morisot, *On the Terrace (Sur la terrasse)*, 1874, 45 × 54, Fuji Art Museum, Tokyo

ifies that the setting is semi-public, the model's eyes are studiously disengaged; the effect is not of eyes averted in modesty when faced with an attentive viewer, but a distancing and inwardness that defuses the whole play of gazes. In her paintings of women at mirrors, the female models do engage actively in looking, but their focused attention once again excludes the viewer of the picture. In another sequence of canvases, those showing pairs of figures in gardens and parks from the early 1880s, the figures rarely interact in any intelligible way, and are often presented in ways that emphasise that their attention is not focused on each other. In the rare appearances of Morisot's husband, Eugène Manet, as a model, he is conspicuously disempowered, notably in *Eugène Manet on the Isle of Wight* of 1875 (pl. 132), in which we view him looking awkwardly through a window at a woman and child passing by on the quay outside.

It is not enough to attribute these devices merely to the constraints imposed on Morisot by her gender; it would have been open to her to reapply the stock formulae

130 Berthe Morisot, *Young Woman at her Window* (*Jeune femme à sa fenêtre*), 1869, 54.8 × 46.3, National Gallery of Art, Washington, Ailsa Mellon Bruce Collection

131 Berthe Morisot, *At the Ball* (*Au bal*), 1875, 62 × 52, Musée Marmottan-Claude Monet, Paris

of genre painting in order to evoke seamless social interchange within the feminine sphere. Yet her rejection of these conventions is quite unlike Manet's emphasis on viewing as fragmented, ruptured and illegible. Rather, the figures that she presented, and the viewing position that she posited for the artist/viewer, seem to withdraw consciously from the male preserve of the active play of gazes and glances, as if to repudiate the notion of *flânerie* as a defining characteristic of modern experience, and to posit an alternative world in which modern woman could wilfully manipulate – and abstain from – the whole business of viewing and being viewed.[56]

One final issue was of central importance in the ways in which the Impressionists' modern life pictures were presented to their viewers – the question of the individualisation of the figures within the picture. In standard nineteenth-century artistic theory, portraiture depicted individuals as individuals, while the figures in genre painting were typical, involved in generic activities and situations.[57] As we have seen, though, Manet, in particular, broke down this distinction in many of his major canvases of the 1860s, by giving distinctively individualised features to the figures in his genre paintings. Discussion of this issue has been complicated by the art-historical exploration of the identity of the models who posed for the Impressionists' paintings, which has at times led any picture whose models have been identified to be treated as a portrait. In this context, the titles that the artists gave to the pictures when they were first exhibited are of central importance, since they indicate the ways in which they wanted the pictures to be viewed and interpreted.

Here, we can begin to draw some conclusions about the approaches of the different artists. Throughout his career, Manet continued to particularise the features of his figures, refusing to subscribe to the stereotypical physiognomies of conventional genre painting. It was in response to this that a puzzled reviewer asked of *The Railway* (pl. 120): 'Is Manet's *The Railway* a double portrait or a subject picture? . . . We lack the information to solve the problem; we are even more uncertain about the young girl, for this would be a portrait seen from the rear.'[58] Although few of his viewers would have recognised his models, their evident individuality consistently worked against the possibility of viewing his canvases as 'typical' scenes. This would have heightened the viewer's sense of being a potential participant in the scene, but at the same time it made that scene harder to interpret, since it could not be decoded in terms of any preordained stereotypes. Moreover, the titles that Manet gave his major pictures consistently identify only the setting or the context of the figures, never giving clues to interpreting their identity or the relationships between them.

For a short period around 1870, Degas treated some of his genre paintings in a similar way, in pictures such as *Bouderie* (pl. 117). In the early 1870s, however, he began consistently to make a clear distinction between his treatment of male and female figures in his multi-figure compositions. Females, such as his ballet dancers, are generally treated as types (e.g. pls 103–4); indeed, it has been shown that their facial features, with their

132 Berthe Morisot, *Eugène Manet on the Isle of Wight* (*Eugène Manet à l'Isle de Wight*), 1875, 38 × 46, Musée Marmottan-Claude Monet, Paris

characteristic snub noses and slightly simian features, conform closely to stereotypical ideas of the physiognomy of the lower classes.[59] This process of typecasting extended, too, to the characteristic movements of other female workers; Edmond de Goncourt visited Degas in 1874 to see his latest work: 'He put before our eyes, in their poses and their graceful foreshortening, laundresses, and more laundresses . . . speaking their language and explaining in technical terms the pressure stroke of the iron, the circular stroke, and so on.'[60]

By contrast, men, when they appear, are recognisable individuals enacting their specific professional or personal roles. In the canvases depicting ballet classes and rehearsals, the ballet masters are always images of specific individuals (e.g. pl. 104). Although the compositions feature views from unexpected angles and the figures are grouped in unconventional ways, the male figures are never treated so that they lose their identity or surrender their authority over the anonymous female dancers.[61] The contrast is still stronger in *The Orchestra of the Opera* (pl. 105), where the male players in the orchestra are highly individualised while the framing of the scene beheads the female dancers on the stage.

The individualisation is more explicit in the pictures of groups of men that Degas entitled *Portraits* in the catalogues of the group exhibitions: *Portraits in an Office (New Orleans)* of 1873 (the so-called *Cotton Bureau*, pl. 133), *Portraits at the Stock Exchange* (Musée d'Orsay, Paris) and *Portraits of Friends, on the Stage* (Musée d'Orsay, Paris) both of *circa* 1879. In these, the men's identities are defined in part by their environments – whether at work, at the stock exchange or in the office, or at leisure, in their privileged place back-stage; but the treatment of the figures emphasises that we are dealing with unique individuals, presented as if observed going about their habitual business or pleasure.

Individuality for Degas was also a matter of social class, as well as sex. In the group exhibition of 1881 he included two pastels titled *Criminal Physiognomy*, apparently derived from images of specific male criminals, but treated in a way that emphasised their conformity to physiognomical stereotypes.[62] Individuality, for Degas, was the province of the male bourgeois alone. In the ballet scenes and the *Portraits* alike, the actual identities of these men would have been known only to a small inner circle among Degas's audience – or to virtually none, in the case of *Portraits in an Office (New Orleans)*. But, beyond these few privileged insiders, it would have been evident to viewers familiar with nineteenth-century conventions of typecasting that these were images of unique individuals.

Renoir and Caillebotte, too, generally used their friends as models. Renoir tended to play down their distinctive features. His use of different models for each figure, instead of resorting to stereotypes like Bouguereau (pl. 125), was a means of giving a sense of liveliness and actuality to a scene such as *Ball at the Moulin de la Galette* (pl. 111), but the slight softening and generalisation of their features ensure that they blend seamlessly into the overall mood of the picture. Caillebotte's treatment of his figures was more varied. In *The Pont de l'Europe* (pl. 109) the individuality of the principal figures is emphasised, but less so in *Paris Street: Rainy Weather* (pl. 107), while his working-class figures are just as typecast as Degas's.

*   *   *

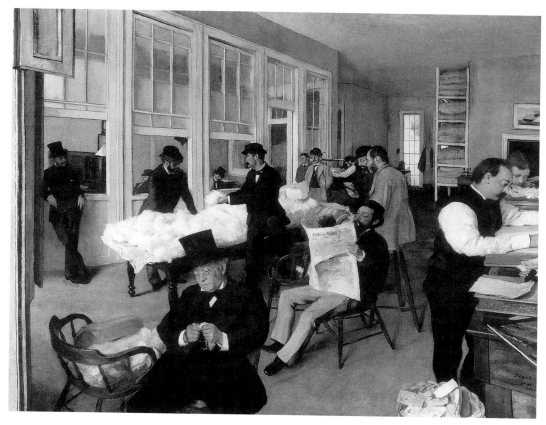

133   Edgar Degas, *Portraits in an Office, New Orleans* (*Portraits dans un bureau, Nouvelle-Orléans*) [known as *The Cotton Bureau*], 1873, 73 × 92, Musée des Beaux-Arts, Pau

We can now return to the broader question of the artists' ways of seeing the modern social scene, and to the viewpoint of the flâneur. All of the Impressionist artists rejected the neat legibility of the figures and situations in conventional urban genre paintings, like Bouguereau's indigents (pl. 125) or Baugniet's bourgeoises (pl. 3), paintings that followed Castagnary's prescription that 'each figure must be in its place, play its part, and so contribute to the expression of the general idea'. Yet the ways in which they challenged the norms and the implications of their solutions were very varied.

At first sight, it is Degas whose compositions are most complex and fragmented, whether by the cut-off forms at their margins or the seemingly incidental figures – like the stretching, scratching dancers – which demand attention and prevent the viewer from clearly identifying the 'general idea'. Yet, apart from the exceptional *Bouderie* and *Interior* (pls 117, 116), these are pictures in which, more broadly, the viewer is given a coherent overview of a world that makes sense, a world in which everyone does know their place. We are invited to imagine that it is the scrutinising eye of the artist that has identified and located them, though of course it is the artist's much-paraded artifice that has created this world; as Degas famously insisted, 'I assure you no art was ever less spontaneous than mine . . . of inspiration, spontaneity, temperament – temperament is the word – I know nothing'.[63] Degas offers us the clues to the identities of the figures and the roles they play, and also weaves their poses – at first sight so disparate and uncoordinated – into an ensemble that gains its own coherence as we scrutinise it.

It is the *flâneur*-detective who is invoked here; his searching eye can find order and meaning in the seeming incoherence of the modern urban environment. As Carol Armstrong has pointed out, the forms of legibility that Degas explored in the mid-1870s have much in common with the vision of the modern world proposed in Duranty's *La nouvelle peinture* of 1876, in their concentration on the multiple clues offered by external appearance and environmental details.[64] The standard markers of difference – class, sex and race[65] – are deployed in order to create a world that the observant viewer can readily decode.

Yet in the later 1860s both Degas and Duranty had been more equivocal about the possibilities of interpreting the modern world. In an essay of 1867 on physiognomy, Duranty revealed misgivings about the whole subject. After paying lip-service to the claims of physiognomy to the status of a science, he admitted the possibility of aberrant individuals whose appearance eluded all systems of classification, and spoke of the powerlessness of the police in the face of such individuals, since the police operate by stereotypes. He concluded by declaring impatiently that the perceptive individual could understand more than any system could teach: 'The best advice to give to those who want to recognise a man or men is to show much spirit and shrewdness in unravelling their complexities, since words are lying, action is hypocritical and physiognomy is deceitful!'[66] It is significant that Duranty's criticisms of physiognomy are couched in terms of the limitations of police methods; it is misleading to posit a simple equation between *flâneur* and detective. This sceptical, ambivalent vision is closer to Degas's *Interior* and *Bouderie*, in which, as we have seen, the paraded clues simply do not add up.

Manet's paintings, through to the end of his career, resist the attentions of the detective. As we have seen, his figure compositions constantly play on a wide range of uncertainties, inviting interpretation but denying any fixed reading. Moreover, he used details sparingly, and, where he did, often included elements that made no obvious sense: why, for example, is there a bunch of grapes on the stone ledge on the right side of *The Railway* (pl. 120)? Although the texture and tonality of his paintings changed during the 1870s, as he adopted higher-key colour and a more broken touch, the basic paradox that underlay his art remained the same. It could be seen, and enjoyed, merely in terms of coloured *taches*; but if its content and meaning were interrogated according to contemporary critical criteria, it revealed a world that was fascinating to the eye, but incoherent and unintelligible. The *flâneur* whose attention Manet's paintings invited was a *curieux* who could delight in the unknowable.

In a sense Renoir's vision of the modern city fell between these two modes, less legible than Degas's paintings of the 1870s, less puzzling than Manet's. But it also rejected the standard critical procedures that both Degas's and Manet's invited, by playing down the detailed clues and markers by which pictures were generally interpreted, and smoothing over signs of difference. Despite the complexity of the figure subject in a canvas such as *Ball at the Moulin de la Galette* (pl. 110), the homogeneity of his picture surfaces, in touch, texture and colour, seems to divert attention from the social content of the pictures and to defuse their more problematic associations. Monet's work follows a comparable track, moving away from the self-conscious foregrounding of the act of viewing in *Boulevard des Capucines* (pl. 89), with the presence of the spectators on the adjacent balcony, to the vibrant overall spectacle of the street scenes of 1878 (pl. 95).

These modes of representing the world of leisure and work of the mid-1870s must be viewed in the wider historical context of the politics of the 'moral order' regime of

Marshal MacMahon. There were two dimensions to this context, both artistic and socio-political. First, in these years the artistic authorities pursued a rigorously conservative policy, seeking to sponsor a revival of traditional history painting, in the face of the ever-increasing commercial success of landscape and genre painting. At the prize-giving ceremony at the end of the Salon of 1876, the Minister's message was unequivocal:

> [The Chamber of Deputies] wants elevated art, which provides the impetus for all other types of art, an art that has momentarily been abandoned by public favour and an art that the State alone can sustain, to continue and to accentuate the excellent movement of renewal that we have witnessed in the last two or three Salons. We are beginning to feel the effects of the salutary emulation that the commissions of paintings and sculptures for our great monuments has begun to awaken in the French school.[67]

By these standards, all the paintings of modern urban life that we have been examining were transgressive – dragging into the world of fine art precisely the corrupt influences that the authorities were at such pains to lock out.

This conclusion becomes all the clearer when their subject matter is framed in the broader context of the social and political constraints of the period. In the severe repression of MacMahon's regime of the mid-1870s, cafés and places of popular entertainment were particular objects of surveillance and controls, since they were regarded as primary focuses of political opposition, alongside the intense moral and political censorship to which all publications were subjected. The controls on alcohol consumption imposed by the *loi Roussel* in February 1873 were followed by a succession of measures against cafés and places of entertainment, the last and most draconian of them in the summer of 1877, just after the government upheavals of the *seize mai*. Many were reopened after the Republican gains in the elections of November 1877, but the formal controls were removed only in July 1880, after the government change of January 1879.[68]

Manet's path is easiest to chart in this context. To the Salon of 1874, the first after MacMahon became President, he submitted *Masked Ball at the Opera* (National Gallery of Art, Washington), an image of one of the most morally equivocal upper-class rituals of the period; the jury rejected it.[69] In February 1874, his *In the Café* lithograph was published in an overtly subversive journal, accompanied by a text that marked out the café as a locus of political debate; this issue of the journal was banned by the French censors.[70] Finally, it was probably in 1877, at the time of the most stringent controls, that he began his first major project to paint a Parisian brasserie, the Brasserie Reichshoffen.[71] At the same time, too, he painted a number of canvases that included beer waitresses – the *femmes de brasserie* whose activities serving beer in the open spaces of these establishments was a central issue in the literature of moral fear at this period (see pl. 112).[72]

Degas's engagement with political issues was predictably more oblique. In the main, as we have seen, the spaces that he chose to paint were the preserve of the privileged *flâneur* in whose world everything could be seen to be in its appointed place. Yet *In a Café* (pl. 115), like Manet's canvases, tackles the problematic aspects of café life. Moreover, the pastel *Women in Front of a Café in the Evening* (Musée d'Orsay, Paris), shown in the third group exhibition in 1877, engages directly with the world of clandestine prostitution, through the costume, physiognomies and body language of the figures, and through the overtly sexual gesture of the central figure, with her thumb to her mouth. Beyond this, as Carol Armstrong has noted, Degas signposted the links between this world and the world of the ballet dancer by including in the same show *The Dance Class* (Corcoran Gallery of Art, Washington), a ballet rehearsal scene in which a resting dancer repeats the same loaded thumb gesture.[73] Certainly, these few examples do not establish Degas as a politically oppositional picture-maker in these years. However, by exhibiting these pictures he revealed his determination that even the most problematic aspects of modern urban life should not be excluded from his public pictorial scrutiny; and by presenting them as 'fine art' he issued an unequivocal challenge to the values of the artistic authorities.

In some ways Renoir's position was the most paradoxical. By exhibiting a picture of one of the public entertainment places of Montmartre in 1877 he was inviting his viewers to view his canvases in political terms, at a time when memories of Montmartre's role in the Paris Commune were still fresh. Yet *Ball at the Moulin de la Galette* (pl. 110) does everything that it can to defuse these associations. Renoir later recalled that 'when he used to go often to the Moulin de la Galette . . . he found many delicate feelings among the people whom Zola described as atrocious beings';[74] his whole image of the Montmartre of the 1870s was one of easy, relaxed sociability. In the immediate context of the 'moral order' regime, this vision might be seen as a celebration of a counter-culture – of the survival of a vibrant urban popular culture in the face of government repression. Yet the blandness and seeming innocence of the pleasures that Renoir's pictures evoke encourage a very different reading – that they are essentially escapist and nostalgic images, that seek to mask the complexities and troubles of modern urban life under a veneer of bonhomie.[75] Indeed, the echoes of Watteau and the *fête champêtre* that permeate *Ball at the Moulin de la Galette* add to this sense of distancing; it was presumably with Renoir's agreement that his friend Rivière compared *The Swing* (Musée d'Orsay, Paris), shown at the same exhibition, with Watteau.[76]

It has recently been argued that in their views of Paris of the early to mid-1870s, after the Commune, the Impressionists 'politicised their creations by reimagining and reconstructing symbolically their partly destroyed country and disrupted social hierarchy', and that their paintings 'establish . . . visual parallels and metaphors for the actual rehabilitation of Third Republic France' by 'representing as bright, flourishing spaces' the 'damaged sites of the Commune'.[77] The argument in this chapter has been that their paintings were more provocative, more controversial in their implications, and far more varied, than this verdict suggests. Within the field of high culture, the whole project of 'viewing modern life' was deeply problematic during the 1870s. From the standpoint of the authorities, renewal lay in *la France profonde*, in the mythic image of an unchanging countryside that underpinned the conservative image of the French nation (pls 53 and 72), and not in the turbulent city of Paris or its surroundings. It was no coincidence that, after the Franco-Prussian War and the Commune, the seat of government did not return from Versailles to Paris until June 1879, after MacMahon's fall from power.

In this context, the Impressionists' consistent choice of problematic or equivocal scenes and sites can be set against the few urban modern life subjects that won success under the 'moral order' regime. Here the careers of Jean Béraud and Henri Gervex are particularly revealing. Béraud's only two Salon pictures of urban street life exhibited at the height of the 'moral order' regime were both scenes with clear moral and religious overtones – a group of upper-class figures leaving a funeral in 1876, and a fashionable congregation leaving church in 1877 (pl. 134);[78] likewise Gervex's first such subject

134 Jean Béraud, *Sunday, near the Church of Saint-Philippe-du-Roule* (*Le Dimanche, près de Saint-Philippe-du-Roule*), 1877, 59.4 × 81, The Metropolitan Museum of Art, New York, Gift of Mr. and Mrs. William B. Jaffe, 1955. (55.35)

depicted religious observance – a scene of a first communion at La Trinité in Paris, bought by the State at the Salon of 1877.[79] As the political climate changed from 1878 onwards, both artists quickly felt able to exhibit contemporary subjects without any such moral justification.

Viewed within this broader context, our analysis of the ways in which the Impressionists' scenes of contemporary life engaged their viewers has shown what diverse types of vision of the modern world they presented. For Degas in the 1870s, as for Duranty, modernity embodied a set of spaces that the privileged viewer could penetrate and signs that the skilled observer – the social detective – could decode. For Renoir, urban life could still sustain a mythic image of wholeness and harmony; there seems no reason to view this as an attempt at reparation after the Commune, for it does not mark a significant change from his pre-1870 work; rather, it was a facet of his larger artistic project. Manet, like Degas, was fascinated by signs, but for him they could not ultimately be resolved into a coherent reading of the modern world. His *curiosité*, and the visual excitement that his pictures register, in their observation and in their facture, were a celebration of a vision of the modern that could not be classified and controlled.

Faced with these pictures, at the Salon and the Impressionist exhibitions, the viewer had nowhere to hide. The landscapes and rural genre scenes that were the staple diet at the Salon offered an imaginative retreat into a seemingly natural unchanging world; historical or mythological scenes created a temporal and emotional distance between the viewer and the image. By contrast, the urban scenes of the Impressionists plunged spectators back into the world that they had left behind them as they entered the gallery from the street outside: fine art offered no sanctuary here. Beyond this, the various ways in which the pictures activated the relationship between the viewer and the canvas made the paintings themselves act in a sense like a mirror – a mirror in which the viewer was forced to imagine himself or herself as an active participant in the scene depicted. Yet in another sense, the scenarios were quite unlike a mirror, since they were carefully staged and constructed so that the viewer's position and role were predetermined, locked into the structure of human and spatial relationships within the picture. If Renoir invited his audience to imagine the possibility of free play in the pleasure grounds of Montmartre, and Degas offered the privilege of visual access to the insider world of Paris's urban entertainments, Manet's canvases, in many different ways, brought their viewers face to face with a vision of a modern urban life that was ultimately illegible.

5   Making a Mark: The Impressionist Brushstroke

Recent research, through the visual examination and technical analysis of paintings, has demonstrated the complexity of the Impressionists' procedures, and has definitively given the lie to the idea that their art was somehow simpler and more 'natural' than that of their predecessors. We now recognise that the informality and seeming improvisation of their paint surfaces were the result of extended exploration of the possibilities of their media, and that the surfaces themselves were often built up by an extended process in order to realise their final effect.[1] Yet, these final effects have received too little attention in this analysis; more emphasis has been placed on the successive stages of execution of their paintings than on the qualities of the finished work, although it was, of course, the finished works that were placed before their viewers. This chapter seeks to redirect attention back onto the effects that the artists achieved in their completed paintings, not in order to question the value of studying their working methods, but because it was by these final effects that the artists wanted their art to be seen and known.

*   *   *

Questions of technique were the central preoccupation of the critics of the early Impressionist exhibitions; it was the artists' handling of paint that marked them out from their contemporaries. The dominant characteristic of this handling was the *tache* – the distinct coloured touch or mark – which played a far more visible and active role in the overall effect of their paintings than it did in the work of their contemporaries. Painting technique has in recent years tended to be studied separately from questions of ideology and meaning;[2] however, for nineteenth-century viewers the physical make-up and execution of a work were integral to its expressive content. When in 1877 Frédéric Chevalier described the impact of the group exhibition on its viewers, he considered that it was the physical qualities of the paintings that generated the 'astonishment, disdain and indignation' that he saw expressed around him:

> ...some young painters...reveal themselves with an effervescence of colour, fantastic effects, an orgy of lines, a fury of brushstrokes, a debauch of impasto, an explosion of light, audacious compositions, outrageous dissonances and impudent harmonies whose combination creates the most unexpected, the most dishevelled and the most disorderly type of painting that one can imagine. An art that is savage, irreverent, undisciplined and heretical.[3]

This chapter will seek to restore the links between Impressionist technique and world view. The relationship was not, of course, static. Alongside the rapidly changing political and artistic contexts that we have already explored, there were fundamental changes in

facing page Claude Monet, *Snow Effect, Sunset (Effet de neige au soleil couchant)* (detail of pl. 144)

the Impressionists' technique and handling of paint between the late 1860s and the early 1880s. Put very crudely at the outset, they moved from a variegated facture that stressed the diversity of the elements within the scene to types of handling that emphasised the overall coherence of the scene – and of the picture itself. At the same time, the status of the individual brushstroke, and its role in the picture, underwent a parallel shift, from a relatively impersonal representational shorthand to distinctively personalised – and sometimes virtuoso – 'signature styles'.

For some decades, technical virtuosity had been seen as a central quality of French painting. Viewed from the standpoint of academic values, this growing preoccupation with manual skill testified to the loss of art's elevated purposes. In 1846, Charles Blanc criticised the new faction, among whom he named Narcisse Diaz de la Peña, who saw nothing in painting beyond 'a sparkling screen': 'a mosaic of dazzling tones is for them the last word in art.' Proceeding solely 'by touches, I was going to say by *taches* . . . , they have depraved the whole family of chaste muses'.[4] Academic theory insisted on invisible execution and the dominance of line over colour – methods that were a visible realisation of the superiority of abstract ideas over sensory experience. However, for many viewers the visible coloured *touche* was a marker of the rejection of academic shackles and demonstrated the painter's concern to translate personal visual experiences into paint.

The issues were summed up in a celebrated interchange of opinions between Ingres and Delacroix. Ingres asked: 'What does this procedure of execution by the *touche* mean? Where do you see the *touche* in nature? It is the quality that false talents use to demonstrate their dexterity with the brush. However skilful it is, the *touche* must not be visible, it hinders the illusion and immobilises everything; instead of the object, it draws attention to the process; instead of thought, it proclaims the hand.'[5] Delacroix responded to this argument in his uncompleted *Dictionnaire des Beaux-Arts*: 'The *touche* is a means, like any other, that contributes to expressing thought in painting . . . What can one say of the masters who dryly emphasise contours while rejecting the *touche*? There are no more contours in nature than there are *touches*. One must always return to the means that best suit each art, that are the language of that art.'[6]

This technical virtuosity served a number of functions. First, it allowed the artist to work quite quickly and informally, to make rapid notations of visual effects and to sketch a composition without elaborate preparatory studies. At the same time, the visible touch could be seen as a marker of the artist's unique personality – of his or her creative presence on the physical surface of the finished work. These two facets, notation and self-expression, are fundamental to the study of Impressionist technique.

Yet in finished paintings, even by artists who were renowned for their visible execution, the *touche* was generally subordinated to the overall effect of the picture. In the completed canvases of artists such as Delacroix (e.g. pl. 135), the size of the individual mark was carefully gauged so that it did not disturb the unity of the ensemble, whether on the scale of the major exhibition painting or the smaller picture designed for the dealer market. Delacroix explained the principles behind his execution in his draft *Dictionnaire*: 'The *touche*, when used as it should be, serves to define more clearly the different planes in which objects are situated. When it is strongly emphasised, it makes them come forward; the opposite sets them back into the distance.'[7] Beyond the role of the *touche* in the spatial organisation of the picture, it was a constantly repeated precept that the more significant elements in a scene should be indicated by being treated with

135   Eugène Delacroix, *Arabs Skirmishing in the Mountains* (*Combadale t d'Arabes dans les montagnes*), 1863, 92 × 74, National Gallery of Art, Washington, Chester Dale Fund

a more emphatic *touche*, so that the technique would offer a readily legible expression of the hierarchy of values that the painting's subject sought to convey.[8]

With Courbet and Manet, critics quickly sensed that things were different. Consistently, both artists were criticised for their failure to observe any such hierarchy – for treating the human figure as if it was no more significant than its surroundings. Courbet's use of the palette knife and Manet's distinctive *taches* led critics to broadly the same conclusions. It was the treatment of Courbet's figures that led Charles Perrier in 1855 to describe his art as 'seditious' (*factieux*): 'Your stonebreaker should not be as insignificant an object as the stone that he is breaking.'[9] For Hippolyte Babou in 1867, Manet's 'mania for *seeing by taches* inevitably leads to a sort of uniform impression that diminishes, effaces and defiles the human figure';[10] as we have seen, in 1869 Thoré saw this as a marker of Manet's 'pantheism'.[11] It was 'pantheism', too, that Camille Lemonnier found in the all-over technique of Courbet's seascapes exhibited at the Salon of 1870 (e.g. pl. 177):

> Courbet is the most voluptuous and the most refined of virtuoso painters. Immersed in a vast pantheism, he views with equal love the star shining in the firmament and the pebble glistening in the weeds. His childlike and corrupted genius plays indiscriminately with the rough textures of broken stones and the brilliance of a sunlit glade. He does not admit that there are trivial things in nature and he treats everything with the same grandeur.[12]

Just as the equally weighted touch could be seen as a challenge to humanistic values, so colour, too, could be subversive if not harnessed by the discipline of line, as Charles

Blanc so vividly declared in the introductory section of his *Grammaire des arts du dessin*:

> Line [*le dessin*] is the male sex in art, and colour the female . . . In painting, colour is essential, but it takes second place. The union of line and colour is necessary to beget painting, just as the union of man and woman is necessary to beget humanity; but line must retain its ascendancy over colour. Otherwise, painting is on the road to ruin; it will be betrayed by colour just as humanity was betrayed by Eve.[13]

Or, as Charles Gleyre, teacher of Monet, Renoir, Sisley and Bazille, put it more succinctly: 'That accursed colour will turn your head.'[14] To these commentators, questions of technique and treatment were clearly not ideologically neutral.

Much of the rhetoric in support of Impressionist technique invoked the idea of the 'natural', presenting it as an attempt to get closer to 'nature' by rejecting the precepts of academic art. For their supporters, this marked the triumph of nature over artifice; for their opponents, by contrast, it marked the loss – or rejection – of the skills and discipline on which 'fine art' should be based. Any discussion of painting technique has to stress at the outset that any such invocation of the 'natural' is purely rhetorical. As Delacroix's comments on *touche* and contour so clearly acknowledge, any visual representation in paint on canvas is based on conventions that view a mark of a particular shape, texture and colour on a two-dimensional surface as the equivalent to something in some notion of the 'real world'. For those who accept a particular convention, it may be seen as reflecting a 'natural' vision, whereas its opponents may see it as a travesty of the idea of 'nature'. The stark contrast between the technique of the Impressionists and the meticulous detailing of the English Pre-Raphaelites (seen by many as the last word in 'realism' on their appearance at the Exposition Universelle of 1855[15]) shows how diverse these conventions might be.

Yet, as we have seen in Chapter One, the notion of the 'innocent eye' was a potent myth. In various forms, it appears as the basis of a number of the formative narratives of the 'new painting'. Francis Wey remembered standing with Courbet in front of a landscape that Courbet had just painted:

> . . . he pointed out an object in the distance and said: 'Look over there, at what I've just painted? I haven't a clue what it is.' It was a greyish block that, at a distance, I couldn't identify; but, casting my eye across the canvas, I saw that it was a heap of logs. 'I didn't need to know that,' he said, 'I painted what I saw without knowing what it was. And then, stepping back from his canvas, he added: 'To be sure, that's right, they were logs.'[16]

In 1876 Frédéric Henriet recorded François Bonvin's version of the same slogan when describing the new generation of artists who had rejected formal training, whom he called *irréguliers*: 'Fanatical believers in *naïveté* in art, they repeat this paradox of Bonvin's: "You want to paint a hand? Well, if you realise that it is a hand, you're f****d"'[17] Monet reiterated the same ideas around 1890 in conversation with the American painter Lilla Cabot Perry: 'He said he wished he had been born blind and then had suddenly gained his sight so that he could have begun to paint . . . without knowing what the objects were that he saw before him.' His instructions to Perry are one of the clearest surviving statements of Impressionist principles: ' "When you go out to paint, try to forget what object you have before you . . . Merely think, here is a little square of blue, here an oblong of pink, here a streak of yellow, and paint it just as it

136 Gustave Courbet, *The Stream of the Puits Noir* (*Le Ruisseau du Puits Noir*), *c.*1860–65, 64.2 × 79.1, The Baltimore Museum of Art, The Cone Collection, formed by Dr. Claribel Cone and Miss Etta Cone of Baltimore, Maryland

looks to you, the exact colour and shape, until it gives your own naïve impression of the scene before you." '[18]

These precepts were phrased in slightly different terms by Cézanne in 1874. Back in his home town of Aix-en-Provence after gaining notoriety in Paris by showing his work in the first group exhibition, he tried to explain to the local museum director the principles that Pissarro had recently taught him when they were working together around Pontoise. He reported on the conversation in a letter to Pissarro: 'I told him that you replace modelling [*le modelé*] by the study of *tons*, and I tried to make him understand this by reference to nature, but he shut his eyes and turned his back.'[19] The term *tons* here encompasses both tone (on the dark–light scale) and colour (hue), and indicates that the world is being viewed in terms of zones or patches of colour; *le modelé*, by contrast, refers to the delicate gradations and invisible facture by which academic technique sought to suggest the fullness of three-dimensional form on the flat surface. The central point in Cézanne's attempted demonstration was the invocation of 'nature' to discredit *le modelé*: it was the individual painter's direct observation of the external world – in Cézanne's regular terminology, the *sensation* – that showed up *le modelé* as nothing more than an academic abstraction. Two years later, on the Mediterranean coast at

L'Estaque in 1876, Cézanne found this principle confirmed by his own experiences while painting *The Sea at L'Estaque* (pl. 45): 'It's like a playing card. Red roofs against the blue sea ... The sun here is so terrifying that it seems to me that the objects are silhouetted not only in white or black, but in blue, red, brown and violet. I may be mistaken, but this seems to me to be the opposite of *modelé*.'[20]

Cézanne's emphasis on the primacy of contrasts of colour pinpoints one fundamental difference between Courbet and the Impressionists. Courbet rendered natural light primarily in terms of tonal oppositions, with sharp illumination set off against dark shadow (see pl. 136), while the Impressionists increasingly sought to recreate the effects of sunlight by relationships and contrasts of hue. Courbet explained why he began his landscapes from a dark priming: 'Nature, without sunlight, is black and obscure; I act as light does; I illuminate the projecting points, and the picture is done.'[21] The Impressionist view, as expressed in Cézanne's famous dictum, was very different: 'I wanted to copy nature, but did not succeed. But I was pleased with myself when I discovered that sunlight ... could not be reproduced, but that it must be *represented* by something else – by colour.'[22] Courbet's comment suggests that in a sense he viewed himself in a quasi-divine role, as the creator of the solidity of the objects that he depicted, through his powers as an artist. By contrast, colour, as discussed by contemporary theorists and as used by the Impressionists, was concerned with surface appearances, and was the vehicle by which the individual artist's sensory experiences could be translated into paint on canvas. The focus of the present chapter is on the brushstroke – the Impressionist 'mark'. However, colour was the constant corollary of the development of the Impressionist *touche*, as the artists gradually abandoned the residue of tonal modelling in favour of the representation of form, space and light through harmonies and contrasts of colour.[23]

A final issue was the notion of 'temperament'. For critics such as Zola, temperament was the marker of the true painter – one who did not subordinate himself to academic rules and conventions. But for critics from an academic standpoint, the pursuit of individual temperament was undermining the discipline and authority of the French school of painting; and the key marker of this temperament was the parading of a distinctive individual facture – the demonstrative personal paint-mark.[24]

*   *   *

The early phases of the Impressionists' *tache*-ist handling can be seen in Monet's *The Quai du Louvre* of 1867 (pl. 90), in which all the diverse elements in the scene are treated in a lively, succinct shorthand. The touch is a little softer in the distance, but otherwise there is no sense of a hierarchy of focus or significance; the eye plays from one accent to the next – from the dome on the horizon to the kiosk on the *quai*, from the equestrian statue of Henri IV to the horses and carriages. The immensely varied brush-marks draw out the distinctive shape and texture of each object and deftly characterise the figures as types. The effect is one of specificity, precision even, as if the artist is insisting 'I was there, at that moment, and it looked just like that'. Yet this effect is achieved without any distracting detail; every element takes its place in the overall tableau, and the zones of the scene in which there is no activity are treated broadly and simply, in relatively undifferentiated sweeps of colour.

Over the next six years, Monet's touch became lighter and still more flexible, and the notation of the diverse elements in his scenes less specific; but, up to around 1873, his more highly finished canvases were treated in an essentially similar way. In *The Prom-*

enade at Argenteuil (pl. 55) of 1872, there is a play on the recurrent vertical accents – the sails, the trees and tree-trunks, the factory chimneys, the little spire on the house and the figures; each is given equivalent weight and significance in the scene, with the figures (conventionally treated as a focal point) relegated to a marginal position beneath the trees. Yet each of these elements is succinctly characterised and delicately differentiated, by constant variation of touch, colour and tone, and set off against areas that are far more broadly painted.

Handling of this type became the hallmark of early Impressionism. It was also adopted by Pissarro and Sisley, and on occasion Renoir, by around 1870, and was common currency in the group until around 1873 or 1874 (see e.g. pls 52, 57, 58). Like Monet, Pissarro and Sisley developed a lighter and more economical touch between 1870 and 1873, but the essentials of their treatment of their subjects remained constant, in their pursuit of a painterly shorthand that succinctly conveyed the diversity of their chosen subjects. The surface of Pissarro's *Spring at Louveciennes* of 1870 (pl. 137) is relatively densely worked; yet the final surface is constantly varied, sometimes quite broadly brushed, sometimes treated in small flecks of paint, thus evoking the diverse textures of

137   Camille Pissarro, *Spring at Louveciennes (Printemps à Louveciennes)*, 1870, 59.5 × 73, Stiftung 'Langmatt', Baden

138   Alfred Sisley, *The Foot-Bridge at Argenteuil (Passerelle d'Argenteuil)*, 1872, 39 × 60, Musée d'Orsay, Paris

the scene, as the *contre-jour* light illuminates the grass in the foreground and catches the fresh foliage of the trees and bushes beyond, while throwing into silhouette the trunks and branches of the chestnut trees that dominate the composition. These trees give the whole picture a taut tonal structure, against which the play of touch and colour in the sunlit zones is played off.

The extreme variety of their mark-making complemented the types of site that they chose. Pissarro's *Pontoise* of 1872 (pl. 57), for example, presents a scene built up from disparate elements and viewed from an unexpected angle, with the church, traditional focus for a rural village *motif*, tucked away beneath the hillside, with a factory chimney alongside it. The flexibility and variegation of the *touche*, softer and less assertive than in *Spring at Louveciennes*, and the lack of any overall rhythm or pattern to either composition or handling, bring out most effectively the calculatedly anti-picturesque qualities of the scene.[25] Likewise in Sisley's *Foot-Bridge at Argenteuil* (pl. 138), painted early in 1872 when the bridge had not yet been fully repaired after its destruction during the Franco-Prussian War, the differentiation of the touch stresses the incoherence of the scene depicted – the contrasts between foliage and houses, stone bridge-piers and wooden railings, roadway and water surface. The viewer's experience of the picture is further dislocated by the foreground figure who has paused to look back in our direction, but why, and what he is looking at, we do not know; his face is virtually blank.

But how does this flexible *touche* relate to the notion of the 'innocent eye'? It is immediately clear that these pictures cannot be viewed literally in terms of the ideal of innocent viewing proposed by Courbet and Bonvin; the diverse ingredients in these scenes are treated in ways that show that the painters well knew what they were, as they sought a representational shorthand that would sum up the essentials of their appearance and communicate these to their viewers. Rather, the pictures show up Courbet's and Bonvin's prescription as a notional ideal, a figure for a type of viewing that sought to focus on the immediate visual experience alone. This demanded that the painter should reject *le modelé* in favour of the study of *tons*; the *tache* was the seemingly neutral unit that could stand as the pictorial equivalent of an optical *sensation* unadulterated by memory and prior knowledge.

Yet there are certain pictures from these years in which issues of visual representation are more problematic. We have already looked at the ambiguous – or rather illegible – gestures of the figures in Monet's two views of La Grenouillère (pls 32, 54; see p. 76); in the London version (pl. 32), in particular, there are other puzzling elements. It is with great difficulty that one can identify the set of vertical accents, mostly dark, above the walkway to the left of centre as another female figure in a bathing costume, or the flurry of coloured touches beneath the tree at far left as a group of figures dappled by sunlight. The dabs and blobs in the water on the right, presumably a cluster of mostly male bathers, are so loosely handled that one cannot fit heads to bodies or count the number of figures there. Through much of the picture, the handling is so calculatedly informal and improvisatory that individual marks cannot readily be matched to specific objects or to specific ingredients in the painter's visual experience.

However, as we have seen, Monet did not regard these canvases as fully complete and ready for public display; thus he felt able to leave certain passages in some sense unresolved. It is in a group of landscapes by Renoir from the early 1870s that such uncertainties play a particularly significant role. *The Seine at Chatou* (pl. 139), though boldly and broadly handled, was signed by Renoir at the time that he painted the picture.[26] In this image of a cluster of nondescript villas by the river, seen *contre-jour*, the sharpest highlights are a blob of white paint to the left of the central house and a string of white touches in the water below this; we read these lower marks as reflections of the accent above, but we cannot tell what is catching the light so sharply – perhaps a glass roof, but we cannot be sure. Seen as it is in the painting, it is simply a visual effect. In the scene that Renoir witnessed, it was a by-product of an optical incident, or accident, but the role that it is given in the painting – a focal point without any declared referent – presents it to us as a marker of the painter's *naïveté*, of the innocence of his eye. Unlike the Courbet/Bonvin topos, presumably Renoir did know what was reflecting this sharp light; the crucial thing was for him to present it to us as if he did not know. Beyond this, he calculatedly used these highlights to overturn any hierarchy of significance within the picture, since they present us with a focal point that – whatever it represents – is something trivial and incidental.

Renoir also abbreviated and fragmented human figures in extreme ways in some of his landscapes in these years. The male field workers in *The Harvesters* (pl. 71) are as summarily treated as the bathers in Monet's La Grenouillère views, but paradoxically, as we have seen (see p. 87), it is they who are indicated by the picture's title. Expectations are undermined still further in *Path Rising through Tall Grass* (pl. 140).[27] Here we recognise a female figure, wearing fashionable summer clothes and holding a red parasol, with a child in front of her – an orthodox protective role, unlike Monet's pictures of Camille and Jean (see pp. 126–8); but the woman's figure is represented by a remarkable configuration of messy, rough *taches*. These can be seen in two ways. Viewed in terms of the 'innocent eye', they blend in with the ebullient, improvised brushwork of the rest of the picture, in which the figures are just another ingredient, of no special

139   Pierre-Auguste Renoir, *The Seine at Chatou (La Seine à Chatou)*, *c*.1871, 46.7 × 56.1, Art Gallery of Ontario, Toronto, Purchase, 1935

significance, alongside the scattering of small trees and the fence-posts at bottom right. But, especially within nineteenth-century terms of reference, this treatment of a bourgeois female figure is a blatant affront to any notion of female elegance and propriety.

This figure makes a fascinating contrast to a story that Renoir later told about his visit to Algeria in the early 1880s. He remembered how, in the dazzling sunlight of Algiers, the sordid rags of a beggar walking towards him came to look like a royal robe of gold and purple; only when he came close did Renoir see him for what he was.[28] There, the sunlight – and Renoir's sunny vision – could transform rags to robes; here, by contrast, in the early 1870s, he could allow his pursuit of the 'innocent eye' to transform a pretty dress into a painted mess, and thus to override the delight in a pretty female figure which was (for better or worse) to become the keynote of his later art.

This flexible, notational technique was a material expression of *curiosité* – of the way of seeing that was alert to everything within the visual field without privileging any one element over the others. Viewed in this way, the modern world was made up of disparate, diverse elements, all of them optically of equal significance, not differentiated by any extraneous value-system, whether theological, moral, political or social. In a sense, the contrast between the clarity of the elements in Monet's *The Quai du Louvre* and the visual uncertainties that we have noted in paintings such as Renoir's *The Seine*

140 Pierre-Auguste Renoir, *Path Rising through Tall Grass* (*Chemin montant dans les hautes herbes*), *c.*1873, 60 × 74, Musée d'Orsay, Paris

at Chatou echoes the distinction that we have drawn between the two different notions of *curiosité*, between the penetrative eye of the detective and the vision that could accept – and celebrate – the unknowable. Beyond this, the implications of *curiosité*, of both types, were of course not morally or politically neutral, since the rejection of preordained hierarchies of value was itself inevitably a political position, and one that, especially in the repressive climate of the early to mid-1870s, was highly loaded.

At this point, though, another distinction must be drawn – between this representational shorthand and the techniques that Manet was developing in the same years. It is easy to juxtapose the paintings that Manet and Monet made when they were working together at Argenteuil in 1874, and to contrast Monet's sustained attention to the play of light and shade and of reflections in water (e.g. pl. 61) with the imprecisions, ambiguities and, at times, downright inaccuracies that characterise even Manet's most 'Impressionist' canvases.[29] Yet, as many witnesses tell us, Manet was wholly unconcerned with accuracy of this sort: '. . . he did not copy nature at all closely; I noted his masterly simplifications . . . Everything was abbreviated . . .'. 'Concision', Manet insisted, was the essence of good art.[30]

A further demonstration of the divergence between Manet's and Monet's attitudes to picture-making can be seen in Manet's *The Painter Claude Monet in his Studio* (pl. 141),

141 Edouard Manet, *The Painter Claude Monet in his Studio* (*Le Peintre Claude Monet dans son atelier*), 1874, 81.3 × 99.7, Bayerische Staatsgemäldesammlungen, Munich, Neue Pinakotek

exhibited in Manet's one-artist show at the offices of *La Vie moderne* in 1880. Monet is depicted at work *devant le motif*, true to his principles. Yet, as Manet depicts him, he is facing in quite the wrong direction to be painting the canvas that we see on his easel – seemingly the same view that acts as the backdrop of Manet's own picture.[31] Manet is indeed representing Monet pursuing his dedication to painting in the open air, but the older artist wittily reveals his own view of the limitations that these principles imposed on a committed plein-airist, and his belief that artistic decisions should be transcendent over natural appearances.

This approach to picture-making is vividly expressed in the handling of the paint surfaces in Manet's paintings. Virtually from the start of his career, he included certain passages in his finished pictures that defy naturalistic interpretation – the cape held by the figure in *Mademoiselle V. in the Costume of an Espada* of 1863, for instance, or the sheet beneath Christ's body in *The Angels at the Tomb of Christ* of 1864 (both Metropolitan Museum of Art, New York). In virtually all of his Salon paintings, throughout his career, there are comparable areas in which the apparently fluent play of the brush cannot be readily interpreted in representational terms, often placed alongside other elements that can be read more illusionistically. In *Luncheon* (pl. 4), this appears especially in the mark-making on the cut face of the lemon and on the coffee pot held by the servant, but in other more prominent areas of the picture, such as the faces of the boy and the servant and the boy's trousers, the modelling is deliberately simplified and schematised.

Such effects are still more marked in Manet's smaller, but complete, paintings of the 1870s. In *The Swallows* (pl. 47), a canvas which, though small and informal, Manet submitted to the Salon of 1874, the dresses of both women are treated with particu-

142 Edouard Manet, *Before the Mirror* (*Devant la glace*), 1877, 92.1 × 71.4, Solomon R. Guggenheim Museum, New York, Thannhauser Collection, Gift, Justin K. Thannhauser, 1978

larly summary strokes; on the right-hand figure the marks are especially assertive. Likewise in *Before the Mirror* (pl. 142), exhibited together with *The Painter Claude Monet in his Studio* in Manet's show at the offices of *La Vie moderne* in 1880, the brushwork on hair, flesh and corset makes no pretence of modelling the form of the figure or her clothing. In the broadest terms, the weight, direction and rhythm of the strokes do suggest the three-dimensionality of the forms, but they do not claim to define or fix either the form of the figure or the lines and folds of her clothing. Looked at one by one, these strokes are seemingly arbitrary – assertively visible as painted marks, and emphatically detached from their representational functions. The *tache* has become disembodied, geared to pictorial effect rather than functioning as a descriptive shorthand.

At the same time Manet plays with the viewer's expectations about the primary focus of the picture, by placing the most intense colour accents – a flurry of strong red strokes – on and below the figure's right elbow, rather than on the parade of exposed flesh of her neck and shoulders.[32]

As has often been stressed, these apparently improvisatory marks were the product of repeated rehearsals and re-paintings, continued until Manet had achieved the appearance of impromptu informality that he sought. At the same time, the resulting pictorial effects highlight the artifice of their making, and parade their identity as *taches* of colour. Yet the pictures cannot be seen merely as demonstrations of Manet's love of the coloured *tache*. Despite their apparent arbitrariness when they are viewed in isolation, taken together these *taches* play an integral part in the overall effect of Manet's canvases, not only as pictorial elements, but as representations of a vision of the modern world.

As we have argued in Chapters One and Four in discussing his Salon paintings after about 1866, Manet was exploring an imagery of the contemporary world that embodied the ambiguities and uncertainties about social order and identity that characterised a particular view of 'modernity'. The uneven focus and irregular rhythms of his technique complemented the subject matter and arrangement of his figure compositions. Beyond this, in paintings such as *Before the Mirror* (pl. 142), the whole surface is treated in an equally informal and sketch-like way, allowing the eye no point of focus or repose; it is as if the technique recreates the effect of a momentary glimpse of the model in the privacy of her toilette. This all-over sketch-like quality was not merely a matter of the scale of the painting; for Manet worked up other modest-sized canvases to a degree of finish comparable to his Salon paintings – among them *The Plum* (National Gallery of Art, Washington), which was exhibited together with *Before the Mirror* in his show of 1880 at *La Vie moderne*. If the more elaborated paintings evoke the equivocality and uncertainties of the modern gaze, *Before the Mirror*, in its technique as well as its subject, hints at a different type of looking, the rapid glance that it is impossible – or inappropriate – for the viewer to hold for longer than a moment.

*   *   *

Significant changes in the Impressionists' painting techniques took place in the mid-1870s, changes that, initially at least, led in different directions, Monet and Renoir developing a finer, more fragmented brushstroke, and Pissarro and Cézanne exploring ways of giving an overall coherence to the whole picture surface. We shall explore each in turn.

Beginning in the autumn of 1873, Monet began increasingly to adopt a smaller, more mobile touch. In *The Sheltered Path* (pl. 143), for instance, the foliage is treated less descriptively; the brush-marks are no longer used to differentiate one object from another, and are less readily identifiable as standing for a particular object in the scene. Instead, the flecks, dabs and dashes of colour that animate the surface, though variegated in shape and direction, are more uniform in scale, giving the whole picture a mobility and shimmer that can more easily be seen as evoking the play of light.

Over the next few years, Monet continued to modify his handling from one picture to the next, according to the subject and effect that he was treating. But his touch consistently fragmented the objects depicted or played down their structure. In *The Tuileries* (pl. 91), the pavilion of the Louvre (though readily recognisable) is given no

143 Claude Monet, *The Sheltered Path* (*Chemin creux*), 1873, 54.5 × 65.5, Philadelphia Museum of Art: Gift of Mr. and Mrs. Hughs Norment in honor of William H. Donner, 1972

more solidity than the trees in the park, and the little figures are no longer deftly characterised, but treated so summarily that they cannot even be counted, let alone classified. One critic in 1877 described the figures in Monet's Tuileries paintings as 'noxious insects'.[33] The varied fleck-like touch that dominates in the foliage is set off against the smoother surfaces of grass and paths, but the keynote of the picture is established by the foliage, expressing the play of light on a still day in early autumn. At the same time, strokes and accents of colour begin to appear that cannot be ascribed any direct representational referent: here, the crisp, deep red strokes on the left side of the bush at lower left, together with the pink accents beneath the bush in the centre of the picture.

The contrasts are far harsher in *Snow Effect, Sunset* of 1875 (pl. 144), and the brushwork calculatedly rough in the foreground, to convey the effect of the aftermath of a snowfall in the ugly backstreets of Argenteuil with their irregular jumble of buildings and open spaces. The broad shapes of the buildings are clearly indicated, but wholly without the suggestion of detail; the grasses in the foreground are notated in crude, rapid dashes of paint, while the figures, though pivotally placed at the centre of the canvas, are treated very summarily, even dismissively. Even a figure that plays a central role in the subject of a painting may be treated just as casually: the race umpire on his

144 Claude Monet, *Snow Effect, Sunset* (*Effet de neige au soleil couchant*), 1875, 53 × 64, Musée Marmottan–Claude Monet, Paris

little boat in *The Boats, Regatta at Argenteuil* (pl. 74) is reduced to a few rapid dashes and flecks of paint.

In some pictures of the later 1870s, this process is carried further. In the most highly worked of the paintings of the Gare Saint-Lazare (e.g. pl. 27), even the linear, geometrical structure of the station roof is softened, while trains, figures and buildings are virtually dissolved into a play of coloured touches. In this group of paintings, too, Monet omitted the station roof entirely at the points where he placed the principal puffs of smoke and steam, so as to allow the light-toned canvas priming to dictate its tonality. This is evidence of the advance planning that he gave to even such ephemeral elements as the placing of puffs of smoke;[34] but, beyond this, it shows that he was no longer thinking of solid material objects as an armature with which to structure his canvases.

Every physical element in the scene is now subordinated to the painter's process of visual dissolution and painterly recreation.

The dissolution of form reached its extreme point in some views of Vétheuil painted around 1879. These mark Monet's return to the traditional motif of the country village crowned by a church, but the treatment of the forms seems to undercut the values that the motif proclaims. In *Vétheuil in Summer* (pl. 145), for instance, the whole village is treated in soft coloured dabs, its buildings given no firmer a structure than the fields and foliage. The forms of the buildings are articulated by the direction of the brush-strokes, and by the contrasts of oranges and pinks set off against blues, conveying the effect of the evening sun; but these never create a sharp contour. When the picture is seen from a distance, the subtle differentiation of colour and touch allows us to imagine the shape of the buildings and their position in space, but, viewed from close to, the effect is confusing, especially in the group of houses below the church. The soft touches do not coalesce into identifiable forms and cannot be recognisably tied to any precise representational role. Moreover, similarly weighted touches appear in different spatial

145 Claude Monet, *Vétheuil in Summer (Vétheuil en été)*, 1879, 68 × 90, Art Gallery of Ontario, Toronto, Purchase, 1929

planes, creating visual equivalences between hillside and houses, hillside and reflections on the water; the whole surface has a remarkable homogeneity. Even the broadest strokes never acquire a dynamic, calligraphic energy of their own; this restraint emphasises further the notional innocence of the artist's eye, face to face with his *sensations*. However, taken one by one, the touches cannot be seen as direct equivalents of elements that Monet observed in the scene before him.

In 1880–81 there was a marked change in the surface qualities of Monet's most fully realised paintings, as he began to animate them with far more assertive, incisive individual strokes. These began to appear in his paintings of the Seine and its banks at Vétheuil of summer 1880, but became far more emphatic in the canvases from his first two spells of work on the Normandy coast, at Les Petites-Dalles in autumn 1880 and Fécamp in spring 1881, and then in the products of his final summer at Vétheuil in 1881.

In *The Sea at Fécamp* (pl. 146), this energised, calligraphic facture is used to provide the visual equivalent to the movement and force of the sea, in sequences of bold hooks for the successive bands of waves sweeping towards the shore, and in the extraordinary fantasia of small-scale calligraphic loops and swirls that evoke the waves as they break against the cliffs. Set against the cursive handling of the sea are the more staccato strokes

146   Claude Monet, *The Sea at Fécamp* (*La Mer à Fécamp*), 1881, 65.5 × 82, Staatsgalerie, Stuttgart

147   Claude Monet, *The Wheatfield* (*Champ de blé*), 1881, 65.5 × 81.5, Cleveland Museum of Art

on the shore, mainly vertical on the foreground rock and the right cliff-face, and insistently horizontal on the jutting cliff beyond. This remarkable array of mark-making is never closely descriptive; yet it succeeds in evoking with great vividness the forces of the elements, seemingly captured at the most fleeting moment.[35]

    This dynamic handling is perhaps the more striking when applied to a subject with less intrinsic dynamism than a stormy sea – as for instance to the meadows around Vétheuil. In *The Wheatfield* (pl. 147), the strokes that animate the picture's surface are again crisp and graphic; hooks and dashes of paint, varied in direction and length, give an insistent pulse of energy to the whole canvas, from the foreground grasses to the bold streaks across the upper sky. The trees are animated by sharp vertical strokes that suggest the direction of their growth and link the two dominant horizontal bands of the composition, but wholly without seeking to describe trunks and branches with any precision. Yet, alongside all this animation, Monet was able to use a far softer, less assertive touch to achieve the final stages of atmospheric harmonisation in the picture, with the

148 Alfred Sisley, *The Fields* (*Les Champs*), 1874, 46 × 61, Leeds Museums and Galleries (City Art Gallery)

sequence of soft pink strokes all along the base of the sky, to the left and right of the main group of trees. Through the mid-1880s, Monet's touch remained assertive and dynamic, but gradually became less crisp and sharply accented, as he came to give an ever more central role to the *enveloppe*, the unifying effect of atmosphere across the whole scene, that was to become the leitmotiv of his series of the 1890s.[36]

At first sight, Sisley's facture appears to have developed in ways parallel to Monet's. From 1874 onwards, his touch became more vigorous, more emphatic, and the overall effect of his canvases more animated and assertive. At the same time, the subjects he chose were often very complex – a weave of contrasting shapes, colours and textures. Yet, unlike Monet's, his variegated touch can still readily be viewed as a shorthand notation for the diversity of the objects within the scene itself. In *The Fields* of 1874 (pl. 148), the subject includes little except foliage and sky, but the crops, bushes, grasses and trees are varied in rhythm, hue and texture, and conveyed with an exceptionally fluent and flexible touch and in constantly varied nuances of green. The scene is far from the unity of conventional images of *la France profonde* (see e.g. pls 53, 72). Instead, we are immersed in a small corner of the countryside, and presented with a whole range of different ingredients; only the stakes and the two sketchy figures silhouetted against the sky suggest any wider space, but we are given no access to this. It is the diversity of the textures and the animation of the marks that energise Sisley's work at this period, rather than the sort of sustained dismantling of forms that we have examined in Monet's canvases of the mid- to later 1870s.

Renoir's technique, at its most extreme, posed just as many problems as Monet's. Yet in each of the first three group exhibitions he took pains to include canvases that showed his art at its most accessible – at the first, genre paintings such as *The Theatre Box* (pl. 121) alongside *Harvesters* (pl. 71); in the second and third, delicately worked female portraits: alongside *Study* (pl. 43) in the show of 1876 was *Portrait of a Young Girl* (the portrait of Mademoiselle Legrand now in the Philadelphia Museum of Art),[37] while in 1877 the *Portrait of Madame A. D.* (pl. 50) and *Portrait of Madame G. C.* (the bust-length portrait of Madame Charpentier now in the Musée d'Orsay) accompanied *The Swing* (Musée d'Orsay) and *Ball at the Moulin de la Galette* (pl. 110). In part, this must be seen as a recognition that different genres demanded different treatment; in part it may have been a desire to deflect criticism from his (in conventional terms) most exper-imental and formless work by demonstrating his mastery of the fluent *belle peinture* that was becoming increasingly successful at the Salon in these years.

However, more perhaps than any other Impressionist paintings of the period, Renoir's experimental works from around 1875–8 reveal a sustained attempt to erase *dessin* and tonal contrast, in favour of an art based on a network of coloured touches alone. The effects of this are especially striking in figure paintings, since conventionally it was in these that the clear delineation of form was expected. In *Study* (pl. 43), painted in the summer of 1875, the form of the naked figure remains relatively intact beneath the var-iegated colour patches that suggest the play of light through foliage onto her skin. Although Albert Wolff famously described the figure as 'a mass of decomposing flesh', other critics praised the light effect and flesh tones when it was exhibited in 1876.[38]

In *The First Step* of 1876 (pl. 149), very possibly exhibited as *Mother and Child* in the group show of that year,[39] the forms remain distinct when the canvas is seen from a distance; however, the contours are never sharply defined, but suggested by contrasts of tone and colour. The surface is constantly variegated, with much small-scale, almost hairline brushwork added at a late stage, on the skirt and the shadows on the flesh, as well as on the hair itself. The forms and the play of light are suggested by these filigree textural effects without being defined with any precision, and some of the last touches added to the canvas appear very improvisatory – such as the highlights in the child's eyes and the sharp white accents (perhaps a handkerchief?) on the left side of the woman's skirt. Yet all these seemingly informal marks, when viewed together, create a composition of real weight and monumentality. Even at the moment when Renoir's tech-nique was most overtly challenging traditional conceptions of drawing and modelling, the figure grouping is a virtual replica, in reverse, of one of the most celebrated acade-mic paradigms in the Louvre, Raphael's Virgin and Child known as *La belle jardinière*.

Renoir took this process of dissolution furthest in canvases such as *Young Woman on a Bench* (pl. 150), probably painted in summer 1876 – a picture that fetched the derisory sum of 31 francs at the Hoschedé auction sale in 1878.[40] Here the figure is given no clearer definition than its surroundings; everything is treated in variegated dabs and flecks of colour. The composition is unobtrusively anchored by the fence at top left, the tree-trunks on the right and the legs of the bench on which the woman sits, and the upper parts of the figure itself are differentiated from the rest by the broader zones of deep blue of the bodice and hat, and the sharply contrasting accents of her eyes and lips. Yet the red of the lips is handled just as loosely as the flecks of bright red that suggest flowers elsewhere in the picture, and the treatment of the face as a whole is just as fragmented in touch as the rest of the canvas; this image of a young girl is in no way prettified. Renoir's repudiation of drawing is further stressed by the visible white priming

149   Pierre-Auguste Renoir, *The First Step* (*Le premier pas*), 1876, 111 × 81, private collection, New York

150 Pierre-Auguste Renoir, *Young Woman on a Bench (Jeune femme au banc)*, c.1876, 64 × 52, Christie's, London, 19 June 1999, lot 14

that is seen between the coloured touches over much of the canvas; it is made very clear that there is no lay-in or underdrawing to structure the image. Renoir insists that his fragmented coloured flecks are the sum of the whole image, and challenges the viewer to make pictorial sense of them.

*   *   *

Pissarro and Cézanne took a rather different path. From late 1873 onwards, they both adopted a denser and more ordered paint handling, giving their paint surfaces a more consistent texture and density across the whole canvas. In Pissarro's work, this new technique begins to appear in *Hoar-Frost* (pl. 79), dated 1873 and included in the first group show in 1874. The touch here is less variegated and more evenly weighted; the paint layers have a consistent density through most of the picture, and the same colours – soft oranges and blues, with a few small flecks of red – recur in many parts of the canvas.

These effects become far more emphatic in Pissarro's peasant scenes of Pontoise and Montfoucault of 1874 and 1875 (e.g. pls 151, 80). In *Peasant Woman Pushing a Wheelbarrow, Maison Rondest, Pontoise* (pl. 151), probably executed in early spring 1874,[41] the shape and direction of the marks remain responsive to the diversity of elements in the scene, but there is a marked homogeneity in their surface quality – a con-

151 Camille Pissarro, *Peasant Woman Pushing a Wheelbarrow, Maison Rondest, Pontoise* (*Paysanne poussant une brouette, Maison Rondest, Pontoise*), 1874, 65 × 51, Nationalmuseum, Stockholm

sistent density and emphasis on their material presence on the canvas surface: a slab of paint on a house in the distance is very similar in weight and texture to one on a wall in the foreground. This can be seen as a return to the thicker paint layers of Pissarro's work up to 1870; but the effect is quite different: in pictures like *Spring at Louveciennes* of 1870 (pl. 137) there is none of the consistency and coherence of surface texture that is so marked in *Peasant Woman Pushing a Wheelbarrow, Maison Rondest, Pontoise*. In another way, too, the various elements in the later picture are locked together, by the close parallels that are stressed between objects located in different spatial planes – between the walls on either side of the peasant woman and the houses beyond, and, most markedly, between some of the tree branches and the clouds in the sky.

All of this was achieved by the brush; but these developments were further accentuated in a group of canvases by both Pissarro and Cézanne from the mid-1870s that were largely executed with the palette knife. Both artists had previously used the palette knife, in a group of canvases of around 1865–7 (as indeed had both Monet and Renoir on occasion in the same years). At that date, it was a technique inseparably linked to Courbet and his reputation (see pl. 136): for Courbet's supporters it was a marker of his potent creative temperament, for his opponents of his wilful rejection of the basic disciplines of the art of painting. Courbet's example was still relevant in the mid-1870s, during his exile in Switzerland after his condemnation for the destruction of the

168

Vendôme Column. In this context, the use of the palette knife could be seen as a gesture of solidarity with the most famous cultural martyr of the aftermath of the Commune. In the early 1870s, too, Daubigny was also on occasion using the palette knife with great breadth and bravura.[42]

In some ways the effect of the palette knife, as it was used by Pissarro and Cézanne in the mid-1870s, is unlike Courbet.[43] Courbet's art, as we have seen, remained strongly tonal, and in his paintings the knife is primarily used descriptively, as a shorthand means of evoking the materiality of the objects represented, and particularly of stones and rocks and the other physical objects that were the focus of his art – the 'representation of real and existing things' that in 1861 he said was the only possible purpose for painting.[44]

By contrast, the knife-strokes in Pissarro's and Cézanne's canvases of the mid-1870s are less directly descriptive and less concerned with suggesting three-dimensional form, but are used, rather, to introduce nuances of variegated colour. The forms of the individual marks do vary according to the shapes and textures of the objects for which they stand, but they are not closely analogous to them. The smooth surfaces made by the knife-strokes create a particularly homogeneous effect across the whole painting.

Pissarro's palette-knife paintings (e.g. pl. 152) were probably all painted in 1875.[45] However, as always, the dating of Cézanne's comparable paintings is more problematic. Traces of knife-work are visible in *The Hanged Man's House at Auvers-sur-Oise* (pl. 41), included in the group exhibition in spring 1874. The encrusted surface and the consistent weight and density of the textures in this painting are closely comparable to Pissarro's *Peasant Woman Pushing a Wheelbarrow, Maison Rondest, Pontoise*, and may indeed have influenced this painting, though without leading Pissarro to take up the knife at this point. Like Pissarro, Cézanne's most extensive work with the knife seems to date from around 1874–5.[46]

Cézanne's marks are generally broader and at times quite crude in effect, Pissarro's smaller in scale and more delicate, but both artists used the knife to achieve a wide range of effects – ranging from simple and unmodulated slabs of colour, such as the façade of the house in Cézanne's *House at Auvers* (pl. 154), to complex and delicate weaves of varied colour, as in the area of foliage just to the right of this same façade. The two painters' palette-knife paintings have a strong two-dimensional presence that establishes a dialogue – or a tension – between the picture surface and the represented space, rather than being experienced primarily within the pictorial space that the picture represents. This emphasis on surface is accentuated by two further means – by giving very much the same texture and density to both foreground and background planes, for instance the foliage to the right of the house and the hill beyond it in *House at Auvers*, and by creating distinctively shaped accents that rhyme with similar shapes in other zones of the canvas, as in the loosely wedge-shaped accents that suggest the foliage of the foreground trees in Cézanne's *The Etang des soeurs, Osny* (pl. 153), in which the sequence of dull green knife-strokes running diagonally across the centre of the picture from the upper left seems particularly remote from any directly representational function.

Pissarro's *The Little Bridge* (pl. 152), dated 1875, is very similar to *The Etang des soeurs, Osny* in tonality and type of subject; indeed the two paintings may well represent the same park and be an example of canvases painted 'side by side'.[47] Like Cézanne's canvas, *The Little Bridge* is almost entirely painted with the knife, with the exception of some of the tree-trunks and the crisp strokes of dark green added at a late stage to

152 Camille Pissarro, *The Little Bridge (Le petit pont)*, 1875, 65.5 × 81.5, Kunsthalle, Mannheim

153 Paul Cézanne, *The Etang des soeurs, Osny (L'Etang des soeurs, Osny)*, 1875, 60 × 73.5, Courtauld Institute Gallery, London

154 Paul Cézanne, *House at Auvers (Maison à Auvers)*, c.1874.5, 60 × 73, Stiftung 'Langmatt', Baden

the foliage at top centre. However, Pissarro's knife-work is finer and less assertive; he used the knife with a finesse and lightness of touch that allowed it to skim across under-lying paint layers without covering them fully, and thus creating complex small-scale variegation of tone and colour. The edges of these small strokes are often quite rough and ragged, thus emphasising still further Pissarro's rejection of conventional notions of modelling and finish.

Both Pissarro's and Cézanne's paint-handling began to change markedly in 1876, in some senses in parallel ways, but without the close community of purpose that marked their work in 1874–5. In 1876–7 Pissarro's brushwork became smaller and more frag-mented. The breadth of treatment of his paintings of 1874–5 gave way to a busy, at times fussy surface, in which every area of the canvas is variegated and animated. In some paintings he seems to have looked to the more emphatic accents of Monet's latest work,[48] while the softer touch in *The Plain of Epluches (Rainbow)*, begun in autumn 1876 (pl. 76),[49] is more reminiscent of Renoir, in the way that the distinct coloured

155 Camille Pissarro, *The Côte des Boeufs at the Hermitage, Pontoise (La Côte des Boeufs à l'Hermitage, Pontoise)*, 1877, 115 × 87.5, National Gallery, London

flecks introduce sequences of related colours throughout the canvas. Yet Pissarro deployed these effects far more thoroughly and consistently than Renoir; the small touches are relatively even in weight all across the foreground of the picture, and the background, though more homogeneous in texture, is still enlivened by constantly varied nuances of colour and touch that pick up the foreground hues.

In 1877, in his more highly finished paintings, Pissarro began to give greater order to these small-scale touches, at times laying them on in sequences of approximately parallel strokes. This can be seen in the foreground of *The Côte des Boeufs at the Hermitage, Pontoise* (pl. 155), an early spring subject dated 1877, one of Pissarro's largest and most ambitious paintings from this period, probably exhibited at the third group exhibition with the title *The Orchard, Côte Saint-Denis, at Pontoise*.[50] However, the upper parts of this canvas are much more thinly painted and far less ordered in their execution – a telling reminder that the complexities of Pissarro's paint surfaces of this period were not part of the initial conception of his pictures, but developed as he worked them up to a higher degree of finish. Two years later, this increasing systematisation of touch led to paintings such as *Kitchen Garden at the Hermitage, Pontoise* (pl. 156). Here the whole canvas, including sky and houses, as well as the foliage and foreground terrain, is animated by small-scale touches equivalent in weight and scale but very varied in detail, running as they do in different directions, some crisper and more linear, some in softer coloured dabs. The following year, in *Landscape at Chaponval* (pl. 157), the

156　Camille Pissarro, *Kitchen Garden at the Hermitage, Pontoise (Jardin potager à l'Hermitage, Pontoise)*, 1879, 55 × 65.5, Musée d'Orsay, Paris

brushwork is relatively even in size and rhythm throughout the painting except for the sky (here again less highly worked), and in some parts of the canvas the strokes run in parallel sequences from lower left to upper right, creating a taut and coherent overall effect. The textures in these paintings may still be seen as a response to the visual stimulus – the *sensation* – of the scene itself; the marks may readily be viewed as standing for the textures of grasses and foliage. Yet, when these small dashes and flecks of colour are carried over into the sky and onto the walls of cottages, as they are in *Kitchen Garden at the Hermitage, Pontoise*, it becomes clear that they have transcended any 'natural' starting point, and have become an organising principle whose prime point of reference is the effect of the finished picture.

Paintings such as *Landscape at Chaponval* have often been compared with Cézanne's contemporary work, and in particular to the so-called constructive stroke, the seemingly systematic parallel hatching that is such a prominent feature in the brushwork of his

157 Camille Pissarro, *Landscape at Chaponval* (*Paysage à Chaponval*), 1880, 54 × 65, Musée d'Orsay, Paris

paintings around 1880. Tracking the development of Cézanne's technique in these years is handicapped – as always – by the lack of securely datable paintings; in addition, discussion is complicated by the relationship between his landscapes and still lifes – paintings done from 'nature' – and the figure subjects that he executed from his imagination. Although Theodore Reff in 1962 argued that the 'constructive stroke' emerged first in his imaginary works and was only later reapplied by Cézanne in his landscapes,[51] recent discussions have tended to the opposite conclusion, that these developments were simultaneous in both categories of work.[52] Indeed, the visual experience of the Cézanne retrospective exhibition of 1995–6 revealed such closely comparable changes in markmaking in the two types of painting that it seems most implausible that these took place at different dates. It seems clear that more fantastic, imaginary scenes continued into the early 1880s alongside his more serene bather compositions.

In 1876 Cézanne, like Pissarro, adopted a vigorous, emphatic touch quite unlike his recent palette-knife work, in paintings such as *The Sea at L'Estaque* (pl. 45), described in his famous letter of July 1876 (see p. 149–50), and included in the group exhibition of 1877. At various points, especially in the foliage, sequences of adjacent strokes run roughly parallel, creating some sense of rhythm in that zone of the canvas, but these run in varied directions, without imposing any dominant rhythm onto the canvas as a whole; the overall effect is of variegated, dynamic coloured touches. The so-called *Fantastic Scene* (pl. 158), the only imaginary figure painting by Cézanne known without doubt to have featured in the 1877 show,[53] has a similarly boldly handled, accented surface.

In *Bathing Women* (pl. 159) and *View of the Surroundings of Auvers* (pl. 160), the brushwork remains blocky and emphatic, but in both pictures – one imaginary, one from nature – there are clearer sequences of parallel strokes in the foliage, mainly running from lower left to upper right. The rhythm and density of the touches in these two paintings are so similar that they seem very likely to be roughly contemporary – the landscape was probably executed in summer 1877.[54] In *The Chaine de l'Etoile with*

158 Paul Cézanne, *Fantastic Scene (Scène fantastique)*, *c.*1876, 54.5 × 81.5, The Metropolitan Museum of Art, New York, Gift of Heather Daniels and Katharine Whild, Promised Gift of Katharine Whild, and Purchase, The Annenberg Foundation Gift, Gift of Joanne Toor Cummings, by exchange, Wolfe Fund, and Ellen Lichtenstein and Joanne Toor Cummings Bequests, Mr. and Mrs. Richard J. Bernhard Gift, Gift of Mr. and Mrs. Richard Rodgers, and Wolfe Fund, by exchange, and funds from various donors, 2001. (2001.473)

the Pilon du Roi (Glasgow Museums: Art Gallery and Museum, Kelvingrove), probably painted in summer 1878, smaller and more regular parallel strokes appear, relatively unobtrusively, across the whole central zone of the painting.[55]

The next landscapes that can be dated with relative confidence are *The Bridge of Maincy* (Musée d'Orsay, Paris), painted near Melun, south-east of Paris, in summer 1879, and *The Château of Médan* (pl. 161), executed while Cézanne was staying with Zola at his new Seine-side country home in summer 1880.[56] The parallel strokes in *The Bridge of Maincy* are looser and heavier, those in *The Château of Médan* exceptionally orderly and evenly weighted along the river bank and across the trees and background hillside. Of the two, *The Bridge of Maincy* is more lightly worked overall, but in both canvases there are areas where there is no such systematic handling – in the very sketchy top left corner of *The Bridge of Maincy* and in the sky in *The Château of Médan*. This shows that Cézanne, like Pissarro in *The Côte des Boeufs at the Hermitage, Pontoise* (pl. 155), began his canvases in a more informal, sketch-like manner, and only gradually imposed this surface ordering onto the canvas as he reworked it. This emerges particularly clearly in *Tall Trees at the Jas de Bouffan* of about 1883 (pl. 163). At bottom right, the initial layers remain visible, thin and un-reworked; in the next stage, seen across much of the foreground, crisper and more distinct brushstrokes begin to intro-

159   Paul Cézanne, *Bathing Women (Baigneuses)*, *c.*1877, 38.1 × 46, The Metropolitan Museum of Art, New York, Bequest of Joan Whitney Payson, 1975. (1976.201.12)

duce variegations of colour; but it is only after this that Cézanne began to introduce the network of rhythmic parallel strokes. With their varied colour, they act at one and the same time to give a sense of light and atmosphere and to impart a shimmer and richness to the whole picture surface.

This order, as in Pissarro's contemporary work, may have its starting point in observed foliage, but its rationale, in the final analysis, is essentially pictorial. Indeed, in its mature form Cézanne's 'constructive stroke' involved a more categorical disjunction between *sensation* and pictorial order than Pissarro's technique in these years, since at many points in his more elaborately worked canvases painted around 1880 the parallel strokes are so regular, in their size, shape and direction, that they no longer have any intelligible point of reference in the natural world. Their dominant direction from lower left to upper right, recurring in picture after picture, is evidently superimposed, not derived from direct observation. At times, too, these strokes are applied to elements in the natural scene whose textures bear no relationship whatsoever to the brush-marks in that area of the canvas – for instance the beige and brown strokes that suggest the bare earth on the river bank across the foreground of *The Château of Médan*.

This disjunction between observation and picture-making is confirmed by the appearance of closely similar effects in the pictures that Cézanne executed from his imagina-

160   Paul Cézanne, *View of the Surroundings of Auvers (Auvers-sur-Oise, vu des environs)*, *c.*1877, 60 × 50, private collection, New York

tion during the same years, where there was no external point of reference that could act as a template for the effects he created. *Three Bathing Women* (Musée du Petit Palais, Paris) shows handling comparable to *The Bridge of Maincy*, and, as has recently been argued, *The Eternal Feminine* (pl. 162) is in parts so close to *The Château of Médan*

161 (*above*)   Paul Cézanne, *The Château of Médan* (*Le Château de Médan*), 1880, 59 × 72, Burrell Collection, Glasgow

162   Paul Cézanne, *The Eternal Feminine* (*L'Eternel féminin*), *c.*1880, 43 × 53, The J. Paul Getty Museum, Los Angeles

163   Paul Cézanne, *Tall Trees at the Jas de Bouffan* (*Grands arbres au Jas de Bouffan*), *c.*1883, 65 × 81, Courtauld Institute Gallery, London

that they must have been executed around the same time.[57] The rather lighter and more fluid version of the 'constructive stroke' in *The Temptation of Saint Anthony* (Musée d'Orsay, Paris) suggests that this, too, was painted at the same period.[58]

This account suggests that in Cézanne's art, as to an extent in the same years in Pissarro's, there was a gradually increasing self-awareness about the integral role of the brush-mark as an ordering principle for the canvas. Their paintings of 1874–5, and their brief re-adoption of the palette knife, had stressed the physicality of the painted surface in new ways. However, it was only when they found ways of combining this sense of surface with the far greater finesse of touch and colour permitted by the brush that they could evolve a manner of painting that could synthesise the delicacy and complexity of their visual *sensations* into a coherent pictorial form. Painting could thus become a 'harmony parallel to nature'.[59]

Phrased in this way, this account of Pissarro's and Cézanne's paint-handling between 1874 and 1880 runs the risk of reducing it to a form of Greenbergian 'modernism', viewing it in terms of a primary concern with the intrinsically two-dimensional qual-ities of the painted mark on the flat canvas surface. Yet this would be to misrepresent their project. First, they remained centrally concerned with refining and analysing their visual *sensations* of the scenes in front of them. Their experiments with different types of facture belong to the second stage in their process that Cézanne, in his later comments on art, took great pains to isolate: *réalisation* – the translation of the *sensation* into coloured paint-marks. In 1906, in one of his last letters to his son, Cézanne described his aims in a way that re-emphasised the centrality and complexity of the *sensation*, and at the same time marked out *réalisation* as a distinct element in his processes: 'As a painter I am becoming more lucid in front of nature, but the realisation of my sensations is always very laborious. I cannot achieve the intensity which opens out before my senses, I do not have that magnificent richness of coloration that animates nature.'[60] *Réalisation*, here, is not an end in itself, but inseparably linked to the *sensations* that were the picture's starting point.

Yet, at a more conceptual level, there appears to have been a significant difference between the ways in which Pissarro and Cézanne conceived their technique. Cézanne left no commentaries on his own technique during these years. But his 'constructive stroke' was a type of mark that established a categorical distinction between the painting and its subject matter, applied as it might be to elements of all sorts within his paintings, regardless of their observed forms or textures, whereas with Pissarro there is always a closer residual link to visual experience. The touch, with Cézanne, can no longer stand as a metaphor for the qualities of the subject itself. This is especially significant in his treatment of the female nude – an insistence that the paintwork could not be seen as standing for the notion of sensual flesh or as invoking male heterosexual desire. It is perhaps in this context that we should view the recurring characterisation of Cézanne's art as 'pure' painting. The first traced example of this seems to be Gauguin's description of Cézanne's Pontoise landscapes in a letter to Pissarro in 1884 as representing 'an essentially pure art', in contrast to the 'astonishing execution' of Monet's recent paintings of the Mediterranean coast.[61]

*   *   *

The years from the mid-1870s to the early 1880s marked an increasing self-awareness about *réalisation* among all the members of the Impressionist group – a self-awareness that marked a definitive recognition of the impossibility of evoking the 'innocent eye'. This involved them in an ever-increasing concern for the qualities of the finished painting. We have no way of telling exactly what elements in the Impressionists' landscapes were executed out of doors and what were the result of studio elaboration.[62] However, it is clear that the changes that we have been describing in the treatment and surface qualities of their finished paintings emerged in the later stages of their execution – at the stage of *réalisation*, when the painters' primary concern was with the overall effect of the picture, rather than with direct notation of a natural effect.

By contrast, the initial lay-in layers of the Impressionists' landscapes were treated in broadly similar ways throughout these years; indeed, even the canvases that Monet left in a lightly worked state in the 1890s (e.g. *Poplars on the Epte*, 1891, Tate, London, on loan to National Gallery, London) are not unlike his more rapidly worked paintings of the 1870s. The initial process of blocking in the essentials of a scene in front of the motif remained relatively constant.[63] Moreover, the changes are far less evident in the canvases that Monet completed and sold as *esquisses* or *pochades* in the 1870s than they are in the fully realised pictures that he completed in the same years. As we have seen in Chapter Two, the Impressionists never exhibited these rapidly worked canvases alone, but always in juxtaposition with more highly finished pictures; while the *esquisses* could stand for the aspirations of the plein-airist, it was the more elaborated and complex surfaces of their *tableaux* that offered the fullest sense of their distinctive artistic personalities.[64]

Up until 1873, the practice of Monet and Pissarro corresponded in its essentials with the instructions that Monet later gave to Lilla Cabot Perry, to translate the shapes before her into coloured touches on the canvas. There was, in principle at least, a correspondence between the unit of vision and the unit of paint; a patch of a particular colour seen in the external world was translated into a patch of colour on the canvas. Of course this oversimplifies their practice, but it is usually possible to view the coloured touches in the paintings as standing for some distinct element in the scene, or for the visual experience (the *sensation*) of it.

After 1873 this was no longer so. Increasingly through the mid- to later 1870s the unit of paint in both Monet's and Pissarro's work became smaller than the unit of vision, and often quite separate from any such unit; it can no longer be directly identified with any distinct visual experience. The painter's vision, as presented to us by the painted marks, is now so subtle, so sensitive, that it can take objects apart and recreate them in coloured touches. We are invited to reconstitute the natural subject by taking these touches together, and viewing the picture as a whole.

So far, we have charted this crucial shift in Impressionist technique primarily in descriptive, visual terms. But how far did the painters and their contemporaries recognise this shift, and how far did they attempt to make sense of it in verbal terms – to theorise it? None of the Impressionist artists left any recorded comment about these changes from the years around 1880. However, a letter that Pissarro wrote in 1890 about the development of his own career gives a valuable clue to their significance: 'When I was about forty [i.e. around 1870], I began to understand my *sensations*, to know what I was seeking, but only vaguely; at fifty, that is in 1880, I formulated the idea of unity, but without being able to render it; now, at sixty, I am beginning to see how to render it.'[65] The phase of understanding his *sensations* coincides with the variegated shorthand that we have described as characterising the technique of all the Impressionists in the early 1870s – a type of handling primarily conceived as a means of translating the visual experience of particular objects into paint. The move beyond *sensation* to the formulation of the 'idea of unity' around 1880 is a move from part to whole – from a preoccupation with the individual elements in the picture to an overriding concern for the overall effect of the whole scene.

Contemporary art-critical writing also offers crucial insights. In the reviews of the group exhibition of 1876, there is a marked change of emphasis. Concerns with lack of finish and the *tache* remain, but a new focus emerges, on the relationship between Impressionist technique and the scientific analysis of sunlight, most notably in Duranty's *La nouvelle peinture*: 'Working by intuition, they have gradually succeeded in decomposing sunlight into its rays, and recomposing its unity through the general harmony of the iridescent colours that they scatter across their canvases. The result is quite extraordinary, in terms of its visual refinement and the subtle interrelationships of colour. The most learned physicist could criticise nothing in their analyses of light.'[66] Comparable references to optical theory were made by a number of other reviewers in 1876; it is unclear whether these derived from Duranty's text, or from some other shared source.[67]

Duranty's line of argument is in part problematic, in part very significant. Taken literally, his invocation of the science of optics is misleading. As has often been shown, his notion of decomposing and recomposing sunlight is based on a confusion between additive and subtractive mixing of colours – between colour as light and colour on canvas.[68] Moreover, the idea that separate coloured touches are recomposed in the eyes of the viewer is based on faulty science: when the painting is seen from a normal viewing distance, the distinct coloured touches remain clearly visible.[69] Rather, Duranty's language needs to be understood metaphorically; the image of decomposing light into its component parts was a means of characterising a mode of painting in which the individual coloured touches appeared to fragment the objects depicted, rather than corresponding in any sense to identifiable units of visual experience. The final passage of Mallarmé's essay of 1876 seems also to be feeling its way towards an analysis of the same technical experiments. The Impressionist, he says, is not seeking to imitate nature (an unrealisable ambition) but rather to express 'the delight of having recreated nature touch by touch', and through this to convey the 'Aspect'.[70]

These developments found a fuller formulation in a number of essays and reviews in the early 1880s. Reviewing the group exhibition of 1880, Charles Ephrussi offered a particularly perceptive and well-informed analysis of the characteristics of Impressionist painting, and concluded: '. . . deliberately neglecting distinct, individual tones in order to achieve a luminous unity whose varied elements blend in an indissoluble ensemble and create an overall harmony through their very dissonances'.[71] In 1881 Paul Bourget developed these ideas in a discussion of Impressionist colour observation that vacillates between the scientific and the metaphorical:

They struggle to render [minute distinctions of colour] and to study the smallest details of their own sensations . . . Our independents . . . hence succeed in perceiving the incessant mobility of light that physics is well able to demonstrate, but cannot make visible to our still crude retinas. A sort of impalpable dust of coloured atoms floats in what we take to be shadow and tints that shadow. They do their utmost to soak their brushes in that dust. It is thus that they achieve the singular colour effects that make inattentive visitors shrug their shoulders . . . Their eye seizes nuances that ours does not perceive – for the moment at least, because they will educate us, you can be sure of that.[72]

Although his imagery is ostensibly scientific, Bourget's 'dust of coloured atoms' is a vivid metaphor for the fragmented touch that we have been examining.

In his essay on Impressionism of 1883, Jules Laforgue reiterated Bourget's point about the exceptional sensitivity of the Impressionist eye, and, like him, used scientific optics as the starting point of his account. However, in a paragraph entitled 'False education of our eyes', he explicitly recognised the categorical distinction between natural light and light as represented in painting, and emphasised that the painter's means of rendering natural light were based on conventions. In analysing the differences between traditional and Impressionist methods, he began by characterising this in terms of the act of vision: '. . . the Impressionist sees [the light] as bathing everything not with dead whiteness, but with a thousand vibrant contrasts and rich prismatic decomposition'. Yet he continued his analysis not in terms of the act of viewing the natural scene, but by describing the ways in which these effects were conveyed in painting. In place of contour, the Impressionist 'sees real living lines without any geometrical form, but made up from

a thousand irregular touches that, from a distance, give a sense of life'; and in place of linear perspective, the Impressionist 'sees perspective created by the thousand minute variations of tone and touch, by the varied atmospheric conditions constantly moving in space'.[73]

As it evolved in the later 1870s, the Impressionists' techniques placed ever greater demands on their viewers. Faced with the complex skein of coloured touches of one of their more elaborated pictures, a critic could no longer reiterate the litany that this was merely an incomplete sketch, presented as if it was a finished painting. The new surface elaboration invited a form of creative viewing, appealing to an initiated elite who could see these touches as standing for the finesse of the painter's vision, and could appreciate the overall unity of the ensemble. For those who could do this, the painting offered special insight into the visual world and the vision of the painter; for those who could not – as many of the Impressionists' first viewers could not – it remained a mass of incoherent coloured marks on the flat canvas.

Yet there remained a central ambiguity about this unity: was it viewed as inherent in the scene itself, or as something imposed on it by the painter, as he or she 'realised' a canvas? In a sense this is a false opposition, since the *sensation*, as we have seen, was something personal and unique, and remained the essential starting point in each painter's creative process. Thus the unity that a painter found in a scene was also inevitably the product of his or her own personal vision and was evoked in his or her individual technique. As if to stress this, alongside the material changes in their technique came an increasing insistence in the early 1880s that each artist's facture – their personal artistic handwriting – was unique and distinctive and that it was the material expression of their temperament and personality. This dual nature of the Impressionists' art was fundamental both to its theoretical grounding and to the material practices involved in its production.

In Monet's work, this insistence on the uniqueness and individuality of his technique emerges with the more dynamic and at times calligraphic stroke that we have seen in his paintings of 1880–81 (see pls 146, 147) – a type of mark-making that parades the virtuosity of the painter just as much as it evokes the visual experience of the scene. It was during the 1880s, too, that Monet began to cultivate his public image as a plein-airist painter, emphasising the machismo of his encounters with the elements as he painted on the coasts of France.[74] His technique, in these pictures, is the material equivalent of the physical, bodily drama of these encounters.

The tone of this writing, and the way in which Monet presented his own image, were evidently masculist. This must be set against recent arguments that have sought to emphasise the 'feminine' qualities of Impressionist technique, with its emphasis on colour at the expense of drawing, when viewed within nineteenth-century critical frameworks.[75] Certainly the colour–line contrast might be viewed in gendered terms, as is shown by Charles Blanc's famous verdict quoted above; and, viewed metaphorically, landscape painting might be described as 'feminine' in contrast to 'masculine' figure painting.[76] But the experiences and practices of the landscape painter, exposed to the elements and seeking to 'master nature', were unequivocally 'masculine' in their implications. The gendering of pictorial practices in the late nineteenth century was a complex and often contradictory business.

If Monet developed an assertive 'signature style' as a visible marker of his own artistic personality during the early 1880s, Renoir in the same years went through a crisis of confidence that led him to reintroduce drawing as the basis for his art. The details of this experiment are beyond the scope of the present book, but its implications in the present context are clear: for the moment, Renoir eschewed the pursuit of a distinctive personalised manner in favour of subordinating himself to authority, in the form of both the linear contour and the example of the old masters.

Pissarro, though, became deeply concerned about the relationship between his facture and his personality. In a number of letters in the early 1880s, he tried to articulate the qualities he was seeking in his paint-handling. In 1883 he commented: 'I am very worried about my harsh and rough execution; I should like to find a smoother handling, but without losing the same savage qualities.'[77] Later in the same year, he defined the prime qualities of his recent paintings of peasant subjects (e.g. pls 177, 178): 'Remember that I have a rustic, melancholic temperament, coarse and savage in appearance. It is only in the long term that I can give pleasure, if the viewer treats me with a little indulgence; for the passer-by, the glance is too rapid and he sees only the surface.'[78] In the first of these letters, Pissarro was concerned about the relationship between the surface qualities of his pictures and their overall mood; in the second, he seemingly accepted this conjunction, and extended it, by writing of himself and his paintings alike in the first person singular, to present his own personality and the mood of his paintings as a single, indivisible whole, 'coarse and savage in appearance', that implicitly encompassed both technique and subject matter. This is an extreme example of the rhetoric of 'temperament' painting, in its remarkable elision of self and art, presenting the painted mark as a transparent marker of the artist's character and identity.

This chapter has charted the move from the *tache*-ist style of the early 1870s, relatively similar among the key members of the group, to modes of painting that stressed the distinctive individuality and the uniquely sensitive personal vision of each artist. This development is closely mirrored in the changing patterns of group activity, and in the loss of the collective spirit of the group itself, in favour of each artist pursuing his own career path; this will be the subject of the final chapter.

6 From the 'Little Church' to the Marketplace: Impressionism around 1880

I N THE YEARS AROUND 1880, transformations occurred in many aspects of the Impressionists' lives and work – in their painting technique, in their choice of subjects, in their personal lives and in the exhibition outlets and markets they sought for their work. The result of this was that the artists who had appeared as a coherent group in 1877 quickly rejected any sense of collective identity, and pursued their own individual paths, at times with real acrimony towards their former colleagues. These developments have come to be described as the 'Crisis of Impressionism'.[1] In order to assess their causes and significance, these changes must be viewed in wider contexts; but, taken together, they pose a central question: is it just a coincidence that all these shifts took place in so short a period?

We have examined the changes in the brushwork of the landscapists in the group, from the flexible system of representation by *taches* towards a more unified, integrated pictorial surface. It was in the same years that all the members of the group gave up painting overtly contemporary subjects. Pissarro, as we have seen, favoured more archetypal images of the agricultural countryside from the mid-1870s onwards; Cézanne from the late 1870s increasingly found his landscape subjects in the surroundings of Aix-en-Provence, while Monet and Sisley came to focus on scenes of rivers flanked by small, archetypal country villages. Monet and Renoir also began to travel in order to paint, focusing when away from home on more obviously touristic themes; both of them painted the cliffs and beaches of the Channel coast and the Mediterranean, and Renoir tackled the celebrated tourist sites of Algiers, Venice and the Bay of Naples (e.g. pl. 164). In his figure paintings, too, Renoir began to turn away from contemporary subjects towards more apparently timeless themes such as the female nude, treated in a technique that in many ways marked a rejection of Impressionism, emphasising the contour and definition of forms. Late in his life, Renoir told the dealer Ambroise Vollard that around 1883 he had 'reached the end of Impressionism' and had 'reached the conclusion that he could neither paint nor draw'.[2]

The changes in subject matter have often been explained piecemeal, in terms of the biographies of the individual artists. Certainly both Monet and Sisley moved their homes away from the towns on the fringes of Paris to far more remote villages unaffected by encroaching urbanisation.[3] But Renoir continued to live in Paris, and Pissarro stayed around Pontoise until 1884.[4] The central issue is not where they lived, but what subjects they chose to paint, and how they chose to depict their surroundings, Pissarro creating an imagery of an archetypal peasant world (pls 177, 178), Monet, by contrast, viewing the countryside and the Channel coast in terms of increasingly bold effects of light and colour, at the expense of the social content of the scenes (e.g. pls 146, 147). Equally Monet's and Renoir's travels did not cause them to change their subject matter;

facing page Claude Monet, *Sunset on the Seine, Winter Effect (Soleil couchant sur la Seine, effet d'hiver)* (detail of pl. 169)

164 Pierre-Auguste Renoir, *View of Venice, Grand Canal* (*Vue de Venise, grand canal*), 1881, 54 × 65.1, Museum of Fine Arts, Boston, Bequest of Alexander Cochrane

rather, it was their wish to extend their range of subjects that led them to travel and dictated their choice of sites to visit.

The changing markets and outlets for their work were a crucial factor in the changes in the Impressionists' artistic position in the years after 1877. At the third group exhibition in 1877, the core of the group, as we now perceive it, was present in force: Monet, Pissarro, Renoir, Sisley, Degas, Morisot, Cézanne and Caillebotte. For all of them, the group exhibition was the outlet for their most significant work. None at this point had regular relations with a dealer, and none was exhibiting at the Salon. The group exhibitions drew tiny numbers of people in comparison with the Salon (around 8,000 in 1877 as against 500,000 at the Salon in these years[5]), but a good proportion of those who did come were genuinely interested in their work, and even their smaller, more informal paintings could be presented in favourable conditions, in contrast to the densely hung big halls of the Salon. Their few regular buyers were by now personal friends whom they saw regularly – a group united by their enthusiasm for Impressionist painting, but notably diverse in social and professional terms.[6]

But the sense that the group exhibitions represented a common cause quickly broke down. In 1878 Degas introduced a clause that exhibitors could not also show at the Salon, which Renoir did from 1878 on; Renoir, Cézanne and Sisley did not exhibit with the group in 1879, 1880 and 1881, nor did Monet in 1880 and 1881; he too submitted to the Salon in 1880.

In the later 1870s Renoir was beginning to be patronised by a circle of collectors whom he had met through the publisher Georges Charpentier and his wife, who was hostess to a celebrated literary *salon*. The Charpentiers apparently encouraged Renoir to send to the Salon (and thus to disqualify himself from the group exhibitions), and at the Salon of 1879 his *Portrait of Madame G. C. . . . and her Children* (pl. 165) was a considerable success – in part, it seems, through Madame Charpentier's insistent lobbying.[7] The Charpentiers introduced Renoir to many other patrons who commissioned portraits from him. The demands of recognisable portraiture – of 'verisimilitude' – were clearly one of the factors that forced him to rethink his painting technique (see p. 64).

165   Pierre-Auguste Renoir, *Portrait of Madame G. C. . . . and her Children* (Portrait de Madame G. C. . . . et de ses enfants), 1878, 154 × 190, The Metropolitan Museum of Art, New York, Catharine Lorillard Wolfe Collection, Wolf Fund, 1907. (07.122)

Renoir's new circle of patrons not only affected his work in the field of portraiture; they may well also have been one of the factors that led him gradually to abandon modern urban subjects. Alongside his portraits, he began to produce saleable types of genre painting, in contrast to his studiedly informal Parisian subjects of the mid-1870s (e.g. pl. 150). Images of appealing young girls with exotic overtones, such as *The Little Gypsy Girl* of 1879 (pl. 166)[8] and *Algerian Girl* of 1881 (Museum of Fine Arts, Boston),[9] have subjects that were much in line with contemporary Salon taste; thematically, Bouguereau offers particularly close parallels (e.g. pl. 167), although of course Renoir's lavish colour and fluent painterly technique marked out his vanguard credentials.

By 1879 Monet was selling the occasional picture to dealers, especially still lifes, and early in 1880, as we have seen (p. 63), he explained to Georges de Bellio, one of his principal supporters, that the dealer Georges Petit had agreed to do business with him, but only on condition that he stopped selling his work cheaply to collectors like de Bellio.[10] Soon afterwards, he explained that he thought that Petit was more likely to buy from him if he submitted to the Salon. Of the two large canvases that he sent to the Salon in 1880, *Lavacourt* (pl. 168) was painted explicitly to please the jury (indeed, this was the only one that the jury accepted); it was, he reported, 'more sensible, more bour-

166 Pierre-Auguste Renoir, *The Little Gypsy Girl* (*La petite bohémienne*), 1879, 73 × 54, private collection, Canada

167 Adolphe-William Bouguereau, *On the Bank of the Stream* (*Au bord du ruisseau*), 1875, 137 × 86, Collection Frederick and Sherry Ross, New Jersey

geois' than a third large canvas that he was sure would be rejected – *Sunset on the Seine, Winter Effect* (pl. 169), with its overt echoes of the notorious *Impression, Sunrise* (pl. 37).[11] In summer 1880 Monet, too, showed his links with the Charpentier circle by mounting a one-man show in the offices of Georges Charpentier's magazine *La Vie moderne*; at this show, Madame Charpentier bought the large canvas that had been rejected by the Salon jury, *The Ice-Floes* (The Shelburne Museum). Monet's move to rural themes untouched by modernisation coincided with his concern to finish his paintings more fully; but it also coincided with his move to cultivate a wider circle of *haut bourgeois* collectors, beyond the small circle of insiders of 'artistic' tastes such as de Bellio who had supported him, and had bought even his roughest *esquisses*, through the 1870s (see Chapter Two).

These tentative steps into the art market were consolidated when in 1880–81 the dealer Paul Durand-Ruel began once again to make extensive purchases from Monet, Renoir, Pissarro and Sisley.[12] Pissarro was the one artist to exhibit in all eight of the Impressionist group exhibitions, and he did not submit to the Salon in these years, but, after Durand-Ruel resumed purchases from him, his letters were full of questions about the types of picture that the dealer would welcome, and Durand-Ruel was always ready to advise him about what might sell best.[13]

Alongside Renoir's abstention from 1879 and Monet's from 1880, a number of new exhibitors were introduced into the group exhibitions, among them protégés of Pissarro such as Paul Gauguin in 1879 and Victor Vignon in 1880, and a number of younger associates of Degas such as Mary Cassatt and Federico Zandomeneghi in 1879 and Jean-François Raffaëlli in 1880. Raffaëlli's inclusion, in particular, aroused the opposition of longstanding members of the group, and was viewed by many critics as inconsistent with the aesthetic position that the previous exhibitions had promoted. However, in 1882 Degas and his band were excluded from the seventh group exhibition, which once again presented the core of the original group. But this show was exceptional, since it was co-ordinated and mounted by Durand-Ruel, and many of the exhibits came from his stock.

* * *

These simultaneous changes in technique, subject matter and outlets cannot be treated as coincidental, or discussed in separate terms: the issues they raise are inseparable. To explore these, we must first return to the group exhibitions. For all the apparent homogeneity of some of the earlier exhibitions, notably the third in 1877, the various artists became involved with the group for different reasons. Zola pinpointed some of these in 1880: Monet, Renoir and Pissarro showed with the group because they could not gain acceptance at the Salon, Degas because his quite small, informal works stood little

168   Claude Monet, *Lavacourt*, 1880, 98.4 × 149.2, Dallas Museum of Art, Munger Fund

169 Claude Monet, *Sunset on the Seine, Winter Effect (Soleil couchant sur la Seine, effet d'hiver)*, 1880, 100 × 152, Musée du Petit Palais, Paris

chance of gaining attention in the huge halls of the Salon, and Caillebotte and Ernest Rouart because, as wealthy amateurs and friends of the other artists, they did not need the publicity of Salon display.[14]

We can refine Zola's account, by emphasising that Monet, Sisley and Pissarro, like Degas, were concentrating in the early 1870s on smaller pictures that would not be noticed at the Salon, even if they had been accepted. It was these that they were selling to Durand-Ruel in 1872–3. Although the organisation of an independent exhibition was under active discussion at least from May 1873 onwards, the charter of the *Société anonyme* was only finalised at the end of December; presumably Durand-Ruel's growing financial problems, which forced him to withdraw his support at the beginning of 1874, were a catalyst that led them finally to turn their plans into reality.[15]

However, Zola's general point is crucial: the group and its exhibitions represented an amalgam of different interests. Discussion of the group's activities in terms of interests highlights the dynamics behind the positions that particular artists took and what they did, and makes sense of individual positions that shifted or seemed inconsistent – most notably, perhaps, Pissarro's. Alternative views of the basic dynamic behind the group were already evident in 1876. Three distinct positions are evident in two key texts published in that year, Stéphane Mallarmé's 'The Impressionists and Edouard Manet' and Duranty's *La nouvelle peinture*.

For Mallarmé, the new art reflected a new, collective vision:

At that critical hour for the human race, when nature desires to work for herself, she requires certain lovers of hers – new and impersonal men placed directly in communion with the sentiment of their time – to loose the restraint of education and . . . thus . . . to reveal herself . . . For the mere pleasure of doing so? Certainly not, but to express herself . . . to those newcomers of tomorrow, of which each one will consent to be an unknown unit in the mighty numbers of an universal suffrage.

'Mere pleasure' is firmly rejected in favour of notions of impersonality and anonymity, which elsewhere in the essay Mallarmé links directly with intransigence – with democratic and radical politics in this period of political repression.[16]

Two very different points of view appear in Duranty's essay. One of these also has a political dimension, but one quite unlike Mallarmé's: 'Do you not see in these efforts the urgent and irresistible need to escape the conventional, the banal, the traditional, and to find oneself again and run far away from this bureaucracy of the spirit, with all its rules, that weighs down on us in this country?'[17] The image of 'finding oneself' expresses a quite different notion of the role of the human subject within society – that of the autonomous, self-determining individual, in contrast to Mallarmé's anonymous and 'impersonal men' and 'unknown unit'. This contrast emerges vividly when Duranty argues against the notion that the group shared a collective purpose and vision: 'They are not people who are clearly and steadfastly pursuing the same goal, but rather above all they are independent temperaments. They come seeking not dogma but examples of liberty.'[18]

The other position that Duranty upheld, as we have seen, was that of true Art (see p. 66). The Impressionists' painting was something that could be appreciated only by fellow artists and viewers of truly artistic tastes: 'The public . . . only understands correctness, and demands finish above all. The artist, charmed by the delicacy or boldness of a colour effect, by the character of a gesture or a grouping, is much less concerned with finish and correctness that are the only qualities appreciated by the inartistic . . . It matters little that the public does not understand; it matters more that the artists understand . . .'.[19] This notion of an art that appealed to an elite viewership was a reiteration of a point recurrently made about the work of the *école des Batignolles* in the late 1860s.[20]

No one of these positions is more correct as an analysis of the group's activities; rather, all three represent different interests that were at work, side by side and interacting, within the group. The basic opposition was between the idea of the group as a collective or as a neutral, independent site where individuality could be cultivated. This contrast is central to debates between entrepreneurial capitalism – the promotion of individual 'free enterprise' – and its socialist opponents. But the third perspective, that of true Art, introduced by Duranty alongside the notion of independence, complicated this opposition, by suggesting that Art lies above commerce and entrepreneurship – that Taste transcends Interest.

All three interests were clearly articulated in these two essays in 1876, and all could still be accommodated together in the exhibition of 1877, perhaps the most comprehensive of all the group's displays. But thereafter these same contrasting interests effectively split the group apart. Before exploring the broader factors behind this, we must examine the way in which they worked against each other between 1878 and 1883.

The change in the names given to the exhibitions hints at wider changes. Only in 1874 did the exhibition catalogues use the group's formal name, *Société anonyme des artistes peintres, sculpteurs, graveurs, etc.*; thereafter they simply described them as *Exposition de peinture*, and listed their number in the sequence. Only in posters and advertising were the shows given more informative titles. In these, the participants were only once, in 1877, given the name 'Impressionists'; in 1879, 1880 and 1881 they were called 'Independents'.[21] This was a crucial shift, rejecting the implied shared programme of 'impressionist' in favour of the autonomy of the individual. It is no coincidence that Degas, Duranty's prime informant for his essay of 1876 in which he promoted the 'independent temperaments' model, was also responsible for the change in naming from 'impressionist' to 'independent'. Degas's friend the Italian critic Diego Martelli spelt this out explicitly in a letter about the exhibition of 1879: 'This year, thanks to Degas, they have introduced an innovation which replaces the question of the restricted character of a research into the means of painting by the broader notion of each painting in his own manner, outside the sphere of official protection and favours.'[22]

In an interview in June 1880, Monet declared a position: 'I am an Impressionist and I want always to be one . . . but I only rarely see my colleagues . . . The little church has become a banal school which opens its doors to the first dauber.'[23] At first sight, it seems as if Monet was here standing up for the old collective spirit against Degas's and Pissarro's recently arrived protégés. But Monet gave this interview while his *Lavacourt* (pl. 168) was on show at the Salon. Many of his colleagues felt that his decision to exhibit there was the most blatant betrayal of the 'Impressionist' spirit, and the most overt assertion of the primacy of individual interest over collective benefit. In 1881, when plans were mooted for reuniting the core of the original group, Pissarro felt that they could not simply drop the artists who had kept to the agreed rules, in favour of the return of Monet and Renoir from the Salon, describing them as motivated by 'an individuality which they apply to all their judgements'.[24]

Two years later, Gauguin summed up the arguments in favour of the collective group enterprise in a letter to Pissarro:

> The Impressionists . . . had a certain clientele that was interested in them and followed their progress each year . . . When you are together, one sees each artist's difference, but separately one thinks you all look the same . . . Apart from the individual talent each can show, what will become of the movement? Now . . . there is only talent, but no movement . . . We were interesting because, with some talent, we formed a phalanx of painters *convinced of their movement* and protesting against the art market.[25]

Gauguin's argument here has a certain irony. He himself was outside the 'market', but Pissarro had been selling to Durand-Ruel for two years; and, at the moment that Gauguin wrote the letter, Durand-Ruel was mounting a series of one-artist shows of the principal artists of the Impressionist group, including Pissarro himself, so as to promote them as individuals, not as members of the group. By 1883 Pissarro, like Monet and Renoir, was firmly locked into the dealer system – site of the entrepreneurial speculation in art that Gauguin was opposing. These five one-artist shows, of Boudin, Monet, Renoir, Pissarro and Sisley, seem to have been the first sequence of such events mounted by a dealer in any major art centre.[26] From the end of the 1880s onwards, the one-artist show came to play an increasingly central role in the art world – a crucial stage in the emergence of individuality and originality as primary criteria in the assessment of modern art.[27]

170 Pierre-Auguste Renoir, *A Box at the Opera* (*Une Loge à l'Opéra*) [now known as *At the Concert*], 1880, 99.2 × 80.6, The Sterling and Francine Clark Art Institute, Williamstown, Mass.

However, as we have seen, the opposition in the early 1880s was not simply a matter of collective as against individual interests – of the group shows, with their small but loyal clientele, against the dealer acting as intermediary between artist and bourgeois buyer. The third crucial viewpoint saw the Impressionist group proper as standing for Art – for aesthetic standards as against bourgeois taste. It was this argument that Caillebotte used in 1881 for readmitting Monet and Renoir – that they belonged in any truly 'artistic' exhibition.[28] And in 1882, when Durand-Ruel was trying to coordinate the seventh group exhibition as a display of the old core group, Renoir agreed to show only if it was a matter of 'pure art', which for him at this point meant the omission of Pissarro, with his radical political views, and of his and Degas's protégés.[29]

Pissarro and Gauguin explicitly opposed the idea of an 'artistic' exhibition in arguing against the reinstatement of Monet and Renoir. Gauguin put this very succinctly: 'It is impossible to create a movement outside the Ecole and the Salon without mutual respect between the exhibitors. You should explain this to Caillebotte, who wants an *artistic exhibition*; this art, if it is meant to be different from the Academy, should not appear in the Salon of the Academy.'[30] In the event, though, Monet and Renoir were included in 1882, along with Pissarro and Gauguin. However, one critic, at least, felt that Renoir's new, fashionable manner was quite out of place in the group. Louis Leroy wrote of his *A Box at the Opera* (pl. 170): 'The little faces of the two young women, their attire, the colour of the ensemble, have bourgeois qualities which Impressionism execrates.'[31]

171 Jean-François Raffaëlli, *The Garlic Seller (Marchand d'ails et d'échalotes)*, 1881, 71.8 × 49, Museum of Fine Arts, Boston, the Henry C. and Martha B. Angell Collection

This distinction between 'bourgeois' and 'artistic' needs to be defined in visual terms. The 'bourgeois' qualities that Leroy found in Renoir's picture related to both technique and subject – to the mellow colouring and comparatively careful finish, and to the prettified faces and fashionable ambience; Leroy explicitly contrasted it with the 'hatched, striped and patched surface' of the water in one of Renoir's views of Venice in the 1882 show (pl. 164).[32] Monet, as we have seen, described his *Lavacourt* (pl. 168), painted for the Salon of 1880, as 'more sensible, more bourgeois' than a painting 'too much to my own taste for it to be accepted'.[33] Presumably the latter picture, *Sunset on the Seine* (pl. 169), with its bold brushwork and vivid light effect and its echoes of *Impression, Sunrise*, represented what he would have been considered 'artistic', in contrast to the comparatively bland and delicately finished *Lavacourt*. Interestingly, Monet included both *Sunset on the Seine* and *The Ice-Floes*, rejected by the jury in 1880, in the 1882 show, but expressly asked Durand-Ruel not to include the 'bourgeois' *Lavacourt*;[34] he clearly wished to show his most 'artistic' side.

Equally the protagonists of 'art' rejected Raffaëlli. The contrasts between his and Degas's modern subjects are revealing. Whereas Raffaëlli focused directly on itemising the details of social types and settings (e.g. pl. 171), Degas was preoccupied with how he saw – with the ways that the modern world looked from the unexpected angles of vision so characteristic of modern city life. Raffaëlli's interests belonged to a long tradition of bourgeois scrutiny and classification of non-bourgeois types – to the lineage of *études de moeurs* that led from Jacques Callot in the seventeenth century and Philippe

196

Mercier in the eighteenth to such popular nineteenth-century *physiologies* as *Les Français peints par eux-mêmes* of the 1840s.[35] Degas too, as we saw in Chapter Four, was attentive to markers of class and status, but at the same time he was constantly concerned with the act of viewing, and with the viewer's complex engagement with the sign languages of the modern city. In 1882 the protagonists of the 'artistic' exhibition would have welcomed Degas if he had abandoned Raffaëlli; he refused to do this.

These debates about the 'artistic' in Impressionist painting in the early 1880s echo the terms of a similar opposition in the early 1870s. Then, we learn in a letter from the art-agent Samuel Avery, the works of 'Millet, Diaz, Daubigny, Delacroix, Decamps, Fromentin, Dupré & &' were being marketed as 'high art', in an explicit attempt 'to put Bouguereau, Merle, and others of "The School of Goupil" as the dealers call it, out of fashion'.[36] In both cases, the notion of 'Art' or 'high art' was associated with sketchier, more personal forms of painting, in contrast to the comparative legibility and accessibility of paintings that appealed to bourgeois taste; it was universally agreed that the artists supported by the dealer Goupil – notably fashionable genre painters such as Toulmouche and Baugniet – were the most blatant example of this in the early 1870s; the rival dealer seeking to market the artists listed by Avery as 'high art' was clearly Durand-Ruel.[37]

In another sense, too, the situation in the early 1870s repeated itself in the early 1880s. In the 1870s the banner of 'high art' was evidently used to boost sales of the less immediately ingratiating art; likewise in the early 1880s it was the 'artistic' Impressionists, notably Monet, Pissarro and Renoir, that Durand-Ruel was seeking to propagate, in order to convert the former elite, minority taste into a real commercial merchandise – to commodify the artistic. Again, though, as in the early 1870s, Durand-Ruel does not seem to have bought their most informal and experimental paintings.

*　　*　　*

No single explanation is adequate to explain why the Impressionist group could accommodate such diverse interests in the years 1874–7, only to be torn apart by them between 1878 and 1882. Biographical factors are relevant; as they approached middle age, the artists were seeking to establish themselves professionally and economically. Likewise, the history of artistic groupings shows a recurrent pattern of short phases of collective action followed by the reassertion of individual positions and interests.[38]

However, this change must be viewed in a wider historical and political context. As we have seen, the years of concerted group activity coincided with the presidency of Marshal MacMahon and the government policy of repression and censorship; at the same time, the Directeur des Beaux-Arts, the Marquis de Chennevières, was following an explicitly conservative and pro-Academic policy.[39] The parliamentary elections of autumn 1877, and particularly the Senate elections of January 1879, drastically shifted the balance towards the committed liberal republicans – the so-called 'opportunists' – and in January 1879 Jules Grévy replaced MacMahon as president.

Over the next six years Jules Ferry was perhaps the dominant figure in the government, twice serving as Prime Minister, besides acting, for much of the time, as Minister of Public Instruction and the Fine Arts. Ferry's views of the status of the fine arts and their purpose in modern France emerge vividly in the speeches he delivered at the annual prize-giving ceremonies at the end of the Salon exhibition.

172 Léon Lhermitte, *The Harvesters' Wages* (*La Paie des moissonneurs*), 1882, 215 × 275, Musée d'Orsay, Paris

As we have seen (see pp. 140–41), the ministerial address in 1876, before the changes, had preached the revival of traditional history painting through the sponsorship of the State, the Academy and the Ecole des Beaux-Arts. In 1879, by contrast, in Ferry's first prize-giving address, the watchwords were freedom and individualism, and the ungovernability of art. For him, history painting meant the celebration of modern heroes; and he explicitly sanctioned open-air painting as one of the central elements in modern French painting – 'a more fugitive, yet more intimate truthfulness, harder to seize, but because of this all the more striking'.[40] This invocation itself may well have been a factor in Monet's decision to submit to the Salon jury the next year. But, more broadly, the pleas to individualism were an explicit attempt to prise the gifted individual away from radical groupings. In a sense, with the demise of repression and censorship, the oppositional group activity of the 1870s lost its purpose and its forum.

In the years around 1880, many former star students from the Ecole des Beaux-Arts turned to contemporary subjects and adopted modified forms of impressionist handling; many of their new works won them medals at the Salon, or were purchased by the State, or both (Albert Besnard, Alfred Roll, Jules Bastien-Lepage, Pascal Dagnan-Bouveret).[41] At the same time, other painters who had been painting modern subjects for longer were now awarded medals (Carolus-Duran, Ernest Duez, and finally, in 1881, Manet).[42]

Two paintings exhibited at the Salon in 1882 demonstrate the change in cultural climate: Léon Lhermitte's *The Harvesters' Wages* (pl. 172) and Alfred Roll's *14 July 1880* (pl. 173). Lhermitte's canvas, purchased by the State in 1882, reinterprets the stock theme of agricultural labour by emphasising issues of proprietorship, economics and class, depicting the payment of the workers' wages, alongside a range of working 'types'.[43] This stands in marked contrast to the seemingly homogeneous world of *la France profonde*, as shown, amongst so many other canvases, in Lhermitte's own *The Harvest* of 1874 (pl. 72). Indeed, from the early 1880s onwards, industrial subjects, extremely unusual in earlier years, also began to appear frequently on the Salon walls and to be purchased by the State, as emblems of the progressivist ethos of the 'opportunist' Republic.[44]

Roll's gigantic *14 July 1880*, a State commission, was in a sense the manifesto painting of the new republicanism,[45] and the key example of the new public painting of con-

173 Alfred Roll, *14 July 1880 (14 juillet 1880)*, 1882, 645 × 980, Musée du Petit Palais, Paris

temporary urban subjects that the new regime fostered. We are faced with a crowd – a mix of sexes and social classes that, at first sight, seems as disruptive as any of the Impressionists' modern life subjects of the 1870s. On the left, a peasant woman pours wine out of a barrel and a couple embrace enthusiastically; on the right, bourgeois and working-class couples stand side by side, and a wealthy man in a carriage stares at we know not what; in the centre, a grimacing boy plays the violin alongside a nursemaid with two babies and an evidently inebriated group of male revellers, while, in the foreground, a roughly dressed young boy gestures in our direction – the very image of the *gamin de Paris* who had been the emblem of working-class defiance in previous generations.[46] But this *gamin* – our point of entry into the picture – has been co-opted by the new regime: he is selling *tricolor* buttonholes; and, behind the crowd, we see the silhouette of the newly erected statue of *La République* on the Place de la République in Paris, and, between the statue and the throng, the bayonets of a march-past of soldiers and the distinctive silhouette of an officer on horseback. The crowd before us is legitimised by the newly established celebrations of 14 July and thus by the Republic itself, but it is also controlled, carefully kept in its place beneath the dual emblems of Republic and Army. Roll, and indeed the Republic itself, have appropriated the oppositional imagery of the 1870s, creating a scenario in which tensions of sex and class can be admitted but ultimately defused.

It was at the same Salon that Manet exhibited his last great urban subject, a year before his death: *A Bar at the Folies-Bergère* (pl. 126). Despite all its social and spatial complexities, by 1882 the subject itself was no longer alien in a fine art context. It seems no coincidence that the members of the Impressionist group who had focused with such critical attention on the imagery of Paris throughout the 1870s all turned their backs on such scenes after the early 1880s, or, in Degas's case, treated the settings of his figures in increasingly generalised and inexplicit terms, so that his paintings can no longer be read as direct visual engagements with specific scenarios. A truly 'modern' painting no longer needed to be a painting of modern life; it was now the artist's powers of transformation – his distinctive mark – that stood as the marker of his vision and creativity.[47]

During the early 1880s there was a crucial shift in the relationship between art and the State. In 1880–81 a wholesale reorganisation of the Salon removed it from State control and placed it in the hands of the artists, renaming it the Salon des artistes français; the State planned to mount more select shows every three or four years.[48] The argument for this was that the real strengths of works could not be gauged amid the immense variety and disorder of the annual exhibition, but only with time.[49] This meant that the everyday running of the fine arts was now pushed into what we should call the 'private sector'. But this raised, in the minds of Ferry and many others, the spectre of fashion, commercialism and speculation. Ferry praised the new body for avoiding this pitfall and maintaining rigorous standards,[50] but other commentators were less convinced, or less tactful, than the Minister.[51]

It was these debates that were being played out in the same years around the Impressionist group exhibitions, between those who saw them as a platform for self-advancement and those who insisted that they should stand for Art. But, as we have seen, Durand-Ruel's decisive intervention in the early 1880s meant that even this Art was explicitly a commodity. Soon after, the fashionable commercial gallery of Georges Petit took the former Impressionists up in earnest, claiming for its exhibitions a 'purely artistic character'.[52]

Monet's and Renoir's response to the predicaments of 1880 was to pursue vigorously individualist paths, both in their exploitation of the art market and in their assertion of the uniqueness of their artistic vision; but they did this in different ways, Renoir by looking to the art of the past, and increasingly presenting himself as an inheritor of a great lineage, and Monet by emphasising the virtuosity of his technique and the free-range bravado of the plein-airist, pursuing his unique *sensations*. Pissarro's position was more equivocal, a complex amalgam of anarchist utopianism and entrepreneurial marketing; at least by the mid-1880s he was committed to a pacifist form of anarchism in which society was decentralised

174 Gustave Courbet, *The Cliff at Etretat after the Storm* (*La Falaise d'Etretat après l'orage*), 1870, 133 × 162, Musée d'Orsay, Paris

175   Claude Monet, *Etretat, Rough Sea* (*Etretat, mer agitée*), 1883, 81 × 100, Musée des Beaux-Arts, Lyon

and the individual retained control of his own rights;[53] yet he engaged with the capitalist art market with just as much commitment as any of his colleagues.

A group of paintings by these artists reveals the distance that each had travelled from the informal, explicitly contemporary imagery that they had explored in their paintings of the early 1870s. Early in 1883 Monet returned to Etretat, the Channel coast village flanked by spectacular rock arches, where he had worked in the late 1860s and where he had painted *Luncheon* (pl. 6). By the 1880s Etretat had become a celebrated site and a popular summer tourist resort, and also carried with it a legacy of past representations – most notably the canvases that Courbet had painted there in the late 1860s, several of which had been exhibited in the Courbet retrospective exhibition at the Ecole des Beaux-Arts in 1882.[54] Soon after arriving in Etretat, Monet wrote to Alice Hoschedé: 'I am planning to paint a large canvas of the cliff at Etretat, though it is terribly impudent of me to do this after Courbet who did it admirably, but I shall try to do it differently.'[55] The resulting picture, *Etretat, Rough Sea* (pl. 175), is an overt reworking of the subject of the most ambitious of Courbet's beach scenes, *The Cliff at Etretat after the Storm* (pl. 174), shown at the Salon of 1870 and again in the show of 1882, with its boats on the beach facing the waves, framed by the grandiose mass of the Porte d'Aval. Monet did indeed 'do it differently'; his parade of virtuoso brushwork is a far

176 Pierre-Auguste Renoir, *Seated Bather (Baigneuse assise)*, *c.*1883–4, 121 × 91, Fogg Art Museums, Harvard University, Cambridge, Mass., Bequest – Collection of Maurice Wertheim, Class of 1906

cry from the materiality of Courbet's palette-knife work, evoking, as it does with such vividness, the varied textures of the scene, ranging from the horizontal striations of the cliff to the fluid, cursive movements of the breaking waves. Yet Monet's canvas is not merely a tribute to Courbet; its theme is the traditional romantic opposition of man against the elements. There is no trace of modernisation here, no hint of Etretat's status as a tourist resort or of the many leading artistic figures who had villas there.[56] Along-side the boats and the fishermen, we see three *caloges*, disused boats now thatched and used for storing fishing materials; a curious synthesis of boat and cottage, they evoke the continuity of life at Etretat and of man's confrontation with the sea.[57] The modernity of Monet's vision here lies, not in his subject matter, but in the identity that the picture claims for him as an artist: master of the elements and master of his brush; his vision and technique marked out his unique artistic personality.

Later in 1883, Renoir spent a month on the island of Guernsey, in the Channel to the west of Normandy; it was probably during the following winter that he painted *Seated Bather* (pl. 176), a nude seated on a rock, set against a background closely reminiscent of the outdoor studies that he had made on Guernsey.[58] Yet he made no effort to integrate this background with the figure; it acts as a backdrop, without any credible relationship to the space in which the figure is set. We are left in no doubt that this is a studio composition – an overt rejection of the ambition to integrate figures and setting that was central to his outdoor figure subjects of the 1870s; and there is nothing contemporary about the figure, except perhaps her bracelets. However, Renoir's visit to Guernsey played a larger role in the genesis of the picture than merely supplying the background. While he was on the island, he described the place in terms of a timeless idyll:

> Here one bathes among the rocks which serve as bathing cabins, because there is nothing else; nothing can be prettier than this mixture of women and men crowded together on the rocks. One would think oneself in a Watteau landscape rather than in reality . . . Just as in Athens, the women are not at all afraid of the proximity of men on the nearby rocks. Nothing is more amusing, when one is strolling through these rocks, than surprising young girls getting ready to bathe; even though they are English, they are not particularly shocked.[59]

His experiences on the beach on Guernsey may well have sanctioned his decision to site his non-modern nude in a specific natural setting. The treatment of the figure, too, is in stark contrast to the dissolved forms of some of his figures of the mid-1870s. In contrast to the loosely handled, brushy background, the woman's body is treated smoothly and simply, emphasising its solidity, and the drapery around her legs is modelled by crisp strokes of clear blue. *Seated Bather* marks a crucial stage in Renoir's wholesale rejection in the mid-1880s of the imagery of modernity, and his increasing disillusion with the modern city itself, and the values associated with it.[60]

At the Impressionist group exhibition of 1882, Pissarro exhibited a pair of paintings, with the titles *Study of Figures in the Open Air, Grey Weather* and *Study of Figures in the Open Air, Sunlight Effect* (pls 177, 178).[61] Both show female peasants among trees, seemingly resting. Commenting on the *Grey Weather* canvas, Pissarro wrote: 'This is the type of picture that I am most interested in exploring; its mood is not gay, but I am following the direction of my own *sensations*, I let myself roll along with them.'[62] There are clear echoes of Millet's work in these paintings, in the scale-relationship between

177 Camille Pissarro, *Peasants Resting (Paysannes au repos)*, 1881, 82 × 66, Toledo Museum of Art, Ohio

figures and backgrounds and in the very generalised figure types. However, the settings in which the peasants are presented are less specific than in most of Millet's works. Neither canvas shows any working context, and in both pictures the women are enclosed by trees in such a way that we gain no sense of a nearby work-space; but the body language of the figures suggests rest after labour, and indeed weariness, rather than leisure.

178 Camille Pissarro, *Two Young Peasants Chatting under the Trees, Pontoise* (*Deux jeunes paysannes causant sous les arbres, Pontoise*), 1881, 81 × 65, private collection

At the same time, the pictures scrupulously avoid any signs that could be interpreted in terms of sentimentality or 'romance' – two qualities that Pissarro explicitly rejected in his art.[63] The backgrounds presumably derive from actual sites and the figures from drawings made from models, but the figures in the paintings were clearly not executed in the open air and were very probably based on drawings, not executed directly from the model. The comparative uniformity of technique throughout the canvases absorbs the peasants into their settings, suggesting that they are inseparable from their rustic surroundings, while the 'harsh and rough execution' that worried Pissarro in these years enhances the sense of rusticity.[64] The effect of the pictures, overall, is of a generalisation and a form of typecasting that invite us to view them in generic terms, as commentaries on the human condition, or rather on the condition of the female 'peasant',[65] and not in any sense as records of direct experience.

One, and probably both, of Pissarro's paintings were bought by Durand-Ruel before they were included in the show of 1882, organised by the dealer. He also bought Monet's *Etretat, Stormy Sea* in December 1883, and sold it to the Musée des Beaux-Arts in Lyon in 1902 – it was the first work by Monet to be purchased by any museum in France. Renoir deposited *Seated Bather* with Durand-Ruel in 1886, and the dealer bought it in 1892. All the paintings paraded the artists' distinctive personalities, expressed through both subject matter and technique; and in all of them technique played an integral part in the expressive content of the painting – the bravura of Monet's confrontation with the elements, Renoir's marriage of Impressionist light with traditional form, and Pissarro's 'rustic and melancholic temperament, coarse and savage in appearance'.[66]

There was no single event or turning point that led to the breakup of the Impressionist group. But the years around 1880 brought a range of interests into conflict that led to the end of the 'little church' – to the dismemberment of the Impressionists as a collective, and perhaps to the end of Impressionism as a movement – in favour of the individual artists' pursuit of their personal fame and fortune, in the marketplaces of the brave new capitalist world of the opportunist Republic. As we have insisted, this individuality was a matter of style and technique as well as markets. It is only by analysing all these aspects of their work together that we have been able to track their evolution from the early 1870s to the early 1880s – from the relative homogeneity of their vision and art and the shared purpose of the first group exhibition in 1874, to their emergence as distinctive independent artistic personalities after 1880. It was through this shift that their work began to be assimilated into the bourgeois canon that it had earlier so vigorously challenged.

Coda: Impressionism's Histories Reviewed

WHEN I BEGAN TO WORK IN THIS FIELD, in the late 1960s, there seemed little challenge to the values of high modernism, and the study of nineteenth-century painting seemed really quite easy. A number of basic assumptions – generally unspoken – underpinned the modernist narrative.

First, modernism stressed the primacy of pictorial, formal qualities. Presented with a comparison between – say – genre paintings by Manet and Alfred Stevens (see pls 4 and 10), we knew what to say. The Stevens was anecdotal and sentimental, appealing to values that had nothing to do with 'true' art; by contrast, the Manet, with its frontality, its bold brush-marks and clear colour, explored the medium of oil paint to the full – rejecting extraneous associations, in favour of asserting the primacy of the coloured painted surface.

Second, the history we wrote was linear and, at least implicitly, teleological, defined in terms of an underlying notion of progress, towards the goal of 'pure painting'. A book might have a sequence of chapters such as this: Realism; Impressionism; Post-Impressionism; Symbolism; Fauvism; Cubism and so on. The values that underpinned accounts like these were determined by hindsight; the position of works of art was determined by place in a temporal chain, in a sequence, detaching them from the immediate circumstances and contexts of their making and initial reception.

Third, the modernist narrative was preoccupied by the notion of the avant-garde. Certainly the history of the emergence of the idea of the avant-garde belongs in this period, and it is a primary focus in the first chapter of the present book. But the modernist version, of self-referential and self-sustaining groups working in virtual isolation from the wider art world, is essentially a twentieth-century phenomenon – if such groups ever existed. The notion of the avant-garde also involves a linear view of history; this linear history is often presented as a succession of avant-garde movements, one supplanting the other when the previous one was exhausted.

The values associated with the avant-garde are also tied up with the fourth key facet of the modernist view of history – *qualitative* judgement. Two examples will illustrate this standpoint. First, John Rewald, doyen of the older generation of scholars of Impressionism, wrote in 1980, in the introduction to the catalogue of the Pissarro retrospective, one of his last and most polemical texts:

Souvenir hunters who are presently 'rediscovering', or even 'rehabilitating', various producers of anaemic Salon wares seem completely unconcerned with the fact that what those people produced were *unnecessary* pictures . . . would it not be simpler to sweep away once and for all the anecdotal productions of anti-monumental practitioners, and turn our attention to those who contributed to the chain of crests whose peaks are still great, luminous and alive?

In this context, these are, of course, the Impressionists. The final phrase there, the 'chain of crests' clearly suggests the notion of linear progress; elsewhere in the essay, Rewald made the linkage between this type of evaluation and the progressivist vision clearer, in writing of 'the powerful flow of the mainstream of history'.[1]

The tone of Rewald's judgements was clearly moral; for him, Salon art was morally corrupt, in playing to debased tastes, as well as being aesthetically inferior; or perhaps we should say that he drew no distinction between aesthetic and moral judgement – within the modernist pantheon, aesthetics and morality were one and the same thing. Yet there was no explicitly political dimension to this notion of value; Rewald invoked generalised notions of progress as against reaction, but without any sustained analysis of how the paintings he valued functioned politically.

A surprisingly similar position was presented in 1996, though in very different intellectual clothing, in Michael Fried's *Manet's Modernism*. Here he insists that Manet's art should be viewed only in relation to the fellow members of his avant-garde grouping; evidently, comparisons between his work and contemporary Salon painting demean Manet's work through contaminating contact: '. . . no doubt Manet held the bulk of [Salon] painting in low esteem; but precisely because he did, he would not have felt it a worthy ambition . . . to seek to overthrow its norms . . .'.[2] As we shall see, many other recent writers also restrict their attention to the Impressionists without viewing them in a broader context, though for less overtly qualitative reasons than Fried.

Since the 1970s this framework of assumptions and values has come under sustained attack, from a number of angles. Recent paperback survey texts on Impressionism are a far cry from Phoebe Pool's much-reprinted volume of 1967 in the World of Art series, both in their intellectual agendas and in their critical perspectives; historical, social, ideological and political contexts are now assumed to be the province of the art historian, in contrast to Pool's narrow focus on pictorial qualities and biographical data.[3]

Beyond this, the door has been opened to the serious study of academic art, although with various different agendas. One strategy has been simply to reverse the modernist scale of values, and to attribute absolute value to academic art, or to a particular academic artist. An example of this was Mark Steven Walker's essay in the catalogue of the Bouguereau exhibition of 1984; Walker presented the experience of looking at Bouguereau's art as a sort of religious pilgrimage:

> To these wonder-struck pilgrims the doors of the tabernacles will be opened. To them will be revealed . . . the whole magic of a mysterious world named illusion. To the young of spirit, to the idealists, to those who refuse to cultivate disdain in order to mask their fatigue, to them alone will be given the power to penetrate into the world of Bouguereau.[4]

Like high modernism, an argument such as this makes the assumption that there is only one true scale of values for evaluating art.

At the opposite end of the spectrum is a pluralism that can find pleasure in the widest range of different types of art. In the re-evaluation of nineteenth-century art, this has been pioneered by Robert Rosenblum in his writings and the exhibitions that he has organised, which have played a crucial role in encouraging the display of nineteenth-century academic art in museum installations as well as temporary exhibitions.[5] Most recently this approach has been seen to spectacular effect in *1900: Art at the Crossroads*, shown in London and New York, a display whose juxtapositions challenged conventional modernist hierarchies of evaluation, and reminded us most vividly just how strange and awkward the late work of Cézanne looked among the paintings of his contemporaries.[6]

However, these approaches raise an issue that is central to the present discussion: the question of values. Any evaluation depends on a system of values. High modernism on the one side, and Mark Steven Walker's position on the other, insist on applying a single, absolute set of values across the spectrum. Both viewpoints avoid the central lessons of history and of the history of art and taste: criteria for value judgements have changed constantly through history, and at any one moment, especially in recent centuries, different value systems can exist side by side. At the Salon of 1873, both Bouguereau's *Nymphs and Satyr* (pl. 179) and Manet's *Le Bon Bock* (pl. 180) won high praise, but evidently not for the same reasons, or when judged by the same criteria.

Rosenblum's position, by contrast, allows free play to an almost infinite number of possible criteria or bases for value judgement, all playing freely alongside each other. But an open-ended pluralism such as this raises its own problems; for the supporters of both Bouguereau and Manet were adopting aesthetic positions that stemmed from a coherent system of values, and these two positions coexisted within the French art world in 1873. These values related to larger questions of belief within that culture – beliefs that were not only aesthetic, but also social, political and religious, as the present book has sought to show. When we analyse the exhibition criticism of the period, our primary source for the contemporary evaluation of nineteenth-century art, we find at every point judgements that are *grounded*: they are attempts to work from some coherent system of beliefs. Today, we may adopt any set of values we choose, but we too are accountable for the bases on which we make our evaluations. When we are dealing with the art of the nineteenth century in historical terms, we cannot impose these values retrospectively, but must engage in a critical re-examination of nineteenth-century systems of values.

On the surface we are dealing with the values – the criteria – that were used to judge art. But, beyond this, how should we place these artistic judgements in a wider historical frame? In what directions should we look, when we are trying to locate appropriate contexts for these aesthetic debates? This is the central question that more recent historians of Impressionism have addressed, as they have sought to go beyond the closed circle of style criticism, connoisseurship and artistic biography.

The possibilities of fresh approaches to the art of the period were opened out in the writing of certain historians in the late 1960s and early 1970s, notably Linda Nochlin and T. J. Clark;[7] more recently a whole range of different perspectives and points of view have been explored, all of which have posed vital questions. The present book would have been impossible without their contributions to our understanding of Impressionist painting within its historical contexts. However, in a number of cases problems are raised by the approaches that have been adopted, primarily through the issues that their accounts do not take into consideration.

Richard Shiff's essay of 1978, 'The End of Impressionism', and his subsequent publications have made a prime contribution by working back from Impressionist painting, and from the language that the painters and critics used to analyse it, to a consideration of the notions of visual perception and knowledge that underpinned it. He very persuasively relates the Impressionists' concern with the *sensation* – the sensory experience – and the *impression* to the branch of positivist philosophy represented by

179 Adolphe-William Bouguereau, *Nymphs and Satyr (Nymphes et satyre)* 1873, 220 × 180, The Sterling and Francine Clark Art Institute, Williamstown, Mass.

Hippolyte Taine and Emile Littré, who emphasised the essential subjectivity of any knowledge based on sense experience. This linkage is fundamental for the understanding of Impressionism, with its emphasis on the central role of the individual artist's temperament and the uniqueness of each artist's *sensations* as well as of their means of transforming these into paint. This argument also effectively counters any attempt to interpret their art in terms of objectivity or of the scientific.[8]

However, Shiff's arguments are left on the level of philosophical ideas, and not grounded in the world of everyday physical, social and political experience. He does not analyse what these values stood for, within broader nineteenth-century debates about art and society, or place the debates around the Impressionists' first group exhibitions of the mid-1870s within the specific context of the repressive early years of the Third Republic.

180   Edouard Manet, *Le Bon Bock*, 1873, 94 × 83, Philadelphia Museum of Art: Mr. and Mrs. Caroll S. Tyson, Jr. Collection

At the opposite end of the spectrum is a form of the social history of art in which the primary point of reference is the material reality behind the image – the actual site or scene depicted.[9] This research, notably by Robert Herbert and his former students, has opened out the 'real world' behind the Impressionists' canvases in richly informative ways. We have learned much about the topography of Argenteuil and Pontoise, and about the uses to which particular buildings were put. However, as I have argued in Chapter Three, we must ask whether the viewers of the paintings would have known these details, since the viewers – the target audience – were in Paris, not at Argenteuil or Pontoise. Indeed, at times the painters themselves may not have known them, either. This issue centrally affects the ways in which the paintings would have been classified and the meanings that would have been found in them.

In these social histories, the information with which paintings are compared is at times presented as if it were objective fact – the hard stuff of material reality – and as if the pictures granted us transparent access to this reality. The sources most often cited are archival or sociological data, and the ostensibly factual information of travel guides – whether in verbal or visual form. Too little attention is paid to the issue of representation. The meanings that the paintings conveyed were generated in part by their physical subjects, but also, crucially, by the ways in which the scenes were organised and by their technique – the brushwork and colour. Moreover, all of the contextual sources are representations, too. Even a body of statistics will generate conclusions that depend on the form in which the information is gathered and the questions that are asked. Likewise, the images in travel guides had their own purposes and related to the conventions and expectations of the genre – a genre very different from fine art easel painting, both in its status and in the assumptions behind it.

There is a further limitation in both Shiff's approach and this form of the social history of art – as, too, in Michael Fried's writing: they limit themselves to considering the artists of the modernist pantheon. Shiff does not explore the very different notions of knowledge and truth that formed the dominant world view in France in the 1870s, and that underpinned both figure paintings such as Bouguereau's and the landscapes that gained success at the Salon. This was essentially the loose form of Roman Catholic neo-platonism known as 'eclecticism'. It is only against the background of this notion of knowledge that we can appreciate the full significance of the alternative proposed by Littré and Taine. Likewise, with the social historians, we gain no sense of what other, non-Impressionist artists were painting at the time – whether they treated comparable themes, if not, why not, and if so, how. This was one of the central questions addressed by the exhibition *Landscapes of France* (in London)/*Impressions of France* (in Boston) of 1995–6 that I organised, presenting Impressionist landscape painting in relation to landscapes displayed at the Paris Salon between 1860 and 1890.[10]

The same criticism can be levelled against another approach, that of T. J. Clark, especially in *The Painting of Modern Life: Paris in the Art of Manet and his Contemporaries* (1984/5). Clark, like Robert Herbert, is concerned about the material realities that lay behind the Impressionists' images, but he relates them not to raw factual data, but rather to the ways in which they were presented and discussed in contemporary verbal sources. In his exploration of the verbal material, Clark cites an extremely wide and illuminating range of different types of source – social commentary, travel writing, Salon criticism and so on. He analyses the positions that these texts take and the values they stand for, without any concern for their 'quality' in artistic or any other terms. Yet when he comes to the art, he engages fully only with paintings that belong to the conventional modernist pantheon; in all parts except one in his book, his citations of non-vanguard pictures are few and relatively perfunctory.

Beyond this, Clark seems at times to equate artistic value with political value. This is a strange reversal of Rewald's position: if Rewald collapsed the political into the artistic, Clark here runs the risk of collapsing the artistic into the political. In this reckoning, Manet comes out positively, but Monet does not.[11] However, in general, the traditional modernist pantheon is retained, but legitimised by different criteria. The one exception to this exclusiveness in Clark's text is the fascinating discussion of Manet's *Olympia* in relation to contemporary academic Salon nudes, and the assumptions that lay behind their making and reception.[12] Few recent texts have engaged as seriously and productively as this with the problems of discussing the relationship between the academic and anti-academic painting of the period.

Clark's book also makes a significant contribution to the understanding of broader ideas and beliefs in the period – the sphere of ideology. Yet again, recent writing in this area has tended to distort these issues through what is omitted. This emerges particularly clearly from Stephen F. Eisenman's contributions to *Nineteenth-Century Art: A Critical History* of 1994. Eisenman makes much of the issues of gender, class and race. Realising that, at first glance, this may look like a parody of late twentieth-century political correctness, he assures us in his introduction that these issues were also central concerns in the nineteenth century, and that there is a real continuity between their pre-occupations and ours.[13] Certainly, gender, class and race were fundamental issues then, as now; but what is missing in his account is one aspect of culture and belief that was fundamental in the nineteenth century, but is largely ignored now: this is religious belief – deeply unfashionable as an object of historical study these days.

This reiterates the point made above in relation to Richard Shiff's work – that the dominant theories of knowledge in the mid-nineteenth century were theologically driven. Models of knowledge based on scientific investigation or on sense perception were widely viewed as 'materialist' and thus as a threat to moral and social values. Only when we have reinstated popular theological belief in its proper and central place can we make sense of the alternative visions of the world that were emerging in the nineteenth century.

The central theme in Clark's discussion of *Olympia*, the representation of women, has also been a central concern in recent feminist scholarship.[14] Much has been done to uncover the underlying assumptions about sexual roles and gender roles that under-pinned the images of the masculine and the feminine in the period, and to ensure that these positions are viewed as historical and culturally relative, not natural. In the context of the present book, the discussions of the gendering of space – both social and pictorial – in the writings of scholars such as Griselda Pollock and Kathleen Adler have been especially significant.[15]

However, a number of interventions have worked, from a late twentieth-century feminist standpoint, seemingly in order simply to condemn both the artist and the art he made. Certainly, historical circumstances cannot validate a totally unacceptable ethical position. But the attitudes to gender roles that, say, Renoir and Gauguin represent were so widely shared in the late nineteenth century that judgements based on these attitudes have little directly to do with Renoir and Gauguin themselves, and still less with their art. Their attitudes towards sexuality and gender were undoubtedly central to their art and need to be explored; but many other aspects of their art are closed off by an immediate condemnation on grounds of gender politics alone.[16]

Clark's discussion of *Olympia* has more to offer, through its insistence that issues of gender and sexuality in fine art are inseparable from an exploration of current artistic conventions, the debates around them and the assumptions behind them. It is ironic that Clark did not carry this contextual awareness over into his discussions of landscape in *The Painting of Modern Life*.

Nicholas Green's path-breaking study of the landscape imagery of the period in *The Spectacle of Nature* (1990) wholly avoids the problems that I have been highlighting.[17] Here, nature is rigorously viewed as a cultural construct; landscape, both in the tourist experience and in visual imagery, is presented as a product of bourgeois disenchantment with urban culture, and specifically with Paris. All the views cited, whether verbal or visual, are dissected as representations, as constructs, and analysed in terms of the values they embody; there is no risk here of images being treated as if they were transparent. Yet there is a fundamental problem in Green's treatment of visual images: he refuses to acknowledge that fine art paintings had a different status from a caricature in a weekly magazine or a vignette in a travel guide. His agenda is clear: he wanted to defuse the mystique of the work of art – to rid it of the seemingly transcendental status that was given it within the modernist tradition. But in this book the corrective goes too far. There is no discussion of the status that fine art was accorded in the nineteenth century, and no recognition that the conventions of fine art painting at the time were very different from those of other visual media. Without reinstating the notion that its value was transcendent, we can analyse the status that fine art paintings occupied within nineteenth-century visual culture, and isolate the distinct assumptions, expectations and values that this carried with it.

Green's other writings played a major role in opening out another significant field, the institutional history of the period; in these articles about art institutions and the art trade, far more note is taken of the distinctive character of the art world and of works of 'fine art' as commodities.[18] Historians have come to see that it is impossible to locate a work historically without considering the physical surroundings in which it was meant to be seen, and the values for which that venue stood, and, more specifically, the fierce competition in the period between the public and the private sectors.

However, the most substantial recent institutional history highlights the problems raised when such a history is taken in isolation. Pierre Vaisse's *La Troisième République et les peintres* of 1995, based on a dissertation of 1980, is a remarkable repository of information and attitudes to art institutions under the early Third Republic, but it has a very specific agenda, to demonstrate that, effectively, the avant-garde did not exist during the period, and that the State authorities were paragons of open-minded liberalism. This is an attempt to reverse traditional modernist values just as comprehensively as Mark Steven Walker's vision of Bouguereau, but seemingly written not from personal aesthetic preference but from the ostensibly documentary standpoint of institutional history. The documentary material in Vaisse's argument is carefully selected to make his case; but, more significantly, he never engages with the works themselves, failing to acknowledge the startling distance in world views between – say – the paintings of peasant subjects by Bouguereau and Pissarro around 1880 (see pls 167 and 177), or to pursue the wider implications of the contrast.[19]

There have been many other significant contributions to the study of art institutions,[20] and gender-based studies have played a major part in this, by emphasising the range of institutional structures that acted to control and restrict women's participation in the nineteenth-century art world.[21] Beyond these, two essays have engaged seriously with the relationship between pictorial practice on the one side and institutional and commercial structures on the other. Louise d'Argencourt's essay of 1984 on Bouguereau and the art market draws compelling links between Bouguereau's stylistic decisions and the markets for which he was working,[22] while Martha Ward's study of 1991 of the Impressionist group exhibitions moves from a discussion of display conditions in different types of venue to a richly documented and nuanced view of the different structures within the art world and the values for which they stood.[23]

The political dimension of the early critical responses to Impressionism was highlighted by Stephen Eisenman in 1986; more recently Philip Nord has relocated the artists' lives and careers in the context of contemporary political history in *Impressionists and Politics* (2000). Nord's book throws a welcome focus on the specific and rapidly changing political circumstances in the years in question, in contrast to the broader socio-political concerns of other recent social historians of art. A central theme of the present book is that these immediate political contexts were of pressing relevance to the painters throughout these years, and are of fundamental importance in understanding not only the subjects they chose but also the markets and outlets they sought and the form their paintings took – the composition and execution of the canvases themselves.

Art criticism – without doubt one of the central archival resources for the art of the period – has also become a focus of study.[25] The criticism of the first two Impressionist group exhibitions has been revealingly analysed in terms of the relationships between aesthetics and politics, the show of 1874 by Virginia Spate, that of 1876 by Hollis Clayson;[26] moreover, criticism has been used with great sophistication in certain monographs on the artists of the period, notably Carol Armstrong's study of Degas.[27] However, in a sense the critical exploration of this writing has been thwarted by the very quantity of the material – the hundreds of long reviews published each year, in an era in which analytical description fulfilled the role now taken by the photograph, or by the hasty glance. The series of bibliographies of Salon criticism, initiated by the volume on the Second Empire edited by Christopher Parsons and Martha Ward, has greatly eased scholarly access to the full range of this material, but unfortunately does not take us beyond 1870.[28] By contrast, the contents of recent anthologies of criticism have been selected either because of the fame of the authors or of the objects of their study.[29] In the Impressionist field, Ruth Berson's comprehensive edition of the criticism of the eight group exhibitions is an indispensable resource,[30] and the present book has gained immeasurably from it; but it does not, of course, offer any comparative insight into the criticism of other exhibitions during the period, and especially of the Salon – the point of comparison and contrast that dictated the terms of reference in which the group exhibitions were reviewed.

Close scrutiny of the paintings themselves has opened out another productive avenue in recent scholarship. These investigations have emphasised the complexities of the painters' procedures and have definitively given the lie to the view that their art was essentially rapid and spontaneous. Yet the most closely focused of these studies, including my own monograph on Monet of 1986, have tended to treat the study of materials, methods and techniques as an end in itself, rather than considering the wider implications of the procedures that the painters adopted; more specifically, they have tended to put means before ends, and to privilege analysis of the processes of making over the effects generated by finished pictures.[31] Anthea Callen's recent book, *The Art of Impressionism: Painting Technique and the Making of Modernity* (2000),[32] seeks to establish links between Impressionist practices and the notion of modernity, but the wider arguments seem less focused than the mass of valuable practical information, and, once again, more attention is paid to processes of making than to the visual qualities of finished pictures. These issues are tackled in Chapter Five above, which argues that it is only through close examination of the finished state of the paintings that the Impressionists put before the public that we can define the characteristics that made their canvases so controversial and problematic to their first viewers.

Finally, a crucial role has been played in the re-examination of the art of the period by museum installations and temporary exhibitions. Exhibitions have tended to be monographic – all the major Impressionists have had ambitious retrospectives since 1980; but inevitably a one-artist show is fundamentally decontextualised, whatever comparative apparatus may appear in the catalogue or other material supporting the exhibition. Yet some of these catalogues have included crucial new research and fresh perspectives on the artist in question.[33] Thematic Impressionist shows have yielded important insights – notably *The New Painting: Impressionism 1874–1886* (1986), whose rooms reconstituting selections from the pictures shown at the eight Impressionist group exhibitions, as well as the catalogue and its accompanying essays, offered a grounded and thought-provoking framework for looking at the pictures – though, of course, deprived of their wider context within the Paris art world.[34] My own show *Landscapes of France/Impressions of France* (1995–6), juxtaposing Impressionist landscapes with a selection of landscapes shown in the same years at the Paris Salon, was an attempt to rectify this imbalance.[35] More recently, *Impression: Painting Quickly in France 1860–1890* (2000–01) offered a salutary reminder of the necessity of close and careful examination of the paintings as a basis for any assessment of their making and meanings.[36]

In the display of permanent museum collections, the opening of the Musée d'Orsay in Paris in 1986 was a major landmark, through the quantity and range of works of art displayed, both vanguard and non-vanguard. Crucial contexts for its Impressionist collection were presented by the displays of Salon paintings from the whole second half of the nineteenth century – most of them purchased directly from the Salon by the French State as exemplary representations of the present state of French art.[37] This initiative by the flagship museum of later nineteenth-century French art has encouraged many other museums, in France, in the United States, and elsewhere, to exhibit many more of their non-Impressionist holdings from the period. It is a matter of the greatest regret that, at the time of writing (December 2003), the Musée d'Orsay has removed most of this material from view; it can only be hoped that it will be reinstated in all its fascinating diversity once the present modifications to the museum are complete. As I emphasised in the Introduction, it is only through close examination of the original works of art, in exhibitions, in auction sales and, most of all, in museums, that our understanding of the art of the Impressionists within their historical contexts can be expanded and deepened.

Notes

Chapter 1

A brief first sketch of this chapter appeared as 'Social Critic or Enfant Terrible: The Avant-Garde Artist in Paris in the 1860s', in Klaus Herding (ed.), *L'Art et les révolutions, Section 2: Changements et continuité dans la création artistique des révolutions politiques*, Actes du XXVIIe congrès international d'histoire de l'art (Strasbourg, 1989), Strasbourg: Société Alsacienne pour le Développement de l'Histoire de l'Art, 1992.

1 See e.g. Fried 1969 (reprinted in Fried 1996), Reff 1969, Reff 1970, Hanson 1977.

2 Manet had no such close affiliations before 1865; for an argument that foregrounds his links with other artists, notably Fantin-Latour and Alphonse Legros, in the early to mid-1860s, see Fried 1996.

3 See Rewald 1973, pp. 234–5; Paris, Grand Palais, *Impressionnisme*, 1994–5, p. 336; Pitman 1998, pp. 185–6, 258 (note 87).

4 Duranty, 'Salon de 1869', *Paris-Journal*, 20, 23 May, 1 June 1869, quoted in Crouzet 1964, pp. 289–90 (like other recent scholars, I have been unable to locate copies of the issues of *Paris-Journal* in which Duranty's reviews of 1869 appeared).

5 Rewald 1973 (the first edition was published in 1946).

6 See letters from Bazille to his parents, April, May 1867, in Bazille 1992, pp. 137, 140; on this project, see Roos 1996, pp. 83–8.

7 For two very different views of Chennevières's achievements, see Roos 1989, and Foucart and Prat, 'Préface', in Chennevières 1979.

8 See e.g. Castagnary 1892, I, pp. 390–91, discussing the Salon of 1870; for a recent reassessment of Napoleon III's 'liberal empire', see McMillan 1991, pp. 126–34.

9 Rewald 1973, pp. 139–249.

10 Rewald in the last edition of *The History of Impressionism* reproduced this as an image of Monet, but without mention of the possible implications of this friendship (Rewald 1973, p. 150).

11 On the Café Guerbois, see Rewald 1973, pp. 197–213, Crouzet 1964, pp. 239–41, and, for a recent and judicious summary of the evidence, Pitman 1998, p. 233 note 5.

12 Astruc 1870, VI, grouped Pissarro, Degas, Bazille and Guillemet together; Burty 1870, V, discussed Jongkind, Guigou, Colin and Boudin as 'réfractaires, indépendants'; and elsewhere placed emphasis on Degas, Eva Gonzalès and Bazille; Duranty in 1869 associated Pissarro and Bazille expressly with the *école des Batignolles*, and linked them to Renoir and Scholderer (cited in Crouzet 1964, pp. 289–90); in 1870 Duranty referred explicitly to Fantin-Latour's *Un Atelier aux Batignolles* in grouping together Guillo[sic]met, Pissarro, Sisley, Bazille and Renoir as 'Les Irréguliers et les Naïfs' (Duranty 1870, XII); Zola 1868 discussed Monet, Bazille and Renoir together as 'Les Actualistes', and elsewhere emphasised the work of Pissarro, Jongkind, Boudin, Morisot and Degas.

13 Castagnary 1892, I, pp. 313–14.

14 My approach is in marked contrast to that adopted in Fried 1996. He argues that Manet's art should be viewed only 'in the context of the work of artists with whom he had most in common', and not in the same frame as more conventional types of Salon painting, since 'he would not have felt it a worthy ambition . . . to seek to overthrow its norms' (Fried 1996, p. 456).

15 Chaumelin 1869: 'Ses deux tableaux . . . ont fortement scandalisé les amateurs de peinture proprette, nette, sentimentale et bourgeoise . . . Pas d'expression, pas de sentiment, pas de composition.'

16 Duranty 1870, III: 'A la peinture raffinée, ficelle, M. Manet oppose une naïveté systématique, le dédain de tous les moyens séducteurs. C'est sur un fond gris sombre, ardoisé, qu'il installe ses personnages, comme s'il protestait puritainement contre ces rideaux trompe-l'oeil, ces mobiliers de bric-à-brac que la grande et la petite *toulmoucheries* . . . entassent de peur de passer pour pauvres.'

17 Castagnary 1892, I, pp. 364–5: 'En regardant ce *Déjeuner* . . . je vois sur une table où le café est servi, un citron à moitié pelé et des huîtres fraîches; ces objets ne marchent guère ensemble. Pourquoi les avoir mis? . . . de même que M. Manet assemble, pour le seul plaisir de frapper les yeux, des natures mortes qui devrai[en]t s'exclure; de même, il distribue ses personnages au hasard, sans que rien de nécessaire et de forcé ne commande leur composition. De là l'incertitude, et souvent l'obscurité dans la pensée. Que fait ce jeune homme du *Déjeuner*, qui est assis au premier plan et qui semble regarder le public? . . . où est-il? Dans la salle à manger? Alors, ayant le dos à la table, il a le mur entre lui et nous, et sa position ne s'explique plus. Sur ce *Balcon* j'aperçois deux femmes dont une toute jeune. Sont-ce les deux soeurs? Est-ce la mère et la fille? Je ne sais. Et puis, l'une est assise et semble s'être placée uniquement pour jouir du spectacle de la rue; l'autre se gante comme si elle allait sortir. Cette attitude contradictoire me déroute. . . . le sentiment des fonctions, . . . le sentiment de la convenance sont choses indispensables. Ni l'écrivain, ni le peintre ne les peuvent supprimer. Comme les personnages dans une comédie, il faut que dans un tableau chaque figure soit à son plan, remplisse son rôle et concoure ainsi à l'expression de l'idée générale. Rien d'ar-

bitraire et rien de superflu, telle est la loi de toute composition artistique.'

18 For instance Castagnary 1892, I, pp. 353–5, in his review of the Salon of 1869.

19 Castagnary 1892, I, pp. 364–5: 'Je le sais bien, le pourquoi. C'est parce que M. Manet a au plus haut point le sentiment de la tache colorante, qu'il excelle à reproduire ce qui est inanimé, et que, se sentant supérieur dans les natures mortes, il se trouve naturellement porté à en faire le plus possible.'

20 Mantz 1869, p. 13: 'Admettons qu'il s'agit d'une combinaison de couleurs.'

21 See also Fried 1996, p. 298.

22 See House 1999; for a wide-ranging discussion of the picture, see Wagner 1994 (for alternative explanations for Monet's decision not to submit it in 1869, see ibid., pp. 618–19).

23 Gautier 1880, p. 285; for discussion of the petit crevé, see Siebecker 1867, pp. 23ff.

24 See for instance Aimé-Martin 1838, pp. 39–43; Romieu 1858, pp. 229ff; Dupanloup 1869, pp. 29ff (essay first published in 1866) and pp. 238ff (essay first published in 1867). Moralists generally argued that there were close links between the world of high fashion and the perils of luxe; for a counter-argument, see Feydeau 1866. The painting is compared to contemporary fashion plates in Roskill 1970; however, the relevance of this context should be viewed as much in social or moral terms as in any direct visual relationships.

25 Gandin: see Chaumelin 1869, and Mantz 1869, p. 13; Arthur: see Gautier 1880, p. 285. The gandin was discussed in a spate of pamphlets published in 1860–61 about student morality in the Quartier Latin (e.g. [anon.], Les Etudiants et les femmes du Quartier Latin en 1860, Paris, 1860, and Sus aux gandins! A propos de la brochure Les Etudiants et les femmes du Quartier Latin en 1860, Paris, 1860). On these, see also John House, 'Manet and the De-Moralised Viewer', in Tucker 1998.

26 For attacks on the education offered by Pensionnats, see Romieu 1858, pp. 231ff; Thévenin 1862, pp. 96–7.

27 See House in Tucker 1998; on such eye contact, see also below, Chapter Four, pp. 129–34.

28 See e.g. du Pays 1859, p. 22; Duret, 'Salon de 1870', in Duret 1998, p. 35.

29 Castagnary 1892, I, pp. 33–42.

30 These Physiologies were literary and pictorial studies of characteristic types, of which the most famous was Les Français peints par eux-mêmes, published in many volumes between 1840 and 1842 (on these, see Le Men and Abélès 1993).

31 See e.g. Hanson 1977, pp. 58–68.

32 Letter from Monet to Gustav Pauli, Director of the Bremen Kunsthalle, 7 May 1906, at the date that the Kunsthalle bought the painting (Wildenstein, IV, 1985, p. 370): 'C'est bien Mme Monet, ma première femme, qui m'a servi de modèle, et, bien que je n'aie pas eu l'intention d'en faire absolument un portrait, mais seulement une figure de Parisienne de cette époque, la ressemblance en est complète.'

33 Zola 15 May 1866, in Zola 1970, p. 81: 'Courbet, pour l'écraser d'un mot, a fait du joli'.

34 The contrast between the eye contact in Phryne and the profile in Penelope was emphasised in Chaumelin 1868.

35 Mauner 1977, p. 136; George Mauner's systematic attempt to read Manet's major canvases in emblematic terms seems to me singularly inappropriate to the nature of Manet's overall artistic project (see also Paris, Musée d'Orsay, 2000). It should be noted that Henri Schlesinger exhibited a picture of The Five Senses at the Salon of 1865 and again in the Exposition Universelle of 1867, showing five cocottes, each representing one of the senses (untraced; described in Thoré 1870, II, p. 430: 'l'une sentant des fleurs, l'autre grignotant un fruit, l'autre lorgnant quelque gentleman, l'autre écoutant une confidence, l'autre palpant je ne sais quoi'); it is possible that Manet's canvas stands in an ironic or parodic relationship to the language of signs that Schlesinger had used.

36 Proust 1897, in Proust 1988, p. 45: 'Alfred Stevens avait peint un tableau représentant une femme qui écartait un rideau. Au pied de ce rideau était un plumeau qui jouait là le rôle de l'adjectif inutile dans une belle phrase ou de la cheville dans un vers bien venu. "Tout s'explique, avait dit Manet, cette femme attend le valet de chambre". Alfred Stevens se montra fort irrité du propos.' If the title by which the picture is known, The Morning Visit, is that given it by Stevens, it indicates that the detail of the feather duster was significant, in indicating the time of day, but not in the precise anecdotal sense that Manet proposed.

37 See Paris, Grand Palais, 1983, p. 288, quoting from Théodore Duret, Histoire d'Edouard Manet, Paris, 1926 edition, pp. 88–9; for a reading of the Duret portrait that views it in terms of the personal relationship between the painter and the critic, see Mauner 1975, pp. 103–8.

38 Mallarmé 1876, reprinted in Berson 1996, I, p. 92.

39 Although these attributes have been seen as belonging more to Manet himself than to Zola, the details in the picture mostly belong generically to the world of the writer (see Reff 1975, pp. 35–44, and Paris, Grand Palais, Impressionnisme, 1994–5, pp. 413–14).

40 Thoré, L'Indépendance belge, 29 June 1868, reprinted in Thoré 1870, II, pp. 531–2: 'Quand il a fait sur sa toile "la tache de couleur" que font sur la nature ambiante un personnage ou un objet, il se tient quitte. Ne lui en demandez pas plus long, – pour le moment. Mais il se débrouillera plus tard, quand il songera à donner leur valeur rélative aux parties essentielles des êtres. Son vice actuel est une sorte de panthéisme qui n'estime pas plus une tête qu'une pantoufle . . . qui peint tout presque uniformément, les meubles, les tapis, les livres, les costumes, les chairs, les accents du visage.'

41 Astruc 1868: 'L'aimable fille de Paris, au bois, – alerte, moqueuse et rieuse, jouant à la grande dame un peu gauchement, chérissant les ombrages non pour la fraîcheur qu'ils donnent et la solitude réalisée, – mais pour les bons divertissements qui s'y trouvent: le bal, la guinguette, les restaurant à la mode, l'arbre phénomène converti en salle à manger . . . L'héroïne n'a rien de champêtre que les traits. C'est une bonne fille colorée, potelée, vigoureuse, bien en chair, non dépourvue d'esprit, je le suppose. Les yeux expriment bien la malice d'origine et l'incisive observation populaire . . .'.

42 Chaumelin 1870: 'franchement moderne'; Duret, 'Salon de

1870', in Duret 1998, p. 40: 'un type réel, une femme vivante, la femme de notre temps'.

43 On the relationship between portraiture and genre painting, see also House in Baltimore 1999–2000, especially pp. 28–32, and Kinney 1987.

44 Letter from Manet to Madame Morisot, 1871, as translated in Rosenfeld 1991, p. 117.

45 Théodore de Banville, in *Le National*, 15 May 1873: 'un caractère intense de *modernité*'; Duvergier de Hauranne, in *Revue des deux mondes*, 1 June 1873: 'ce barbouillage malpropre et barbare' (quoted in Tabarant 1947, pp. 206, 210).

46 T. J. Clark's discussion of *Olympia* in Clark 1984/5 is a pioneering exploration of such links between technique and content.

47 Zola 1867, in Zola 1970, p. 107: 'Si j'avais été là, j'aurais prié l'amateur de se mettre à une distance respectueuse, et il aurait vu que ces taches vivaient, que la foule parlait . . .'.

48 Duranty, 'Salon de 1869', *Paris-Journal*, 12 May 1869, as quoted in Crouzet 1964, pp. 289–90: 'Si l'on voyait vite en passant des gens à un balcon, on aurait une impression assez égale à celle du tableau de M. Manet . . . Il a toujours saisi une impression de la nature plus vite, et par conséquent autrement que ses critiques.' Duranty 1870: 'L'effet violent de la nature, l'intense cruauté de ses aspects, de ses notes opposées, le saisissent, le dominent.'

49 Astruc 1870, IV: 'Dans un milieu fade, il apparaît barbare – conservant à la nature, à l'extérieur, cette crudité qui lui est propre et qui ne traduit qu'une expression à la fois energique et profonde. Dans les choses de mouvement, il met sa verve étincelante, fixant les foules, déployant une gamme de tons d'une extraordinaire distinction.'

50 Duret 1885/1998.

51 Spencer 1987, p. 61.

52 For instance Smith 1997. Ward 1996, pp. 263–5, engages with some of the main conceptual issues but without historicising the usage of the term. For a thoughtful analysis of the uses of the term in an early twentieth-century context, see Cottington 1998, especially pp. 37–53; some important distinctions are also made in Wood 1999, pp. 23–55.

53 Pollock 1992, p. 14.

54 See e.g. [Anon.], *La Politique d'avant-garde*, Paris, 1865; for a valuable anthology of contemporary uses of the term (none of them artistic), see Larousse, I, 1866, p. 1033, s.v. 'avant-garde'.

55 Olinde Rodrigues, 'L'Artiste, le Savant et l'Industriel', in *Opinions littéraires, philosophiques et industrielles*, Paris, 1825 (quoted in Hadjinicolaou 1978, pp. 51–2): 'Let us unite; and we each have a different task to fulfil in order to reach the same goal. It is we, the artists, who will act as your avant-garde: the power of the arts is the most immediate and the most rapid.' ('Unissons-nous; et pour parvenir au même but nous avons chacun une tâche différante à remplir. C'est nous, artistes, qui vous servirons d'avant-garde: la puissance des arts est en effet la plus immédiate et la plus rapide.')

Gabriel-Désiré Laverdant, *De la mission de l'art et du rôle des artistes*, Paris, 1845 (quoted in Hadjinicolaou 1978, p. 53): 'Art, as the expression of society, expresses, at its most elevated level, the most advanced social tendencies; it acts as precursor and revelation. In order to find out whether art is worthily fulfilling its initiatory role, whether the artist is truly in the avant-garde, one must know where Humanity is going, what the destiny of the Species is.' ('L'art, expression de la Société, exprime, dans son essor le plus élevé, les tendances sociales les plus avancées; il est précurseur et révélateur. Or, pour savoir si l'art remplit dignement son rôle d'initiateur, si l'artiste est bien à l'avant-garde, il est nécessaire de savoir où va l'Humanité, quelle est la destinée de l'Espèce.') Smith 1998, p. 20, cites Saint-Simon's *Lettres d'un habitant de Genève à ses contemporains* (Paris, 1803) in a discussion of the term; however, while the notion of the avant-garde is clearly implicit in this text, the term itself is not used.

56 Hadjinicolaou 1978, pp. 53 ff.

57 I am indebted to previous writers for these examples, and especially to Calinescu 1987; see also Riout in Duret 1998, pp. 18–22.

58 Balzac, *Les Comédiens sans le savoir*, 1846 (quoted in Calinescu 1987, p. 109), speech by Publicola Masson: 'Everything is conspiring in our favour. Thus all those who pity the people, and brawl over the question of the proletariat and salaries, or write against the Jesuits, or are concerned with the improvement of anything at all . . . Communists, Humanitarians, philanthropists, you understand, all these people are our avant-garde. While we store up the powder, they are braiding the fuse, which will be set alight by the spark of circumstance.' ('Tout conspire pour nous. Ainsi tous ceux qui plaignent les peuples, qui *braillent* sur la question des prolétaires et des salaires, qui font des ouvrages contre les Jésuites, qui s'occupent de l'amélioration de n'importe quoi . . . les Communistes, les Humanitaires, les philanthropes . . . vous comprenez, tous ces gens-là sont notre avant-garde. Pendant que nous amassons de la poudre, ils tressent la mèche à laquelle l'étincelle d'une circonstance mettra le feu.')

59 Hugo 1862, Part IV, Book 7, Chapter III, 'Argot qui pleure et argot qui rit' (quoted in Calinescu 1987, p. 108): 'Les encyclopédistes, Diderot en tête, les physiocrates, Turgot en tête, les philosophes, Voltaire en tête, les utopistes, Rousseau en tête, ce sont là quatre légions sacrées. L'immense avance de l'humanité leur est due. Ce sont les quatre avant-gardes du genre humain allant aux quatre points cardinaux du progrès, Diderot vers le beau, Turgot vers l'utile, Voltaire vers le vrai, Rousseau vers le juste.'

60 Cousin 1855, especially pp. 133 ff.; I am indebted to Stephen Bann for insisting on the relevance of Cousin's discussion of 'le beau' in the context of Hugo's text.

61 Etienne Pasquier (1529–1615), *Recherches de la France*, reprinted in *Oeuvres choisies*, Paris, 1849, II, p. 21 (quoted in Calinescu 1987, pp. 97–8, 327): 'A glorious war was then being waged against ignorance, a war in which, I would say, Scève, Bèze and Pelletier constituted the avant-garde; or, if you prefer, they were the fore-runners of the other poets.' ('Ce fut une belle guerre que l'on entreprit lors contre l'ignorance, dont j'attribue l'avant-garde à Scève, Bèze et Pelletier; ou si le voulez autrement, ce furent les avant-coureurs des autres poëtes.') The passage origi-

nally appeared in Book 6, Chapter 7 of *Recherches de la France* (Estienne Pasquier, *Recherches de la France*, Paris, 1607, p. 868).

62 C.-A. Sainte-Beuve, 'Histoire de la querelle des anciens et des modernes par M. Hippolyte Rigault', II, 22 December 1856, reprinted in Sainte-Beuve, *Causeries de lundi*, XIII, n.d., pp. 150–52 (quoted in Calinescu 1987, pp. 109–10).

63 Baudelaire, 'Mon coeur mis à nu', in Baudelaire 1961, p. 1285 (quoted in Calinescu 1987, pp. 110–11): 'Concerning the love, the predilection of the French for military metaphors . . . Add to the military metaphors: Combative poets. Avant-garde men of letters. The use of military metaphors does not indicate militant spirits, but rather spirits made for discipline, that is to say for conformity . . .' ('De l'amour, de la prédilection des Français pour les métaphores militaires . . . A ajouter aux métaphores militaires: Les poëtes de combat. Les littérateurs d'avant-garde. Ces habitudes de métaphores militaires dénotent des esprits, non pas militants, mais faits pour la discipline, c'est-à-dire pour la conformité . . .').

64 Silvestre 1874: 'un artiste d'avant-garde de l'Art moderne, resté par son savoir fidèle à la grande tradition magistrale, et l'esprit ouvert à tous les souffles novateurs.'

65 Jules Claretie, 'Salon de 1875', in Claretie 1876, p. 338: 'Let us not protest too much. Perhaps some absolute progress will come out of this. These intransigents have no real knowledge, but their methods are curious, and who knows whether, one day, they may not be applied by some master who will at least unite the solidity of true study to the curiosity of these would-be artists, whose eccentricity has the excuse, and the merit, that they are attempting something new and that they are fighting in the avant-garde.' ('Ne protestons pas trop. Peut-être sortira-t-il de là un absolut progrès. La science de ces intransigents est nul, mais leurs procédés . . . sont curieux, et qui sait s'ils ne seront pas appliqués, un jour, par quelque maître qui unira au moins la solidité de l'étude à la curiosité de ces essais d'artistes, dont l'excentricité a pour excuse et pour mérite qu'ils tentent du moins quelque chose de nouveau et qu'ils combattent à l'avant-garde.')

66 Jacques 11 April 1877, reprinted in Berson 1996, I, p. 155: 'This year, in total, the avant-garde painters are eighteen in number.' ('Ils sont, au total, les peintres d'avant-garde, dix-huit, cette année.')

67 Massarani 1880, II, p. 244: 'Et en effet, même l'avant-garde la plus audacieuse, celle qui s'est baptisée toute seule la légion des impressionistes [sic], ne le récuse pas pour patron. Ce n'est qu'un petit groupe hardi, faisant secte à part.' Massarani goes on to describe the Impressionists as 'foragers and pioneers of painting' ('forrageurs et pionniers de la peinture'). I am indebted for this reference to Louise Straarup-Hansen.

68 'Un Amateur', 'A travers l'art . . . Exposition des oeuvres de M. Claude Monet', *L'Art moderne*, April 1883, quoted in Duret 1998, p. 21: 'The soldiers of the avant-garde are always those who have the least chance of being there when the flag is planted on the citadel and the medals are distributed.' ('Les soldats d'avant-garde sont toujours ceux qui ont le moins de chance d'être là quand on plante le drapeau sur la citadelle et qu'on distribue les croix.')

69 Fénéon, 'Les Impressionnistes', 1886, reprinted in Fénéon 1970, I, p. 49: 'M. Dubois-Pillet must appear here. With the four artists whom we have just discussed, he is in the avant-garde of Impressionism.' ('M. Dubois-Pillet doit figurer ici. Il est, avec les quatre artistes dont nous venons de parler, à l'avant-garde de l'impressionnisme.') The responses to this generated a letter from Seurat to Signac, 16 June 1886, first published in Dorra and Rewald 1959, p. xlix: 'Guillaumin got angry with Fénéon (the article) because he chose to speak of Dubois-Pillet, to wish to place him in the avant-garde of Impressionism. Having misread the article, Guillaumin said to me: "Dubois-Pillet is no more in the avant-garde than you or Signac." ' ('Guillaumin . . . s'est mis en colère contre Fénéon (l'article) parce qu'il lui a plu de parler de Dubois-Pillet, de le souhaiter à *l'avant-garde* de l'impressionnisme. Ayant mal lu, Guillaumin me dit: "Dubois-Pillet n'est pas plus à l'avant-garde *que vous et que Signac*." ') On this, see also Smith 1997, pp. 65–6.

70 In these terms, 'avant-garde' seems inappropriate for Courbet, who presented himself, and was perceived by his contemporaries, very much as a 'one-man band'. In 1852 Courbet's friend Champfleury chose *Les Excentriques* as the title for his collection of studies of unique and aberrant individuals in modern society (I am indebted to Richard Hobbs for drawing attention to the issue of the 'excentrique', in the conference on the 'Avant-Garde' that he organised at the University of Bristol in 2002).

71 Proudhon 1865, p. 375: '[le] perfectionnement physique, intellectuel et moral de l'humanité'. 'Nous avons à instruire le peuple, à lui donner, avec le goût de la science, l'intelligence de l'histoire, de la philosophie, le culte de la justice, les vraies joies du travail et de la société.'

72 See Grate 1959, especially pp. 152–60, 172–3; Snell 1982, especially pp. 209–11; Jowell 1977, especially pp. 76–92.

73 'Avant-Garde and Kitsch', first published in *Partisan Review*, Fall 1939; 'Towards a Newer Laocoon', first published in *Partisan Review*, July–August 1940; both reprinted in Greenberg 1986.

74 See e.g. Castagnary 1892, I, pp. 256, 274–5 (on the Salon of 1868), 328–30 (on the Salon of 1869).

75 Duranty 1876, in Berson 1996, I, p. 80: 'Est-ce que ces artistes seront les primitifs d'un grand mouvement de rénovation artistique . . . ? Seront-ils simplement des fascines; seront-ils les sacrifiés du premier rang tombant en marchant au feu devant tous et dont les corps comblant le fossé feront le pont sur lequel doivent passer les combattants qui viendront derrière?' For further discussion of Duranty's position, see below, Chapter Six.

76 See note 68 above.

77 'Les influences de l'Hollande sur le paysage français', in Fromentin 1876.

78 Reprinted in Denis 1912.

79 Anon., *Progrès*, 1869, p. 29; '. . . d'exciter, par ses encouragements, le zèle et l'émulation entre les jeunes artistes'; for a mocking attack on this document, see About 1869, pp. 725 ff.

80 Larousse, XIII, 1875, pp. 224–6.

81 Baudelaire 1855, in Baudelaire 1971, I, p. 382: 'Transportée dans l'ordre de l'imagination, l'idée du progrès . . .

se dresse avec une absurdité gigantesque, une grotesquerie qui monte jusqu'à l'épouvante . . . Dans l'ordre poétique et artistique, tout révélateur a rarement un précurseur.'

82 Zola 1970, pp. 55, 67, 73–4, reprinting articles in *L'Evénement*, 30 April, 7, 11 May 1866.

83 'Motifs d'une exposition particulière', reprinted in Courthion 1953, I, pp. 134–6: 'L'artiste ne dit aujourd'hui: venez voir des oeuvres sans défauts, mais: venez voir des oeuvres sincères. C'est l'effet de la sincérité de donner aux oeuvres un caractère qui les fait ressembler à une protestation, alors que le peintre n'a songé qu'à rendre son impression.'

84 Zola 1867, reprinted in Zola 1970, pp. 96–7.

85 See e.g. Baudelaire 1863, in Baudelaire 1971, II, p. 144.

86 Mallarmé 1876 and Duranty 1876 (quoting Constable), both reprinted in Berson 1996, I, pp. 92, 80; see Isaacson 1994.

87 Goodman 1976, p. 7.

88 Babou 1867, pp. 287–8: 'Cette intelligence, déjà fort exercée par la curiosité, la méditation et l'étude, cette intelligence alerte me plaît, parce qu'elle échappe de plus en plus à l'insouciance étourdie qui passe si souvent pour l'originalité . . ., parce qu'elle est d'une nature essentiellement *suggestive* . . .'.

89 Babou 1867, p. 289.

90 Castagnary 1892, I, pp. 364–5, quoted above, note 17; Mantz 1869, p. 13: 'L'accentuation d'un type, la caractérisation d'un sentiment ou d'une idée, seraient vainement cherchées dans ce tableau sans pensée. Admettons qu'il s'agit d'une combinaison de couleurs et regardons-le comme nous regarderions les folles arabesques d'une faïence persane, l'harmonie d'un bouquet, l'éclat décoratif d'une teinture de papier peint.'

91 Zola 1867, in Zola 1970, p. 110: 'Il vous fallait une femme nue, et vous avez choisi Olympia, la première venue; il vous fallait des taches claires et lumineuses, et vous avez mis un bouquet; il vous fallait des taches noires, et vous avez placé dans un coin une négresse et un chat.'

92 See Zola 1867, in Zola 1970, pp. 104, 111.

93 For the documents concerning the suppression of the lithograph and the painting, see Paris, Grand Palais, 1983, pp. 531–4; cf. also London, National Gallery, 1992.

94 Pitman 1998, pp. 1–2, 60–66. Gustave Planche's comments on Delacroix's *Women of Algiers* are particularly relevant here (Planche 1855, I, pp. 217–18, as quoted in Pitman 1998, pp. 63–4 and 242 note 42): 'Ce morceau capital, qui n'intéresse que par la peinture, et n'a rien à faire avec la niaiserie littéraire des badauds ou la sentimentalité des femmes frivoles, marque dans la vie intellectuelle de M. Delacroix un moment grave . . . Intéresser par la peinture réduite à ses seules ressources, sans le secours d'un sujet qui s'interprète de mille façons, et trop souvent distrait l'oeil des spectateurs superficiels, pour n'occuper que leur pensée qui estime le tableau selon ses rêves ou ses conjectures, c'est une tâche difficile, et M. Delacroix l'a remplie . . . C'est de la peinture et rien de plus.'

95 Mantz 1868, p. 362: '. . . la nature l'intéresse peu; les spectacles de la vie ne l'émeuvent pas. Cette indifférence sera son châtiment. M. Manet nous paraît avoir moins d'ent-

housiasme que de dilletantisme. S'il avait tant soit peu de passion, il passionnerait quelqu'un, car nous sommes encore une vingtaine en France qui avons le goût des nouveautés et des hardiesses.'

96 Thoré, *L'Indépendance belge*, 29 June 1868, reprinted in Thoré 1870, pp. 531–2, quoted above, note 40.

97 Baudelaire 1863, in Baudelaire 1971, II, especially pp. 141–4: 'Mais le génie n'est que *l'enfance retrouvée à volonté* . . . C'est à cette curiosité profonde et joyeuse qu'il faut attribuer l'oeil fixe et animalement extatique des enfants devant le *nouveau*, quel qu'il soit . . .'. For further discussion of *curiosité* in the context of the cultural politics of the 1860s, see John House, '*Curiosité*', in Hobbs 1998. On the gendering of the *flâneur*, see Wolff 1989; see also the essays in Tester 1994. However, the possibilities for a *flâneuse* have been discussed in Wilson 1991, pp. 47–64, Nord 1995 and Nead 2000 (the last two focusing on Victorian London); see also below, p. 228 note 25. An interesting and extended essay on the *flâneur* appears in Larousse, VIII, 1872, p. 436.

98 Fournel 1858, 1867 edition, pp. 268–82, especially pp. 277–80.

99 Baudelaire 1971, II, p. 184: 'D'ailleurs, dans la collection de ses oeuvres comme dans le fourmillement de la vie humaine, les différences de caste et de race, sous quelque appareil de luxe que les sujets se présentent, sautent immédiatement à l'oeil du spectateur.'

100 See especially Clark 1984/5, pp. 79ff.

101 Poe's 'The Man of the Crowd' was first published in 1840; Baudelaire's French translation, 'L'Homme des foules', first appeared in book form in *Nouvelles histoires extraordinaires*, Paris, 1857.

102 See e.g. Clark 1984/5.

103 Fried 1996, pp. 258–60.

104 See Le Play 1855; Le Play's monumental study of the working populations of Europe was published by the Imprimerie impériale, and it was noted on the title page that it was 'imprimé par l'autorisation de l'Empereur'. Le Play made it clear that his aim was to help governments and authorities – implicitly, the French government – to ensure 'the morality and well-being of families and the mutual affection of masters and workers [*la moralité et le bien-être des familles, ainsi que l'affection mutuelle des maîtres et des ouvriers*]', in the changing labour conditions precipitated by industrialisation.

105 Manet was actively involved with oppositional republican meetings after their legalisation in 1868, but there is little evidence that Monet shared these interests; Zola wrote for opposition journals, but Astruc, though apparently a republican by conviction, wrote most of his criticism for the staunchly imperialist *L'Etendard* and *Le Dix Décembre*; on the politics of the Impressionists, see Nord 2000.

106 See e.g. Sennett 1977, 1986 edition, especially pp. 161–74.

107 For the repeated opinion that the fashionable world had come to ape the demi-monde, see e.g. Romieu 1858, pp. 170–74, and the much-discussed *Opinion de M. le Procureur Général Dupin sur le luxe effréné des femmes*, delivered in the Senate on 22 June 1865 (reprinted in Feydeau 1866, pp. 195–204). Dupin's homily elicited many responses, among them Feydeau 1866, written from

the point of view of a fashionable boulevardier, and Audouard 1865, from the point of view of a feminist *femme du monde*. See also House, '*Curiosité*', in Hobbs 1998.

108 See London, National Gallery, 1992, and especially John House, 'Manet's Maximilian: History Painting, Censorship and Ambiguity' therein, for an elaboration of these arguments.

109 On these issues, see especially Kinney 1987.

110 For instance, Privat 1865, pp. 64–5; Castagnary 1892, I, p. 313, reviewing the Salon of 1868; Astruc 1870, IV; Burty 1870, III.

111 Burty 1870, IX: 'Le choix du sujet aura toujours une grande influence sur une foule française. Les abstractions de la forme ou de la couleur, considérées comme agents spéciaux, n'ont guère de prise sur un public qui préfère, en musique, Offenbach à Wagner.'

112 [Delord, Frémy and Texier] 1854; for an important discussion of the identities that Monet constructed for himself during the 1860s, see Wagner 1994, especially pp. 620 ff.

113 See especially Seigel 1986; Brown 1985 is an indispensable discussion of bohemianism and the visual arts; see also Clark 1973, especially pp. 33–4, 44–6; Wilson 2000.

114 [Delord, Frémy and Texier] 1854, p. 10; Mürger's *Scènes* appeared on the stage in 1849 and in book form in 1851; on *Physiologies*, see Le Men and Abélès 1993.

115 On this, see House, 'Censorship', 1997; Kinney 1987.

116 Letter from Courbet to Francis and Marie Wey, 31 July 1850, in Chu 1996, p. 92: 'Oui, cher ami, dans votre société si bien civilisée, il faut que je mène une vie de sauvage. Il faut que je m'affranchisse des gouvernements. Le peuple jouit de mes sympathies. Il faut que je m'adresse à lui directement, que j'en tire ma science, et qu'il me fasse vivre. Pour cela, je viens donc de débuter dans la grande vie vagabonde et indépendante du bohémien.'

117 Letter from Courbet to his parents, 5 August 1850, in Chu 1996, p. 93.

118 On the censorship of Courbet's titles, see House 1989, p. 165; the original title of the Journet portrait, *L'Apôtre Jean Journet*, with the subtitle *Partant pour la conquête de l'harmonie universelle*, appeared only in the lithograph that Courbet published of it, with accompanying verses, very much in the form of a popular *Image d'Epinal* (on this, see Clark 1973, pp. 139, 157, and plate 6).

119 For Cézanne's occasional appearance at the Café Guerbois, see Rewald 1973, p. 200.

120 For a range of readings of Cézanne's early work, see London, Royal Academy, 1988–9. Most studies of Cézanne's early career have been closely centred on the artist's biography and personality; it is in need of detailed reassessment in the broader contexts of oppositional painting in Paris in these years.

121 Stock 1870, as quoted in Cézanne 1978, p. 135, and Paris, Grand Palais, 1995–6, p. 120: 'Oui, mon cher monsieur Stock, je peins comme je vois, comme je sens – et j'ai les sensations très fortes –, eux aussi, ils sentent et voient comme moi, mais ils n'osent pas . . . ils font de la peinture de Salon . . . Moi, j'ose, M. Stock, j'ose . . . J'ai le courage de mes opinions . . . et rira bien qui rira le dernier.' Stock's caricature is reproduced in Rewald 1973, p. 246, and London, Royal Academy, 1988–9, p. 14.

122 On the Impressionists' political allegiances, see Nord 2000 (on Manet, especially pp. 19–22, 31–3; on Monet, p. 30; on Cézanne, pp. 27–8); on Manet, see also Hutton 1987.

123 Mallarmé 1876, in Berson 1996, I, p. 92.

124 Bertall's cartoon, '*Jésus peignant au milieu de ses disciples*', ou '*La divine école de Manet*', tableau religieux par *Fantin-Latour*, was accompanied by a parody of a biblical text which makes the missionary, prophetic implications of the cartoon still more explicit: 'En ce temps-là, J. Manet disait à ses disciples: En vérité, en vérité, je vous le dis, Celui qui a ce truc pour peindre est un grand peintre. Allez et peignez, et vous éclairerez le monde, et vos verries seront des lanternes.'

Chapter 2

1 Zola 1880, in Zola 1970, p. 341: 'Ce que je puis dire, c'est que M. Monet a trop cédé à sa facilité de production. Bien des ébauches sont sorties de son atelier, dans des heures difficiles, et cela ne vaut rien, cela pousse un peintre sur la pente de la pacotille. Quand on se satisfait trop aisément, quand on livre une esquisse à peine sèche, on perd le goût des morceaux longuement étudiés; c'est l'étude qui fait les oeuvres solides. M. Monet porte aujourd'hui la peine de sa hâte, de son besoin de vendre. S'il veut conquérir la haute place qu'il mérite, s'il veut être un des maîtres que nous attendons, il lui faut résolument se donner à des toiles importantes, étudiées pendant des saisons.'

2 Castagnary 1874, in Berson 1996, I, p. 17: 'Les plus forts, ceux qui ont de la race et du sang, auront reconnu que, s'il est des sujets qui s'accommodent de l'état d'impression, se contentent des dehors de l'ébauche, il en est d'autres et en bien plus grand nombre, qui réclament une expression nette, demandent une exécution précise; que la supériorité du peintre consiste précisément à traiter chaque sujet suivant le mode qui lui convient . . . Ceux-là, qui chemin faisant auront perfectionné leur dessin, laisseront là l'impressionnisme, devenu pour eux un art véritablement trop superficiel.'

3 Gautier 1861, pp. 119–20: 'Il est vraiment dommage que M. Daubigny, ce paysagiste d'un sentiment si vrai, si juste et si naturel, se contente d'une première impression et néglige à ce point les détails. Ses tableaux ne sont que des ébauches, et des ébauches peu avancés. Ce n'est le temps qui lui est manqué, car il n'a pas exposé moins de cinq toiles assez importantes; c'est donc à un système qu'on doit attribuer cette manière lâchée . . . Il n'eût cependant fallu que quelques jours de travail pour faire des tableaux excellents de ces préparations insuffisantes.'

4 Monet's notebooks are conserved in the Musée Marmottan, Paris; they are extensively used, but not published in full, in Wildenstein 1974–91.

5 The second *esquisse* (*Chemin de fer*) bought by Caillebotte is Wildenstein, I, 1974, no. 447 (reproduced in Paris, Musée d'Orsay, 1998, p. 119) – broadly and sketchily treated, but not so crude and summary as *The Signal*.

6 For more detail, see House, *Monet*, 1986, pp. 157 ff.

7 Fried 1996, pp. 214, 303–5, misleadingly suggests that there was no clear distinction between the *ébauche* and the *esquisse*.

8 Léon Lagrange in 1865 described Daubigny as leader of the 'school of the *impression*' (Lagrange 1865, pp. 152–3), and in 1866 Charles Blanc criticised certain followers of Corot for being satisfied with 'rendering the *impression*', commenting that 'this is the big word in a certain camp' (Blanc 1866, p. 40).

9 For Monet's normal use of *étude*, see House, *Monet*, 1986, pp. 158–9. In 1879 Monet exhibited a canvas as *Etude de mer* (unidentified, but a possible identification with Wildenstein, I, 1974, no. 112 is suggested in Berson 1996, II, p. 116). Wildenstein, I, 1974, no. 649, a view from the cliffs near Fécamp, was exhibited in the Impressionist group exhibition of 1882 with the title *Etude de mer vue des hauteurs*; Monet sold this canvas to Durand-Ruel in May 1881 with the same title, and, quite exceptionally for Monet, it was sold unsigned. In his retrospective at Georges Petit's Gallery in 1889, a canvas of 1873 was shown as *Etude de bateaux; Havre* (unidentified, but possibly Wildenstein, I, 1974, no. 259, whose early provenance is unclear) and one of his Creuse canvases of 1889 as *Etude d'eau* (probably either Wildenstein, III, 1979, no. 1239 or 1240). In his exhibition of the *Meules* series at Durand-Ruel's Gallery in 1891 he included *Etude de rochers; Creuse*, lent by G. Clemenceau; the identification of this canvas remains a puzzle; although the title seems most appropriate for *Le Bloc*, Wildenstein, III, 1979, no. 1228, later owned by Georges Clemenceau, which is also clearly described in Gustave Geffroy's introduction to the exhibition catalogue of 1891 (reprinted Geffroy 1892, p. 27), documents seem to show unequivocally that Monet did not give this to Clemenceau until December 1899 (see Wildenstein, III, 1979, pp. 300–01, pièce justificative 133, and Wildenstein, IV, 1985, pp. 339–40, letters 1482 and 1485).

10 For instance, in 1859 Corot exhibited *Etude à Ville d'Avray*, and in 1861 *Etude à Ville d'Avray* and *Etude à Méry, près La Ferté-sous-Jouarre*, on both occasions alongside more ambitious subject pictures. Three examples of academic figure studies are Hippolyte Flandrin's *Figure d'étude* at the Exposition Universelle of 1855 (a seated figure of a boy painted in 1835–6; Louvre, Paris); Amaury-Duval's *Etude d'enfant* at the Salon of 1864 (destroyed; see Paris, Grand Palais, 1974, pp. 18–19) and Jules Lefebvre's *Femme couchée; étude* at the Salon of 1868, a much-discussed but now lost 'modern' nude (reproduced from a photograph of 1878 in Clayson 1991, p. 36).

11 Letters from Monet to Bazille, 14 and 16 October 1864, in Wildenstein, I, 1974, letters 11 and 12, p. 421.

12 See letter from Marie le Coeur to Jules le Coeur, 6 April 1866, in Anon., 'L'Eternel Jury', 1921, between pp. 100 and 101. '... l'autre [the smaller painting, accepted by the jury] a été fait à Marlotte en 15 jours, il appelle cela une pochade, il ne l'a envoyé à l'exposition que parce qu'il en avait un autre qui avait plus de valeur, sans cela il aurait trouvé qu'il ne fallait pas l'exposer.'

13 'J'ai bien un rêve, un tableau, les bains de la Grenouillère, pour lequel j'ai fait des mauvaises pochades, mais c'est un rêve. Renoir ... veut aussi faire ce tableau.' Letter from Monet to Bazille, 25 September 1869, in Wildenstein, I, 1974, letter 53, p. 427.

14 The early history of both paintings is unclear; see Wildenstein, I, 1974, nos. 134, 135. The handwritten signature on pl. 31, very unlike Monet's standard script, may imply that it went to a friend (on this signature, identical to those on two other paintings, of 1870 and 1874, Wildenstein, I, 1974, nos. 155 and 313, see House 2001, p. 104, where it is suggested that Manet may have been the first owner of the canvas).

15 Wildenstein, I, 1974, no. 136; reproduced in House, *Monet*, 1986, p. 207.

16 Astruc 1870, I; a few of Monet's Argenteuil river scenes were exhibited during the 1870s as *marines*; however, Burty's description of Monet's technique in his review of the Salon of 1870 strongly suggests that the rejected picture was a seascape: 'M. Monet est un indiscipliné, un peintre lourd, souvent énergique, toujours convaincu. Il recherche les oppositions violentes du ciel bleu avec la grève blanche, de la mer, sillonnée comme par un soc par les bateaux à vapeur aux longs panaches noirs ... Cette rudesse de matelot fraîchement débarqué a paru indécente au jury ...' (Burty 1870, I).

17 I am deeply indebted to the late Charles Durand-Ruel, and to Madame Caroline Durand-Ruel Godfroy, for granting me access to the Durand-Ruel stock books; details later in this chapter derive from the same source.

18 See House, *Renoir*, 1997, pp. 10–12, 46–8; for the dog, see Thomson 1982, p. 328.

19 We await Linda Whiteley's book on the emergence of the art dealer in nineteenth-century Paris.

20 Letter from François Bonvin to Louis Martinet, 22 April 1861, in Moreau-Nélaton 1927, p. 58: 'Encore un bon point pour la bonne pensée que vous avez eue d'une exposition permanente! Ce tableau, que je vous ai porté il y a huit jours, vient d'attirer sur moi l'attention du ministère. Placée à la grande exposition, où elle a eu souvent son équivalent, cette toile n'eût peut-être pas été remarquée. La peinture intime, grande ou petite, a besoin d'un local comme le vôtre: plus grand, c'est trop grand.'

21 Gautier in 1858 described the experience of viewing pictures in the shop windows of Rue Laffitte as 'a sort of permanent Salon [*une sorte de salon permanente*]' (Gautier 1858, p. 10); for descriptions of dealers' shops and windows in these years, see also Henriet 1854, de Lépinois 1860 and Burty 1867.

22 The *Angelus* measures 55 × 66 cm; *Gleaners* (*Des Glaneuses*) 83.5 × 111 cm.

23 For instance, see the contents of his one-artist shows *chez* Martinet in 1863 (see Paris, Grand Palais, 1983, p. 507) and in the offices of *La Vie moderne* in 1880 (see Wilson-Bareau 1991, p. 245).

24 For Boudin, see Jean-Aubry 1922, especially pp. 48–9, 72; for Jongkind, see Hefting 1968, especially pp. 3–4, 32–3.

25 Musée d'Orsay, Paris; Sammlung Oskar Reinhart aus Römerholz, Winterthur. The acceptance of these two paintings at the Salon of 1870 is the only clear instance when smaller paintings of this type were exhibited at the Salon by a member of the Impressionist circle.

26 Wildenstein, I, 1974, p. 424, letter 33, to Bazille 25 June 1867.

27 See House, *Renoir*, 1997, pp. 17–20.

28 Randall 1979, II, p. 313 (Lucas's diary entry for 7 January 1870); see London, Hayward Gallery, 1980–81, p. 80.

29 See Elder 1924, p. 69.

30 They are listed in Monet's carnet as '2 pochades Argenteuil', sold for 400 francs the pair; the titles in Durand-Ruel's stock books do not correspond with those in Monet's carnet, but they can be identified from the prices paid as *Coteaux de Sanois* and *Marine (Argenteuil)*. *Coteaux de Sanois* can very probably be identified as *Vue de la plaine d'Argenteuil* (Wildenstein, I, 1974, no. 220; Musée d'Orsay, Paris), a canvas that is more loosely handled than the others that Monet sold to the dealer during 1872.

31 Guillemot 1898, p. [1]: '... j'avais envoyé une chose faite au Havre, de ma fenêtre, du soleil dans la buée et au premier plan quelques navires pointant... On me demande le titre pour le catalogue, ça ne pouvait vraiment pas passer pour une vue du Havre: je répondis: "Mettez Impression."'

32 Close examination confirms that the picture was executed in a single session, since even the foreground boats and the sun with its reflections were executed wet-in-wet (see House 2001, p. 105).

33 See e.g. Antoine Chintreuil's *The First Dawn, after a Stormy Night* (Salon of 1868) and Jules Noel's *The Port of Brest* (Salon of 1864) in London, Hayward Gallery, 1995–6, pp. 78–9, 94–5; Joseph Vernet's series of monumental canvases of the ports of France in the 1750s and 1760s remained the yardstick against which artists measured their own port scenes throughout the nineteenth century.

34 In this context, it is hard to imagine that any of its original viewers in 1874 could have viewed *Impression, Sunrise* in the terms suggested by Paul Tucker, as 'Monet's vision of a new day dawning for a revivified France' after the disasters of the Franco-Prussian War and the Commune, in the way in which it combines 'the evidence of industrial–commercial activity with the beauties of nature' (See Tucker in San Francisco 1986, p. 110, and also Tucker 1984).

35 Chesneau 1874, in Berson 1996, I, p. 18: 'cette merveilleuse ébauche...'.

36 The other version of the subject, Rewald 1996, no. 171, was clearly painted first of the two.

37 This identification is suggested in Rewald 1996, no. 201, p. 152, and, more confidently, in London, National Gallery, 2000–01, pp. 24–6. The identification of *Etude: Paysage à Auvers* with *Le Quartier du four à Auvers-sur-Oise* (Philadelphia Museum of Art; Rewald 1996, no. 198), proposed in San Francisco 1986, p. 126, is implausible, since parts of this canvas are conspicuously unresolved and the most highly worked areas show a firmer, more ordered touch that suggests a later dating, perhaps as late as 1875–6 (on this canvas, see London, Hayward Gallery, 1995–6, pp. 210–11).

38 Rivière 6 May 1877, in Berson 1996, I, p. 181; the elaborated version is Wildenstein, I, 1974, no. 402 (reproduced in colour in Wildenstein, II, 1996, p. 164).

39 Paris, Grand Palais, 1980, p. 176.

40 Wildenstein, I, 1974, nos. 418, 420, 433.

41 Although *The Signal* (pl. 28) is even rougher and more summary than any other canvas that we know Monet to have exhibited in these years, Georges Rivière's retrospective comments on this show seem to indicate that it was indeed exhibited: 'Un autre tableau ne contient que des disques, le train vient de passer et la fumée tournoie sur la voie en grosses nuées lourdes...' (Rivière 1 November 1877, reprinted in Berson 1996, I, p. 185). Frédéric Chevalier's mention of a canvas 'dont un disque menaçant et farouche domine le premier plan' seems to refer to the same picture (Chevalier 1877, reprinted in Berson 1996, I, p. 139). However, it remains possible that both critics were referring to the other Gare Saint-Lazare canvas with a disc, Wildenstein, I, 1974, no. 445, which, though very sketchily treated, is somewhat more resolved, and has a more formally scripted signature.

42 See also House, *Monet*, 1986, pp. 194, 206–8.

43 Two of the others were probably Rewald 1996, nos. 268 and 275; see also below, p. 174.

44 Probably two from among Rewald 1996, nos. 265, 315 and 316.

45 Probably Rewald 1996, nos. 329, 337 and 348.

46 Rewald 1996, no. 292.

47 Perhaps Rewald 1983, nos. 10 and 17.

48 The small version is Rewald 1996, no. 259 (Musée d'Art et d'Histoire, Geneva), the large one no. 261 (Barnes Foundation); for both sides of the argument about which was exhibited, see Rewald 1996, pp. 178, 180. Two little-noted comments in the criticism of the 1877 show lend further support to the argument that the exhibited picture was indeed the large one. Léon de Lora wrote of the 'ventres bleus' (blue bellies) of his *Bathers* and the 'nuages d'un blanc de faïence' (white pottery clouds) above them, while the critic of *La petite république française* spoke of it as 'des *baigneurs* en plâtre' (bathers made of plaster) (Berson 1996, I, pp. 163, 176); both comments seem far more applicable to the large, densely worked version.

49 Degas's exhibits in 1876 included *Portrait de femme (ébauche)*, in 1879 *Blanchisseuses portant du linge en ville. (Esquisse à l'essence)*; Morisot in 1881 showed *Etude de plein air* (identifiable as *Dame à l'ombrelle*; see Berson 1996, II, pp. 182, 192); Pissarro in 1879 showed *Effet de soleil. Boulevard Clichy. (Esquisse)*, and in 1882 four figure paintings subtitled *étude* (probably Pissarro and Venturi 1939, nos. 513, 530, 541 and 542; see Berson 1996, II, pp. 208, 225–6; on these figure paintings, see below, pp. 203–5).

50 The practice seems to have been pioneered by the landscapists Eugène Ciceri, Charles Hoguet, Narcisse Diaz and Théodore Rousseau around 1850, and spread during the 1860s; see Sensier 1872, pp. 204, 256–7, 273; Thoré 1870, I, pp. 48–9; Jean-Aubry 1922, pp. 53–4, 66–7 (for two sales of Boudin's work during the 1860s); Burty 1867. For the significance of auctions in the period, see Green, 'Dealing in Temperaments', 1987, pp. 62–7; further research is urgently needed on the auction sales of the period and the ways in which artists used them; but see Simon Kelly's essay on the sales organised by Diaz and Rousseau, in Fowle 2003.

51 Letter from Duret to Pissarro, 15 February 1874, in

Pissarro and Venturi 1939, I, pp. 33–4: '. . . un public mêlé et nombreux'.

52 Burty April 1875, p. III: 'Il n'existe malheureusement pas encore à Paris d'endroit discrète et commode où l'on puisse, sans prétention comme sans réticence, accrocher quelques centaines d'études ou de dessins, – voire de tableaux – se complétant et s'expliquant les uns par les autres. L'hôtel Drouot seul offre cet avantage d'attirer journellement la foule et par conséquent de provoquer la critique à fond.' Burty's preface indicates that this sale included 'des fusains, des ébauches et des compositions à l'huile'; it is intersting that the status of the works is not indicated in the titles that Gautier gave them in the sale catalogue.

53 On this auction, see Rewald 1973, pp. 351–4, and Bodelsen 1968. Burty's preface (Burty March 1875), the nearest thing to a manifesto for the Impressionist group, is reprinted in Riout 1989, pp. 47–9.

54 See London, Hayward Gallery, 1985–6, p. 202.

55 Catalogue reprinted in Bodelsen 1968, pp. 336–9.

56 Ward 1991, pp. 605–8; on the cercles, see also Garb 1994, pp. 32–41.

57 Champier 1880, pp. 173–4, quoted in Ward 1991, p. 607: 'Les amateurs, que rebutent un peu les fatigues du Salon . . . préfèrent ces expositions intimes qui paraissent improvisées . . . Les artistes y envoient librement le morceau qu'ils ont sous la main: une esquisse bien venue, une pochade curieuse, une indication de paysage, aussi bien qu'un tableau poussé à la perfection.'

58 Houssaye 1880, pp. 193–4: 'Mais le malheur pour les cercles est que les peintres n'y exposent pas des tableaux pris au hasard dans l'atelier. Ils choisissent, non point en aveugles, et leurs meilleures choses sont réservées pour le Salon. Au Salon, les tableaux qui fondent la réputation, les oeuvres les plus achevées et les plus durables; aux cercles, les portraits de commande ou de complaisance, les tableaux faits vite, les ébauches bien venues.'

59 See Wilson-Bareau 1991, pp. 242–5, where the catalogue is reproduced.

60 In this context, the difficulties of hanging Manet's A Bar at the Folies-Bergère (pl. 126) in the Courtauld Institute Gallery are revealing. The only Salon painting in the Courtauld collection, it consistently diminishes the effect of any smaller painting hung alongside it.

61 Letter from Duret to Pissarro, 15 February 1874, in Pissarro and Venturi 1939, I, pp. 33–4, translated in part in Rewald 1973, p. 310: 'Il vous reste un pas à franchir, c'est d'arriver à être connu du public et à être accepté de tous les marchands et amateurs. Pour cela il n'y a que les ventes à l'Hôtel Drouot et la grande exposition du Palais de l'Industrie. Vous avez maintenant un groupe d'amateurs et de collectionneurs qui vous sont [sic] acquis et vous soutiennent. Votre nom est connu des artistes, des critiques, du public spécial. Mais il faut faire un pas de plus et arriver à la grande notoriété. Vous n'y arriverez point par des expositions des sociétés particulières. Le public ne va pas à ces expositions, il n'y a que le même noyau d'artistes et d'amateurs qui vous connaît d'avance . . . A l'exposition, vous serez vu, sur les 40000 [sic] personnes qui, je suppose, visitent l'exposition, par 50

marchands, amateurs, critiques, qui n'iraient jamais vous chercher et vous trouver ailleurs . . . Je vous engage à exposer; il faut arriver à faire du bruit, à braver, à attirer la critique, à se mettre en face du grand public. Vous ne pourrez arriver à tout cela qu'au Palais de l'Industrie.' The Salon catalogues of the mid-1870s record annual attendance figures of around 500,000.

62 Ibid.: 'Je vous engage à choisir des tableaux où il y ait un sujet, quelque chose ressemblant à une composition, des tableaux pas trop frais peints, et déjà un peu faits.'

63 Letter from Monet to Théodore Duret, 8 March 1880, in Wildenstein, I, 1974, letter 173, p. 438.

64 Letter from Monet to Georges de Bellio, 8 January 1880, in Wildenstein, I, 1974, letter 170, p. 438: 'Je viens vous annoncer une bonne nouvelle, j'ai vendu à M. Petit au prix de 500 francs la nature morte que vouz avez vue puis deux effets de neige au prix de 300 francs avec promesse de nouveaux achats; c'est là une bonne chose, car M. Petit a trouvé mes toiles très à son goût. Je dois seulement vous prévenir qu'il m'a bien recommandé de ne plus vendre à bon marché; c'est à cette condition qu'il fera de nouvelles affaires avec moi.'

65 On Monet's still lifes, see House, Monet, 1986, pp. 40–43.

66 Huysmans 1883, reprinted in Berson 1996, I, p. 398: 'M. Monet a longtemps bafouillé, lâchant de courtes improvisations, bâclant des bouts de paysages . . . il y avait chez lui un laisser-aller, un manque d'études trop manifestes. En dépit du talent que dénotaient certaines esquisses, je me désintéressais, de plus en plus, je l'avoue, de cette peinture brouillonne et hâtive . . . M. Monet est certainement l'homme qui a le plus contribué à persuader le public que le mot "impressionnisme" désignait une peinture demeurée à l'état de confus rudiment, de vague ébauche. Un revirement s'est heureusement produit chez cet artiste; il paraît s'être décidé de ne plus peinturlurer, au petit bonheur, des tas de toiles . . . il nous a servi, cette fois, de très beaux et de très complètes paysages.'

67 Burty 1883: 'M. Claude Monet notamment a accompli sur lui-même d'incontestables progrès. Il n'est plus l'esclave d'une production hâtive provoquée par la nécessité de vendre au jour le jour . . . En vendant plus cher, il peut travailler plus longtemps une toile, en dégager des intentions plus nettes, se reposer même les jours où le rêverie et la fatigue l'emportent.'

68 Blanche 1933, p. 292: '[I]l faut que la maman reconnaisse sa fille.'

69 Letter from Monet to Alice Hoschedé, 13 October 1886, in Wildenstein, II, 1979, letter 711, p. 280: '. . . je persiste à travailler, non pas à mes études commencées depuis longtemps, mais à des tentatives de pochades . . .'. See also letter 713, p. 281. Two of the pochades are Wildenstein, II, 1979, nos. 1116 (Musée d'Orsay, Paris) and 1117.

70 The fullest version of the story, though with impossible dates, is in Clemenceau 1928, pp. 64–5; see also House, Monet, 1986, pp. 164, 221–2.

71 It is noteworthy that Monet exhibited other canvases as impressions in these years: Temps de pluie (impression) and Marine (impression) at Petit's gallery in 1886.

72 Le Roux 1889.

73 Duranty 1876, in Berson 1996, I, pp. 79–80: 'Le public

. . . ne comprend que la correction, il veut le fini avant tout. L'artiste, charmé des délicatesses ou des éclats de la coloration, du caractère d'un geste, d'un groupement, s'inquiète beaucoup moins de ce fini, de cette correction, les seules qualités de ceux qui ne sont point artistes . . . D'ailleurs, il importe peu que le public ne comprenne pas; il importe davantage que les artistes comprennent, et devant eux on peut exposer des esquisses, des préparations, des dessous, où la pensé, le dessein et le dessin du peintre s'expriment souvent avec plus de rapidité, plus de concentration . . .'.

74 Letter to Durand-Ruel, 30 June 1891, in Wildenstein, III, 1979, p. 262, letter 1116: 'Je vends quelquefois certaines esquisses un peu moins cher, mais c'est alors à des artistes ou des amis.'

75 Letter to Durand-Ruel, 22 January 1886, in Wildenstein, II, 1979, p. 271, letter 650: '. . . trop incomplètes pour l'amateur'.

76 Paillet, as translated in Wilhelm 1962, p. 520; among the paintings in the Varanchan sale in 1777 was Fragonard's *Bathers* (Musée du Louvre, Paris). Paillet's comments on sketches pick up on a passage in Diderot's 'Salon de 1767': 'Pourquoi une belle esquisse nous plaît-il plus qu'un beau tableau? C'est qu'il y a plus de vie et moins de formes. . . . l'esquisse est l'ouvrage de la chaleur et du génie, et le tableau l'ouvrage du travail, de la patience, des longues études et d'une expérience consommée de l'art' (Diderot 1983, p. 241). For an extended discussion of the terms *esquisse* and *étude*, see Larousse, VII, 1870, pp. 934–5, 1083.

77 See especially Vaisse 1985 and Berhaut 1985.

78 Robinson, 'Diary', 3 June 1892; see House, *Monet*, 1986, pp. 201, 220 ff.

79 Shiff 1984, pp. 1–38.

80 See Ward 1991, especially pp. 613–18. In this context, Burty's descriptions of the installation of the first group show are relevant. The works were hung on red-brown fabric (Burty, 'Chronique du jour', 16 April 1874, reprinted in Berson 1996, I, p. 36: 'laine brun-rouge'); 'They have hung up draperies as if in a private gallery . . . The paintings are presented to their best advantage; lit almost as they would be in a moderate-sized apartment, isolated, not too numerous, not harming each other by being near other works that are either too bright or too dull.' (Burty, 'Exposition', 25 April 1874, reprinted in Berson 1996, I, pp. 36–7: 'Ils ont fait tendre des draperies comme dans une galerie privée . . . Les peintures se présentent tout à leur avantage; éclairées à peu près comme dans un appartement moyen, isolées, pas trop nombreuses, ne se nuisant pas par des voisinages trop bruyants ou trop ternes.')

Chapter 3

1 See e.g. Herbert 1988; Tucker 1982; Brettell 1990.

2 Bigot 1877, reprinted in Berson 1996, I, p. 134: 'Au fond, ce n'est pas la véritable nature qu'ils ont regardée et qu'ils s'efforcent de rendre, c'est surtout la nature telle qu'on l'entrevoit par échappées dans la grande ville ou dans ses environs, là où les notes criardes des maisons, des murailles blanches, rouges ou jaunes, avec leurs volets verts, viennent se mêler à la végétation des arbres et former avec elle des contrastes violents. Ah! Que les Hollandais, ah! Que nos paysagistes modernes, les Rousseau, les Corot, les Daubigny, ont su exprimer non pas seulement la poésie, mais aussi la vérité de la nature! Qu'ils ont mieux représenté la campagne, avec ses eaux, ses bois, ses champs et ses prairies, avec ses lointains et calmes horizons!'

3 Joanne 1881, pp. xxv–xxvi (preface dated 1877): 'Les Parisiens surtout ignorent l'art de se promener avec profit. Parviennent-ils un jour s'échapper pour quelques heures de ces affreuses prisons de pierre ou de plâtre dans lesquelles ils s'achètent trop chèrement le droit d'être enfermés sans air, sans espace et sans lumière, ils se précipitent par bandes vers certains points où de perfides réclames attirent incessamment leur trop naïve curiosité; ils s'y entassent pêle-mêle dans des établissements publics, encore moins salubres et moins séduisants que leurs demeures, pour y chercher surtout des distractions banales qui n'ont absolument rien de champêtre et qu'ils se fussent procurées à moins de frais dans l'enceinte même de la grande ville.'

4 Henriet 1876, pp. 96–7; see also pp. 81–3 (a version of this part of the book was first published in 1867): '. . . le paysagiste . . . aime avec passion les chaumes rongés des mousses, les mares bourbeuses, les routes défoncées, les chemins creux aux flancs qui s'éboulent. Le crayon à la main, il pousse jusqu'à la férocité son amour du pittoresque; mais, – il le constate avec douleur, – tous ces aspects sauvages ou grandioses de la nature tendent à s'effacer à mesure que la science ne laisse plus aucune richesse du sol inexploitée; à mesure que la civilisation . . . uniformise tout sous un niveau: moeurs, costumes, usages, habitations! Il n'est pas une conquête de l'industrie, pas une amélioration matérielle qui ne coûte en effet quelques sacrifices à la poésie des souvenirs ou à l'ordre des beautés pittoresques . . . La Poésie! Elle est dans le coeur de l'artiste; et . . . nous dirons aux fervents de l'art pur . . . : Retrempez-vous sans cesse au vivifiant contact de la nature, source éternelle du vrai, du beau, du fort. Chantez encore les bois et les vallons, les naïfs épisodes de la vie des champs, les belles moissons d'or et les eaux paresseuses qui bercent la rêverie. Il ne manque point de sentiers perdus, de coins oubliés, où votre inspiration ne risquera pas de meurtrir son aile contre la cheminée de l'usine, le poteau du télégraphe ou les noirs tuyaux de la locomotive!' Green 1990 is a crucial study of the role of the urban viewer in landscape imagery, though focusing on an earlier period.

5 About 1868, pp. 738–9: 'Forêts, rochers, rivages, vallons, troupeaux, palais, ruines, chaumières, costumes, types, étaient les matériaux dont on composait un paysage. Les artistes pensaient à tort ou à raison que le premier coin de terre venu n'est pas l'étoffe d'un tableau et qu'avant de prendre la brosse il faut avoir en provision tout un choix d'objets intéressans. Lorsqu'on rencontrait par hasard dans la nature une réunion de belles choses bien groupées, on disait: "Voilà un site pittoresque," c'est à dire digne d'être peint, semblable à ceux qui fixent le choix des vrais artistes.'

6 Lagrange 1865; see London, Hayward Gallery, 1995–6, pp. 21–3.

7 It is noteworthy that the invading Prussian armies had indeed passed directly through Lavardin, the village presented as so pristine and undisturbed in Busson's canvas, pl. 53 (see House, 'Busson', 2000). *The Village of Lavardin* was one of only three landscapes purchased by the State from the Salon of 1877, at the height of the 'moral order' regime – a testimony to the picture's effectiveness as an expression of conservative aesthetic and political values.

8 'The Environs of Paris', in Clark 1984/5.

9 As is done frequently in Tucker 1982.

10 Rouart 1950, pp. 19–20: 'On dit que c'est un petit rendez-vous très agreste d'un monde très léger et que, si l'on y va seul, on revient au moins deux.'

11 Lenoir 1872, pp. 254–5: ' "Lorsque vous passerez par Bougival, lui répondîmes nous, nous vous ferons canoter, et nous vous présenterons *à la Grenouillère*." Persuadé que c'était une personne de haut parage, le bon Père nous exprima toute sa reconnaissance pour une faveur dont il se croyait indigne.'

12 Notably by John Rewald, e.g. in Rewald 1973; for a recent and very literal exploration of this approach, see White 1996.

13 Sardou 1867, p. 1457, quoted in part in Clark 1984/5, p. 298 note 7: 'Voici le vrai village! Tu peux entrer; ôte ton habit, si tu as chaud . . . chante, si tu es gai! – Tu n'offenseras ici personne! . . . Chatou est loin; et ces petits tourbillons blancs, que le vent soulève autour de toi, sur la route, ce n'est pas le la poudre de riz . . . C'est de la vraie poussière!'

14 The topographical layout of this area remains a puzzle. Presumably, the painter's viewpoint in pl. 62 was closer to Argenteuil, and thus beyond the trees seen on the right in pl. 61, though the trees on the left and the town seem to be viewed from much the same angle in both. A further canvas, Wildenstein, I, 1974, no. 197, seemingly from the identical viewpoint as pl. 62 and painted in the same year, omits the prominent white house. This group of pictures emphasises the liberties that Monet was prepared to take with his chosen subjects, even at this period (for comparable modifications later in his career, see House, *Monet*, 1986, pp. 185–8). The details of the topography of this area are not discussed in Tucker 1982.

15 Tucker 1982, pp. 20, 96, makes the comparison with Daubigny, but sees Monet's views of the backwater, overall, as a 'modern pastoral retreat', and ignores the intrusive elements in pl. 64.

16 On these factory paintings, see Brettell 1990, pp. 73–97; the larger factory, seen in pls 67 and 68, was an industrial distillery (see Brettell 1990, pp. 23–5), although few viewers of Pissarro's paintings would have known this.

17 As suggested in Adler 2000, p. 257.

18 Sardou 1867, p. 1468.

19 Barron 1889, pp. 312–13: 'Ecoutez, en ramant lentement, le conducteur du tramway longeant le fleuve, nommer ces radieux paysages: Louveciennes, – et vous pensez à la Dubarry, à Louis xv, au négrillon Zamore, châtelaine, hôte et gouverneur du riche et discret château d'où la favorite

un jour partit, oh! Bien malgré elle, tirer un numéro fatal à la loterie de sainte Guillotine; – Marly, – et vous seriez tenté d'aller chercher, sous les herbes folles, dans les allées confondues du parc, les vestiges presque introuvables du splendide palais . . . De ces magnificences si vantées . . . , il ne reste guère que l'emplacement, des portes vermoulues, et le mélancolique abreuvoir où se cabraient jadis les chevaux de Coustou.'

20 See e.g. Mayeur and Rebérioux 1984, pp. 18 ff.

21 See Brettell 1990, pp. 160–71; for charts of the topographical distribution of Pissarro's Pontoise sites in the years 1872–6, see ibid., pp. 151, 165, 173.

22 On Pissarro's houses at Pontoise, see Shikes and Harper 1980, pp. 115, 123, and Bailly-Herzberg, I, 1980, p. 81.

23 Letter from Duret to Pissarro, 6 December 1873, in Pissarro and Venturi 1939, p. 26: 'Je persiste à penser que la nature agreste, rustique avec animaux est ce qui correspond le mieux à votre talent.'

24 Letter from Pissarro to Duret, 8 December 1873, in Bailly-Herzberg, I, 1980, pp. 87–8.

25 Brettell 1990, p. 122.

26 Tucker 1982, pp. 169–86.

27 On this type of imagery, see Tucker 1982, pp. 70–76.

28 For a salutary warning about the notion of 'influence' in this context, see Varnedoe 1990, Chapter Two; however, the present account finds more relevance in stereoscopic photographs than Varnedoe allows (see also below, pp. 111–13).

29 Reclus 1866, pp. 365–71. For ecological concerns about Argenteuil in the 1870s, see Tucker 1982, pp. 152, 176–81; for a broader consideration of environmentalist issues in relation to the painting of the period, see House, 'Landscape', 2000.

30 Reclus 1866, pp. 377–80.

31 Ibid., pp. 380–81.

32 Chevalier 1877, reprinted in Berson 1996, I, p. 139: 'Les caractères qui distinguent les intransigeants, la facture brutale, le terre à terre des sujets qu'ils affectionnent, l'apparence de spontanéité qu'ils recherchent avant tout, l'incohérence voulue, les hardiesses de coloris, le mépris de la forme, les naïvetés puériles qu'ils mêlent insouciamment à des raffinements exquis, cette ensemble inquiétant de qualités et de défauts contradictoires n'est pas sans analogie avec le chaos des forces antagonistes qui troublent notre époque. Un art dont l'idéal est vague et l'exécution rudimentaire est celui qui doit refléter le plus fidèlement nos incertitudes et notre prosaïsme actuels.'

Chapter 4

1 Notably Herbert 1988; see also Clayson 1991.

2 Castagnary 1892, I, pp. 364–5: 'Comme les personnages dans une comédie, il faut que dans un tableau chaque figure soit à son plan, remplisse son rôle et concoure ainsi à l'expression de l'idée générale. Rien d'arbitraire et rien de superflu, telle est la loi de toute composition artistique.'

3 Fried 1980.

4 Chambers 1999, p. 45; see also pp. 54–5.

5 Renoir 1879: 'Ce qu'il a peint nous le voyons tous les

jours; c'est notre existence propre qu'il a enregistrée dans des pages qui resteront à coup sûr parmi les plus vivantes et les plus harmonieuses de l'époque.'

6 Fried 1996, p. 17 and passim.

7 I would point to this as a fundamental difference between the present book and Fried 1996; the two texts seek to historicise the viewer/subject in very different ways.

8 Cf. e.g. Ségalen 1983, pp. 78–111. Ségalen's important analyses of the patterns and rituals of peasant life are compromised by the value that she accords to the paintings of Jean-François Millet as documentary evidence (Ségalen 1983, pp. 6, 95–9).

9 For this emphasis on the relativity of notions of work and leisure, I am indebted to Chambers 1999, p. xi.

10 Duranty 1876, reprinted in Berson 1996, i, p. 78: 'Les aspects des choses et des gens ont mille manières d'être imprévues, dans la réalité.'

11 See e.g. Comment 1993/9.

12 Gavarni 1845–6, 1868 edition, p. 42: '. . . prudent de flâner un peu au-dessus de la grande fourmilière parisienne pour en reconnaître les abords'; for the overview of Paris, see especially pp. 41–8.

13 For a rich and thought-provoking discussion of the high viewpoint, see Prendergast 1992, pp. 46–73.

14 Letter from Monet to Nieuwerkerke, 27 April 1867, Wildenstein, v, 1991, letter 2687 (30a), p. 188.

15 Clark 1984/5, pp. 70–72.

16 Leroy 1874, reprinted in Berson 1996, i, p. 25: 'Seulement veuillez me dire ce que représentent ces innombrables lichettes noires dans le bas du tableau? . . . Alors je ressemble à ça quand je me promène sur le boulevard des Capucines? . . . Vous moquez-vous de moi à la fin?'

17 At its south end, the Tuileries Palace abutted directly on to the Pavillon de Flore (see pl. 92). This end of the palace was demolished before Monet painted the canvas, presumably to allow restoration of the Pavillon, since the north face of the Pavillon is here unobscured (this partial demolition is corroborated by Ten Cate's canvas of 1883, *Les Ruines des Tuileries et la Place du Carrousel*, Musée Carnavalet, Paris, P594). Tucker 1982, p. 163, views the canvas as evidence of Monet avoiding 'the ruins and politics, and immersing himself in the natural beauties of the site', while Spate 1992, p. 118, does note the presence of the 'fragment of the bare north face of the Pavillon' in *The Tuileries*.

18 Close examination of contemporary maps (e.g. in Joanne 1863) enables one to reconstruct Monet's angle of vision, looking south-west from Victor Chocquet's apartment on the Rue de Rivoli, and make it clear that the building on the left is indeed the Cour des Comptes.

19 De Nittis's canvas shows that a section at the north end of the Tuileries Palace was also demolished to enable the restoration of the Pavillon de Marsan.

20 See Roos 1988; this article is an exemplary exploration of the relationship between politics and picture-making. On the 14 July celebrations, see below, Chapter Six.

21 See Paris, Grand Palais, 1983, p. 396.

22 There is, as yet, no thorough history of the French stereoscopic photograph, despite the vast popularity of the medium between about 1855 and 1875; for a brief overview, see Pellerin 1995. The classic, though very problematic, comparison of Impressionism with photography is Scharf 1968, pp. 125–61.

23 Varnedoe 1980, p. 67; for a more wide-ranging presentation of these arguments, see Varnedoe 1990, Chapter Two.

24 Varnedoe 1980, p. 71.

25 In this context, it is worth noting that a photograph such as plate 99 offers unequivocal evidence that bourgeois women did move around the streets unaccompanied. Although the viewpoints of such photographs were carefully chosen, the figures that appear in them, down on the street, were clearly in no way posed or arranged, but represent the people who happened to be passing at that moment. While men certainly enjoyed a freedom in the streets denied to women, the contemporary texts that emphasise the moral inappropriateness of women walking alone in public spaces need to be read as prescriptive, not descriptive.

26 For a rich reading of the picture that differs in its focus from mine, see Fried 1999, pp. 2–11; Herbert 1988, p. 19, sees the female figure as 'the psychological focus of René Caillebotte's gaze, therefore of ours', a reading that ignores both the uncertainties about the angles of vision and the anonymity of the 'young man' as he is presented to the viewer.

27 On the privileged position implied by Degas's viewpoints, see Armstrong 1991, pp. 58–62; see also pp. 22–3.

28 See Mayne 1966 and Paris, Grand Palais, 1988–9, pp. 171–3, 269–70.

29 The class contrast in *House-Painters* is also stressed in Fried 1999, pp. 23–4, though the picture is interpreted in somewhat different terms.

30 As emphasised in Fried 1999, p. 27.

31 Herbert 1988, p. 23.

32 Boime 1995, p. 84.

33 Fried 1999, pp. 22–3.

34 [Vassy] 1877, reprinted in Berson 1996, i, p. 145: 'Le principal personnage est le peintre lui-même, causant de près avec une très jolie femme, – encore un portrait, sans doute. Nos compliments, monsieur Caillebotte . . . Vous deviez avoir, ce jour-là, des *impressions* gaies.'

35 'Jacques' 12 April 1877, reprinted in Berson 1996, i, p. 156: '. . . un jeune oisif, précédant une élégante, exquise sous la transparence de son voile moucheté: petite comédie commune, que nous avons tous observée, avec un sourire discret et bienveillante'.

36 As assumed in Varnedoe 1987, p. 74.

37 As suggested by Julia Sagraves in Chicago 1995, p. 102; however, she also rightly acknowledges the ambiguity of the direction of the man's gaze (this discussion does not appear in full in Paris, Grand Palais, 1994–5, p. 140). The mythic image of the *passante* was established by Baudelaire's poem 'A une passante', first published in 1860.

38 Boime 1995, pp. 116–17; see Rivière 1921, pp. 136–7.

39 Boime 1995, pp. 114–17, emphasises both biographical and political dimensions of the image. For a detailed study of the picture in these contexts, see Collins 2001; we await John Collins's book about the picture.

40 See Gronberg 1984, Clayson 1991, pp. 133–53; Carel

1884 is the key nineteenth-century account of *femmes de brasserie*.

41 The picture's title *In the Conservatory* indicates that it should be viewed as a genre painting, and not in any sense as a portrait of the couple who acted as models for it, M. and Mme Jules Guillemet, or as a reflection of the state of their marriage.

42 As noted in Herbert 1988, p. 68.

43 Chevalier 1877, reprinted in Berson 1996, I, p. 139; on the picture and its titles, see Paris, Grand Palais, 1988–9, pp. 286–8.

44 For more detailed discussion of the problems of interpreting *Interior*, see House, 'Degas's "Tableaux de genre"' in Kendall and Pollock 1992; for a persuasive elaboration of a similar argument, see Sidlauskas 1993, and see also Armstrong 1991, pp. 93–100. For details of the picture's execution, see Paris, Grand Palais, 1988–9, pp. 143–6.

45 The picture was titled *Bouderie*, presumably by Degas himself, when he deposited it with Durand-Ruel in 1885; see Paris, Grand Palais, 1988–9, pp. 146–8.

46 As it is in Tucker 1982, pp. 138–9; for a thoughtful corrective, see Spate 1992, pp. 108–12.

47 This canvas is unsigned and perhaps not fully resolved in parts; it was in Monet's studio at his death. We do not know whether he kept it because he considered it in some sense unfinished or because it held special significance for him. For an interesting discussion of this picture, see Spate 1992, pp. 108–12.

48 Montifaud 1874, reprinted in Berson 1996, I, p. 29: 'Cette figure empruntée au monde élégant . . .'; de Gantès 1874 and Prouvaire 1874, reprinted in Berson 1996, I, pp. 23, 34. On Montifaud, see Dawkins 2002, pp. 134 ff.

49 The x-ray was first published and discussed in Wilson Bareau 1986, pp. 79–80; see also House, 'In Front of Manet's Bar', in Collins 1996, pp. 237–40.

50 Emile Bergerat, Le Senne and Charles Flor, all as quoted in Clark 1984/5, p. 242; see also House in Collins 1996, for a more extended discussion of the picture from these points of view. Collins 1996 offers twelve very different approaches to the form and imagery of the *Bar*.

51 See House in Collins 1996, p. 237.

52 On this aspect of the *Déjeuner*, see House, 'Manet and the De-moralised Viewer', in Tucker 1998; on *Olympia*, see especially Clark 1984/5 and Reff 1976.

53 On this, see Deborah Bershad, 'Looking, Power and Sexuality: Degas's *Woman with a Lorgnette*' and Griselda Pollock, 'The Gaze and the Look: Women with Binoculars – A Question of Difference', both in Kendall and Pollock 1992.

54 See also e.g. *View of Paris from the Trocadéro*, 1871–2, Santa Barbara Museum of Art, in which the figures turn their backs on the panorama of Paris, and *Reading*, 1873, Cleveland Museum of Art, in which the single female figure sits absorbed in her book and oblivious to the broad sweep of countryside seen beyond the garden fence. On these issues, see Pollock 1988.

55 Morisot's model was her sister Edma, recently married, and frustrated that her marriage necessitated abandoning her own practice as an artist (see Higonnet 1990,

especially pp. 47–54). However, the picture should not be seen as a portrait or analysed in biographical terms; its generic title, when it was shown at the Salon, demanded that it be viewed as a typical, not a specific figure.

56 For thoughtful discussions of these issues, see Higonnet 1992, especially pp. 70–72, 108–15, 149–50, and Lindsay 1988.

57 For further discussion of this issue in the context of portraiture, see House in Baltimore 1999–2000.

58 Duvergier de Hauranne 1874, p. 671: 'Est-ce un portrait à deux personnages ou un tableau de style que le Chemin de fer de M. Manet . . . ? Les informations nous manquent pour résoudre ce problème; nous hésitons d'autant plus qu'en ce qui concerne la jeune fille, ce serait au moins un portrait vu du dos.'

59 See especially Callen 1995, pp. 1–35.

60 Edmond de Goncourt, *Journal*, 13 February 1874, in Goncourt and Goncourt 1989, II, pp. 569–70: 'Il nous met sous les yeux, dans leurs poses et leurs raccourcis de grâce, des blanchisseuses, des blanchisseuses . . . parlant leur langue et nous expliquant techniquement le coup de fer *appuyé*, le coup de fer *circulaire*, etc.'

61 My argument here runs counter to Lipton 1986, pp. 110–13, who sees these compositions as undermining the authority of the ballet masters.

62 See Douglas W. Druick and Peter Zegers in Paris, Grand Palais, 1988–9, pp. 207–10; Callen 1995, pp. 26–8.

63 Moore 1890, p. 423, reprinted in Moore 1891, 1913 edition, p. 229.

64 See Armstrong 1991, pp. 83–7.

65 Stereotypes of Jewish identity were also part of Degas's repertoire of markers of difference; see Nochlin 1987.

66 Duranty 1867, p. 523: 'Mais le meilleur conseil à donner à ceux qui veulent reconnaître un homme ou les hommes, c'est d'avoir beaucoup d'esprit et de sagacité à démêler l'embrouillé, car la parole est menteuse, l'action est hypocrite et la physionomie est trompeuse!'

67 Speech of M. Waddington, Ministre de l'Instruction Publique et des Beaux-Arts, delivered 12 August 1876, published in Paris, Salon Catalogue, 1877, p. vii: '[The Chamber of Deputies] veut que l'art supérieur qui donne le branle à tous les autres, art momentanément délaissée par la faveur publique, et que l'Etat seul peut entretenir, puisse continuer et accentuer l'excellent mouvement d'une renaissance à laquelle nous assistons depuis deux ou trois Salons. Nous commençons à ressentir les effets de la salutaire émulation qu'ont su éveiller dans l'école française les commandes de peintures et de sculptures destinées à nos grands monuments.' On the cultural politics of the mid-1870s, see also Mainardi 1993.

68 See Barrows 1979, Barrows, 'Cafés', 1991, and Barrows, 'Parliaments', 1991.

69 See Nochlin 1983; Hutton 1987.

70 See Abbeel and Wilson-Bareau 1989; Hutton 1987 presents a valuable account of the specific political circumstances of this moment.

71 See Wilson Bareau 1986, pp. 65–76. Herbert 1988, p. 310 (note 62) associates the Impressionists' café subjects of the later 1870s with the 'euphoria' of 1878 (the Exposition Universelle and the prospect of a change of government);

my argument, by contrast, locates these canvases in the context of the repressions of the 'moral order' regime, and views them as more provocative and challenging than celebratory.

72 See note 40.

73 See Armstrong 1991, pp. 54–6; on *Women in Front of a Café*, see also Clayson 1991, pp. 103–11. Berson 1996, II, 72, questions the identification of the Corcoran picture with that shown as no. 38 in the 1877 show; however, the catalogue lists this as lent by M. H.H., and the Corcoran picture was owned at this date by the English collector Henry Hill.

74 Manet 1979, p. 150, Diary for 20 January 1898: 'Puis il dit qu'il remarquait justement autrefois lorsqu'il allait souvent au Moulin de la Galette où se réunissaient toutes les familles de Montmartre combien il y avait de sentiments délicats chez ces gens dont Zola parlait comme d'êtres atroces.'

75 See House 1985; House, 'Renoir: Between City and Country', in Brisbane 1994.

76 Rivière, 'Les Intransigeants', 1 November 1877, reprinted in Berson 1996, I, p. 186: 'Il faut remonter jusqu'à Watteau pour retrouver un charme analogue à celui dont *la Balançoire* est empreinte. On y reconnît quelque chose du *Voyage à Cythère* avec une note particulière du XIXe siècle.'

77 Boime 1995, pp. 11, 45.

78 *Le Retour de l'enterrement* was shown in 1876 (Private Collection; Offenstadt 1999, no. 326), *Le Dimanche, près de Saint-Philippe-du-Roule* in 1877 (pl. 134; Offenstadt 1999, no. 19).

79 *La Communion à l'église de la Trinité* (Musée des Beaux-Arts, Dijon; see Bordeaux 1992–3, pp. 28–9).

Chapter 5

1 See e.g. Ratcliffe 1961; Callen 1982; House, *Monet*, 1986; London, National Gallery, 1990–91; Callen 2000. I remain indebted to Robert Ratcliffe for his sustained insistence on the need of continual close scrutiny of original works of art.

2 An exception in the study of Impressionism is some of the more recent work of Anthea Callen (see Callen 1991 and Callen 1995), though this pursues different paths from the present chapter.

3 Chevalier 1877, in Berson 1996, I, p. 138: '...de jeunes peintres...se révèlent par une effervescence de couleur, une fantasmagorie d'effets, une bachanale de lignes, une furie de coups de brosse, une débauche d'empâtements, une explosion de lumière, des audaces de composition, des dissonances inouïes et des harmonies insolentes dont l'association forme la peinture la plus imprévue, la plus échevelée et la plus dithyrambique qui se puisse imaginer. Un art farouche, irrévérencieux, déréglé, hérétique.'

4 Blanc 1846: 'Les plus habiles de ce nouveau camp ne voient dans la peinture qu'un étincelant écrin; une mosaïque de tons éclatans est pour eux le dernier mot de l'art. Il est vrai qu'ils ont soin pour la plupart de glisser par dessous quelque poésie, et que tout en ayant l'air de

procéder uniquement [the text reads roniquement] par touches, j'allais dire par *taches*, ils ont mis dans leur intérêt tout ce qui a le privilège d'enchanter les hommes, le soleil, les fées et l'amour... que dis-je? Ils ont débauché toute la famille des chastes muses.'

5 Balze 1880, p. 10: 'Que signifie ce procédé d'exécution par la touche? où donc voyez-vous la touche dans la nature? C'est la qualité des faux talents pour montrer leur adresse de pinceaux. Si habile qu'elle soit, la touche ne doit pas être apparente, elle empêche l'illusion, immobilise tout[;] au lieu de l'objet, elle fait voir le procédé; au lieu de la pensée, elle dénonce la main.'

6 Delacroix 1980, p. 612, Journal entry for 13 January 1857: 'La touche est un moyen comme un autre de contribuer à rendre la pensée dans la peinture... Que dira-t-on des maîtres qui prononcent sèchement les contours tout en s'abstenant de la touche? Il n'y a pas plus de contours qu'il n'y a de touches dans la nature. Il faut toujours en revenir à des moyens convenus dans chaque art, qui sont le langage de cet art.'

7 Delacroix 1980, p. 612, Journal entry for 13 January 1857: 'La *touche* employée comme il convient sert à prononcer plus convenablement les différents plans des objets. Fortement accusée, elle les fait venir en avant: le contraire les recule.'

8 See e.g. Blanc 1867 (1886 edition, pp. 577–8).

9 Perrier 1855, p. 88, quoted in Weinberg 1937, p. 112: 'Mais... que votre casseur ne soit pas lui-même un objet aussi insignifiant que la pierre qu'il casse.'

10 Babou 1867, p. 289: '...cette manie de *voir par taches* conduit nécessairement à une sorte d'impression uniforme qui rapetisse, efface ou avilit la figure humaine.' For an early example of this sort of criticism of Manet, see e.g. Thoré 1870, I, pp. 424–5, reviewing Manet's Spanish costume pieces at the Salon des Refusés of 1863: '...sous ces brillants costumes, manque un peu la personne elle-même; les têtes devraient être peintes autrement que les draperies, avec plus d'accent et de profondeur'.

11 Thoré 1870, II, pp. 531–2; see above, pp. 24–5 and p. 218 note 40.

12 Lemonnier 1870, p. 209: 'Courbet est le plus voluptueux et le plus raffiné des peintres d'exécution. Couché dans un vaste panthéisme, il voit avec un égal amour resplendir l'étoile au firmament et luire le caillou dans les herbes. Son génie enfantin et corrompu joue indifféremment avec le grume écailleux d'une pierraille et le luisarnement d'une clairière au soleil. Il n'admet pas qu'il y ait des petites choses dans la nature et il traite tout avec une même grandeur.'

13 Blanc 1867 (1886 edition, pp. 21–2): 'Le dessin est le sexe masculin de l'art; la couleur en est le sexe féminin... En peinture... la couleur... est essentielle, bien qu'elle occupe le second rang. L'union du dessin et de la couleur est nécessaire pour engendrer la peinture, comme l'union de l'homme et de la femme pour engendrer l'humanité; mais il faut que le dessin conserve sa prépondérance sur la couleur. S'il en est autrement, la peinture court à sa ruine; elle sera perdue par la couleur comme l'humanité fut perdue par Eve.'

14 Clément 1878, p. 176: 'Cette satanée couleur va vous

tourner la tête.' Remarks such as this, together with the reminiscences of many of Gleyre's students, show that the methods he advocated were fundamentally academic; his reputation for liberalism seems to have been founded largely on his laissez-faire attitude to teaching, rather than on any active encouragement he gave his students; for a different view, see Boime 1971, pp. 58–65.

15 For a comparison of the 'realism' of Courbet and the Pre-Raphaelites, see Thoré 1870, I, pp. 277–9 (discussing the London International Exhibition of 1862).

16 Reminiscences of Francis Wey, published in Courthion 1950, II, pp. 190–91: '... il me désigna au loin un objet en disant; "Regardez donc là-bas, ce que je viens de faire? Je n'en sais rien de tout." C'était un certain bloc grisâtre, dont, à distance, je ne me rendis pas compte; mais jetant les yeux sur la toile, je vis que c'était un massif de fagots. "Je n'avais pas besoin de le savoir, dit-il, j'ai fait ce que j'ai vu sans m'en rendre compte" (puis, se reculant devant son tableau), il ajouta: "Tiens, c'est vrai, c'étaient des fagots."'

17 Henriet 1876, p. 149 (in 'Impressions et souvenirs', the section of the book that Henriet added in 1876): 'Fanatiques de la naïveté dans l'art, ils répètent ce paradox de Bonvin: "Tu veux peindre une main, n'est-ce pas? Eh bien, si tu sais que c'est une main t'es f..."'.

18 Perry 1927, p. 120.

19 Letter from Cézanne to Pissarro, 24 June 1874, in Cézanne 1978, p. 147: '... lorsque je lui disais ... que vous remplaciez par l'étude des tons le modèle, et que je tâchais de lui faire comprendre sur nature, il termait les yeux et tournait le dos'. (The published text reads 'modelé', not 'modèle'; however, this would make no sense in this context, and is presumably either an editorial error, or one made by Cézanne himself; John Rewald translated it as 'modeling' in Rewald 1973, p. 336.)

20 Letter from Cézanne to Pissarro, 2 July 1876, in Cézanne 1978, p. 152: 'C'est comme une carte à jouer. Des toits rouges sur la mer bleue ... Le soleil y est si effrayant qu'il me semble que les objets s'enlèvent en silhouette non pas seulement en blanc ou noir, mais en bleu, en rouge, en brun, en violet. Je puis me tromper, mais il me semble que c'est l'antipode du modèle.'

21 Riat 1906, pp. 218–19: 'Vous vous étonnez que ma toile soit noire. Cependant, la nature, sans le soleil, est noire et obscure; je fais comme la lumière; j'éclaire les points saillants, et le tableau est fait.'

22 Denis 1912 (1920 edition, p. 253): 'La nature, disait Cézanne, j'ai voulu la copier, je n'arrivai pas. Mais j'ai été content de moi lorsque j'ai découvert que le soleil ... ne se pouvait pas reproduire, mais qu'il fallait le représenter par autre chose ... par de la couleur.'

23 For detailed analysis of this development, focusing on the work of Monet, see House, Monet, 1986, pp. 114–33.

24 Cf. e.g. Zola 1866, reprinted in Zola 1970, p. 60; Vinet 1866, p. 433: 'What word do our art-critics use to indicate the special genius of the artist? A word from the language of M. Purgon, the word "tempérament." Even the language of the kitchen does not affright them; thus, when a painting is warmly executed and coloured, they say that it has "du ragoût".'

25 On this, see too Brettell 1990, pp. 49–50.

26 The form of the signature belongs to the early 1870s.

27 The original title of this picture is unknown; it corresponds in size to the canvas sold as Paysage d'été in the Impressionist auction sale of 1875 (see Bodelsen 1968, p. 336, lot no. 59), but this identification cannot be confidently made.

28 Rivière 1921, p. 190.

29 For instance, the ambiguous lighting and impossible reflections in Banks of the Seine at Argenteuil, 1874 (Private Collection, on extended loan to the Courtauld Institute Gallery, London).

30 Jeanniot 1907, p. 853: 'Manet ... ne copiait pas du tout la nature; je me rendis compte de ses magistrales simplifications ... Tout était abrégé ...'.

31 Herbert 1988, p. 235, comments on the similarity of these views, but without noting that Monet, as he is presented, cannot be painting this scene.

32 For a richly nuanced account of the handling of Before the Mirror, see Armstrong 1995. A comparably playful challenge to viewing habits, used in the opposite way, occurs in A Bar at the Folies-Bergère (pl. 126), in which the most summarily treated zone is the little bouquet, painted directly on the primed canvas, placed in the barmaid's cleavage – conventionally the focal point of images of barmaids (see House, 'In Front of Manet's Bar', in Collins 1996, p. 239).

33 C. D., in Berson 1996, I, p. 142: 'insectes nuisibles'.

34 On this, see House, Monet, 1986, pp. 67–8.

35 The status of The Sea at Fécamp is complicated by the existence of another version of the scene, very similar but slightly smaller (Wildenstein, I, 1974, no. 659); only a close examination of this canvas will clarify the relationship between the two versions.

36 In House, Monet, 1986, pp. 86–91, the contrast between the two versions of The Manneporte, Etretat of 1883 and 1886 in the Metropolitan Museum, New York, was attributed to Monet's wish to coordinate his treatment of the rock faces with the different states of the sea in each, stormy in the former, calm in the latter. Without discounting this, I would now place greater emphasis on the overall shift in Monet's work of the mid-1880s towards a softer, more harmonised type of mark-making. On the series, see also House, 'Time's Cycles', 1992.

37 See Ottawa 1997–8, pp. 142–4.

38 Wolff, in Berson 1996, I, p. 110: 'un amas de chairs en décomposition'; Emile Blémont wrote of it as 'bien posée et bien éclairée', while Armand Silvestre praised the colour of his flesh painting and described Etude as 'un morceau de coloriste' (Berson 1996, I, pp. 63, 110).

39 The First Step, dated '76', is wrongly dated to 1880 in Daulte 1971, no. 347, and its provenance incorrectly recorded there. Together with many other earlier Impressionist canvases, it was re-registered in Durand-Ruel's stock in 1891, with the title Le premier pas. Although it cannot be definitively identified in the firm's earlier stock books, it seems very likely to have been the canvas that was registered as Femme et enfant in a Durand-Ruel stock list of 1876, and then again as Femme tenant un enfant in 1881 (there is no consistency of titles between Durand-

Ruel stock lists in these years). In both of these lists, a canvas titled *Femme au piano* also appears, which, as Anne Distel has argued (London, Hayward Gallery, 1985–6, no. 35), is very probably the canvas now in Chicago (pl. 44). In the exhibition of 1876, this was listed as being loaned by M. Poupin, an associate of Durand-Ruel (see ibid., p. 27 note 22); Poupin was also listed as the owner of a canvas titled *Femme et enfant* in the same show. Although no reviews allow us to identify this definitively with *The First Step*, it seems very likely that this was the picture shown in 1876: no other painting of a similar subject from these years is a plausible candidate.

40 Although this canvas is traditionally dated to 1875, the fragmented technique is far closer to his handling of similar subjects in 1876; on the sale, see Bodelsen 1968, pp. 339–40; Sale catalogue, Christie's, London, 29 June 1999, lot 14.

41 Pissarro spent the late autumn of 1874 with Ludovic Piette at Montfoucault.

42 E.g. *L'Hiver*, Salon of 1873, Musée d'Orsay, Paris.

43 However, Brettell 1990, pp. 40–41, draws a persuasive comparison between Courbet and Pissarro's *The Little Bridge* of 1875.

44 For this central concern, see Courbet's open letter of 1861 to his pupils: '. . . la peinture est un art essentiellement *concret* et ne peut consister que dans la représentation des choses *réelles et existantes* . . . L'imagination dans l'art consiste à savoir trouver l'expression la plus complète d'une chose existante . . .' (Aux jeunes artistes de Paris, 25 December 1861, in Chu 1996, p. 184).

45 Four of Pissarro's palette-knife paintings are dated 1875, and it seems likely that a fifth, though often placed around 1874, was executed in the same year (see London, Hayward Gallery, 1980–81, nos. 39–42, pp. 104–7, and *The Little Bridge*, pl. 152). No palette-knife work has been identified in any of Pissarro's paintings dated 1874.

46 *House and Tree: Hermitage Quarter at Pontoise*, very extensively executed with the knife, is plausibly dated to 1874 in Rewald 1996, no. 222; seemingly an early spring subject, with leaf-less trees but a flowering fruit tree, it cannot be contemporary with Pissarro's view of the same subject dated 1874, since this shows fully foliated trees; although noting this difference, Barbara White proposes that the two paintings were executed side by side (White 1996, pp. 122–3). The often-reproduced pairing of the two artists' views of Les Mathurins and the Saint-Antoine road – both extensively executed with the knife – is, however, persuasive (see White 1996, pp. 126–7); Pissarro's canvas is dated 1875.

47 The subject of *The Little Bridge* was located by Leopold Reidemeister in the park of a château at Osny, on the outskirts of Pontoise (Reidemeister 1963, p. 74; see also Brettell 1990, pp. 40–41); although the Etang des soeurs at Osny has not been precisely located, it seems very likely that it was in the same park. This pairing is not mentioned in White 1996. Cézanne's *L'Etang des soeurs, Osny* has traditionally been dated to 1877, on the basis of the memories of Lucien Pissarro, but it is quite unlike any other work by Cézanne that can plausibly be attributed to that year.

48 Most obviously in *Le Jardin des Mathurins, Pontoise, 1876*, Nelson Gallery and Atkins Museum, Kansas City, which bears a close resemblance to Monet's recent Argenteuil garden pictures, such as *Gladioli*, 1876, Detroit Institute of Arts; see also Brettell 1990, pp. 174–6.

49 This autumnal effect is dated 1877, but the fact that it was included in the third group exhibition in spring 1877 shows that it was begun the previous autumn (the effect represented is clearly grounded in direct observation); it was presumably completed in the studio early in 1877.

50 As suggested by Richard Brettell in San Francisco 1986, p. 195.

51 See Reff 1962.

52 E.g. Harvey 1998, p. 314.

53 It is described in detail in Rivière's review of the show (Rivière 14 May 1877, reprinted in Berson 1996, I, p. 182) and is dated *circa* 1875 in Rewald 1996, no. 237. This is one of the strangest pictures of Cézanne's career, with its very diverse figures – fishermen, bourgeois women and children, and man in a black coat and hat – scattered across a riverside or seaside landscape. Rivière wrote of its 'astonishing grandeur and extraordinary calm', and described it as 'vast and sublime like a beautiful memory' ('C'est d'une grandeur étonnante et d'un calme inouï . . . C'est vaste et sublime comme un beau souvenir . . .'). Recent commentators have viewed it as marking Cézanne's abandonment of the 'nightmarish imaginings' and 'disturbing imagery' of his earlier work (Lewis 1989, p. 204), and have found 'a new serenity' in it (Rewald 1996, I, no. 237, p. 169). However, the conjunctions of figures are disconcerting: the two girls on the bank on the left, who seem to be falling or throwing themselves to the ground, rather than playing; the strange solemnity of the group of fishermen; and the dark silhouette of the wanderer figure at bottom left with his stick, described by Rivière as 'Asverhus' (Ahasuerus, the Wandering Jew, and presumably a surrogate for the artist; on the imagery of the Wandering Jew, though not in the context of Cézanne's picture, see Nochlin 1967; Brown 1985, especially pp. 36–7). Rivière's emphasis on the role of memory in the picture seems crucial; it cannot readily be viewed in the same terms as any of the 'modern life' paintings discussed above, in Chapter Four.

54 *View of the Surroundings of Auvers* has recently been proposed as one of the landscapes that Cézanne exhibited in spring 1877 (see Brettell in San Francisco 1986, p. 196). However, if it was exhibited, it must date from 1875 at the latest, since it is a summer subject and Cézanne was not at Auvers in summer 1876; its treatment is conspicuously unlike the other Auvers canvas, largely executed with the palette knife and very plausibly of 1875, that was probably exhibited in 1877 (Rewald 1996, no. 312, there dated c. 1877; reproduced in White 1996, p. 132). *View of the Surroundings of Auvers* belongs far more plausibly in 1877, the date of the very comparable canvas by Pissarro that appears to show the same subject (reproduced in White 1996, p. 135). Another Auvers landscape by Cézanne that seems to belong to the same summer is *Auvers-sur-Oise* (Ashmolean Museum, Oxford; Rewald 1996, no. 401, there dated 1879–80).

55 See London, Hayward Gallery, 1995–6, pp. 240–41; in Paris, Grand Palais, 1995–6, pp. 182–3, *Le Bassin du jas de Bouffan* (Rewald 1996, no. 350) is dated to 1878; however, the broad sweeps of paint in it, and especially the treatment of the foliage on the left, make it far more likely to belong to 1876, the same summer as *The Sea at L'Estaque* (pl. 45).

56 For their dating, see Rewald 1996, nos. 436, 437.

57 See Harvey 1998, p. 314.

58 This is dated *circa* 1875–7 in Paris, Grand Palais, 1995–6, pp. 156–8, and in Rewald 1996, no. 300; surprisingly, Harvey 1998 does not propose that it should be re-dated.

59 Letter from Cézanne to Joachim Gasquet, 26 September 1897, in Cézanne 1978, p. 262: 'une harmonie parallèle à la nature'.

60 Letter from Cézanne to his son, 8 September 1906, in Cézanne 1978, p. 324: '. . . je deviens, comme peintre, plus lucide devant la nature, mais . . . chez moi, la réalisation de mes sensations est toujours très pénible. Je ne puis arriver à l'intensité qui se développe à mes sens, je n'ai pas cette magnifique richesse de coloration qui anime la nature.'

61 Letter from Gauguin to Pissarro, around 10 July 1884, in Merlhès 1984, letter 49, p. 65: 'un art essentiellement pur', 'd'une exécution étonnante'. Georges Rivière may have been hinting at something of this quality in Cézanne's art in 1877 in describing him as 'in his work a Greek of the best period' ('dans ses oeuvres, un grec de la belle époque'; Rivière 14 May 1877, reprinted in Berson 1996, I, p. 182). A rather different notion of 'purity' in painting is explored in Pitman 1998.

62 For discussion of Monet's use of the studio, see House, *Monet*, 1986, pp. 147–56, 170–82.

63 For Monet's later lightly-worked canvases, see House, *Monet*, 1986, especially pp. 167–70. The same is not true of Pissarro. His canvases of the 1870s that were not fully realised show similar initial layers to Monet's – rapidly and broadly brushed in (e.g. *Piette's House at Montfoucault*, 1874, Fitzwilliam Museum, Cambridge, Pissarro and Venturi 1939, no. 285); however, some unfinished paintings of the mid-1880s show far more schematic and seemingly artificial initial layers, with broad, parallel hatching strokes more like Cézanne's 'constructive stroke' (e.g. *Landscape at Osny*, c. 1884, Columbus Museum of Art, Ohio, Pissarro and Venturi 1939, no. 629), perhaps a reflection of his increasing dissatisfaction with open-air sketching in these years.

64 Thus the recent exhibition *Impression: Painting Quickly in France 1860–1890* (see London, National Gallery, 2000–01) misrepresented their overall project by focusing on their more rapidly worked canvases alone; on this, see House 2001.

65 Letter from Pissarro to Esther Isaacson, 5 May 1890, in Bailly-Herzberg, II, 1986, letter 587, p. 349: 'J'ai commencé à *comprendre mes sensations*, à savoir ce que je voulais, vers les quarante ans, mais vaguement; à cinquante ans, c'est en 1880, je formule l'idée d'unité, sans pouvoir la rendre; à soixante ans, je commence à voir la possibilité de rendre.'

66 Duranty 1876, reprinted in Berson 1996, I, p. 76: 'D'intuition en intuition, ils en sont arrivés peu à peu à décomposer la lueur solaire en ses rayons, en ses éléments, et à recomposer son unité par l'harmonie générale des irisations qu'ils répandent sur leurs toiles. Au point de vue de la délicatesse de l'oeil, de la subtile pénétration du coloris, c'est un résultat tout à fait extraordinaire. Le plus savant physicien ne pourrait rien reprocher à leurs analyses de la lumière.'

67 See e.g. Schop 1876, Enault 1876, Olby 1876, reprinted in Berson 1996, I, pp. 107, 81, 100; these texts were published between 7 and 10 April 1876; Duranty's pamphlet was published around mid-April; the copy deposited with the authorities as *dépôt légal* is dated 12 April (see Crouzet 1964, p. 332 and note 82).

68 See e.g. Roque 1997, pp. 242–3.

69 This was first clarified in Webster 1944; around 1888 Pissarro recommended that his paintings should be viewed from a distance of three times the diagonal of the picture (Sheldon [1889?], p. 160), a distance greater than that demanded by post-Renaissance academic theory, but still close enough for the individual touches to remain visually distinct.

70 Mallarmé 1876, reprinted in Berson 1996, I, p. 97; for a persuasive insistence that this text is concerned with the painter's exploration of his experiences of the external world, rather than a proto-modernist plea for aesthetic autonomy, see Isaacson 1994, p. 431, and especially note 15 there.

71 Ephrussi 1880, reprinted in Berson 1996, I, p. 277: 'négliger à dessein les tons particuliers pour atteindre une unité lumineuse dont les éléments divers se fondent dans un ensemble indécomposable et arrivent par les dissonances mêmes à l'harmonie générale'.

72 Bourget 1881, reprinted in Riout 1989, pp. 317–18: 'Eux s'acharnent à rendre cet infiniment petit, et . . . à étudier le menu détail de leurs sensations . . . Nos indépendants . . . en arrivent à percevoir cet mobilité incessante de la lumière que la physique peut bien démontrer, mais non pas rendre réelle pour nos rétines encore frustes. Une sorte d'impalpable poussière d'atomes colorés flotte dans ce que nous prenons pour de l'ombre et teinte cet ombre. Eux s'efforcent à tremper leurs pinceaux dans cette poussière-là. C'est ainsi qu'ils obtiennent ces colorations singulières qui font hausser les épaules au visiteur inattentif . . . leur oeil, à eux, saisit des nuances que le nôtre ne saisit pas – pour l'instant du moins, car ils feront notre éducation, soyez-en sûr.' I am indebted to Juliet Simpson for drawing my attention to Bourget's text and helping me to realise its relevance to my argument; see Simpson 2001.

73 Laforgue 1883, reprinted in Riout 1989, pp. 335–7; translated in London, National Gallery, 2000–01: 'l'impressionniste . . . voit [la lumière] baignant tout non de morte blancheur, mais de mille combats vibrants, de riches décompositions prismatiques . . . il voit les réelles lignes vivants sans forme géométrique mais bâties de mille touches irrégulières qui, de loin, établissent la vie . . . il voit la perspective établie par les mille riens de tons et de touches, par les variétés d'états d'air suivant leur plan non immobile mais remuant'.

74 See especially Maupassant 1886 and Le Roux 1889 (both

describing him at Etretat in the mid-1880s), Geffroy 1897, p. 261 (describing his activities on Belle-Isle in 1886).

75   See e.g. Callen 2000, p. 204; Tamar Garb, 'Berthe Morisot and the Feminizing of Impressionism', in Edelstein 1990.

76   See Broude 1991, p. 151.

77   Letter from Pissarro to Lucien Pissarro, 4 May 1883, in Bailly-Herzberg, I, 1980, letter 144, p. 202: 'Je suis fort troublé de mon exécution rude et râpeuse, je voudrais bien avoir un faire plus aplani, réunissant cependant les mêmes qualités sauvages . . .'.

78   Letter from Pissarro to Lucien Pissarro, 20 November 1883, in Bailly-Herzberg, I, 1980, letter 190, p. 252: 'Rappelle-toi que je suis de tempérament rustique, mélancolique, d'aspect grossier et sauvage, ce n'est qu'à la longue que je puis plaire s'il y a dans celui qui me regarde un grain d'indulgence; mais pour le passant, le coup d'oeil est trop prompt, il ne perçoit que la surface . . .'.

Chapter 6

1   See especially Ann Arbor 1979–80.

2   Vollard 1938, p. 213: 'J'étais allé jusqu'au bout de l' "impressionnisme", et j'arrivais à cette constatation que je ne savais ni peindre, ni dessiner.'

3   Monet moved to Vétheuil, a village on a remote loop of the Seine over thirty miles north-west of Paris, in August 1878; after a brief spell at Poissy, on the Seine nearer to Paris, he settled definitively in 1883 at Giverny, a short distance further down the Seine valley from Vétheuil. Sisley moved to Moret-sur-Loing, on the south-eastern edge of the Forêt de Fontainebleau, in 1880, and remained based in this area until his death in 1899.

4   Pissarro remained in the Pontoise area, around twenty miles north-west of Paris, until 1884, when he moved definitively to the small village of Eragny, on the river Epte around forty miles north-west of Paris.

5   Salon attendances for 1875 (496,000) and 1876 (518,892) are given in Paris, Salon Catalogue, 1877, pp. v–vi; for the Impressionist exhibition of 1877, see San Francisco 1986, p. 192.

6   There was no consistent pattern of background or occupation among the Impressionists' first collectors: Victor Chocquet was an employee in the state Customs House, Ernest Hoschedé the spendthrift proprietor of a wholesale fabric firm, Eugène Murer a pastrycook, Théodore Duret a journalist and art critic, Jean-Baptiste Faure a celebrated operatic baritone, Georges de Bellio an expatriate Romanian homeopathic doctor, Georges Charpentier the leading publisher of 'naturalist' fiction. On these and other collectors, see Distel 1990.

7   See Ottawa 1997–8, pp. 161–7, 296–9.

8   On this, see Brisbane 1994, p. 78; Ottawa 1997–8, pp. 168–9, 300–01.

9   During his second visit to Algeria in spring 1882, Renoir told Durand-Ruel that he was hoping to bring back some figure paintings, 'which I was not able to do on my last trip' (letter from Renoir to Durand-Ruel, March 1882, in Venturi 1939, I, pp. 124). This makes it very possible that *Algerian Girl*, which is clearly dated '81', was painted

when Renoir was back in Paris, from a model wearing Algerian costume and seated on North African fabrics.

10   Letter from Monet to Georges de Bellio, 8 January 1880, in Wildenstein, I, 1974, letter 170, p. 438.

11   Letter from Monet to Duret, 8 March 1880, in Wildenstein, I, 1974, letter 173, p. 438: 'Je travaille à force à trois grandes toiles dont deux seulement pour le Salon, car l'une des trois est trop de mon goût à moi pour l'envoyer et elle serait refusée, et j'ai dû en place faire une chose plus sage, plus bourgeoise.'

12   Durand-Ruel resumed his purchases from Sisley in April 1880, from Pissarro in December 1880, from Renoir in January 1881, and from Monet in February 1881 (Wildenstein, I, 1974, p. 117, mistakenly states that his purchases from Monet resumed in October 1880, a mistake repeated in Wildenstein 1996; on this, see House 1978, p. 679).

13   For Durand-Ruel's advice to Pissarro in the years 1882–5, see Ward 1996, p. 277 (note 13).

14   Zola 1880, reprinted in Zola 1970, p. 332.

15   See Rewald 1973, pp. 309–16; Rewald links the realisation of their plans to Durand-Ruel's problems. It has recently been argued that the group shows should be viewed as an implementation of an idea proposed in December 1871 by Charles Blanc, then Director of Fine Arts, that exhibitions 'designed to attract buyers' should be the result of 'artists' private or collective initiative' (Jane Mayo Roos, 'Herbivores versus Herbiphobes', in London, Hayward Gallery, 1995–6, p. 49). However, Blanc's comparison was with the artist-controlled Royal Academy in London (Blanc 1871, in Paris, Salon Catalogue, 1872, p. cxix); what he had in mind seems to have been not a set of splinter groups but rather a single large artist-run exhibition (this is what came into being when the Salon was transferred to the control of the artists in 1880–81).

16   Mallarmé 1876, reprinted in Berson 1996, I, p. 97; on the explicitly political label 'intransigent', used frequently by critics in reviews of the group exhibitions of 1874 and 1876, see Stephen F. Eisenman, 'The Intransigent Artist or How the Impressionists Got Their Name', in San Francisco 1986.

17   Duranty 1876, reprinted in Berson 1996, I, p. 80: 'Ne voyez-vous pas dans ces tentatives le besoin nerveux et irrésistible d'échapper au convenu, au banal, au traditionnel, de se retrouver soi-même, de courir loin de cette bureaucratie de l'esprit, tout en règlements, qui pèse sur nous en ce pays?'

18   Duranty 1876, reprinted in Berson 1996, I, p. 79: 'Ce sont moins gens voulant tout nettement et fermement la même chose . . . que des tempéraments avant tout indépendants. Ils n'y viennent pas non plus chercher des dogmes, mais des exemples de liberté.'

19   Duranty 1876, reprinted in Berson 1996, I, p. 79: 'Le public . . . ne comprend que la correction, il veut le fini avant tout. L'artiste, charmé des délicatesses ou des éclats de la coloration, du caractère d'un geste, d'un groupement, s'inquiète beaucoup moins de ce fini, de cette correction, les seules qualités de ceux qui ne sont point artistes . . . D'ailleurs, il importe peu que le public ne comprenne pas; il importe davantage que les artistes comprennent . . .'.

20   See above, p. 40 and p. 222 note 110.

21 On the naming of the shows, see San Francisco 1986.

22 Letter from Diego Martelli to Francesco Gioli, March/April 1879, translated from the French translation in Martelli 1979, p. 39; see also Martelli's published review of the 1879 show, in which this initiative is not attributed to Degas (Berson 1996, I, p. 230).

23 Taboureux 1880: 'Je suis et je veux toujours être impressionniste . . . mais je ne vois plus que très rarement mes confrères . . . La petite église est devenue une école banale qui ouvre ses portes au premier barbouilleur venu . . .'.

24 Letter from Pissarro to Caillebotte, 27 January 1881, in Bailly-Herzberg, I, 1980, letter 86, p. 145: 'une individualité qu'ils appliquent à tous leurs jugements'.

25 Letter from Gauguin to Pissarro, January/February 1883, in Merlhès 1984, letter 32, pp. 39–40: 'Les impressionnistes . . . avaient une certaine clientèle s'intéressant à eux suivant leur progrès chaque année . . . lorsque vous êtes ensemble on voit la différence de chacun mais à part on croira que vous vous ressemblez tous . . . En outre du talent *particulier* que chacun peut montrer que devient dans tout celà le mouvement . . . maintenant . . . il n'y a que talent et pas de mouvement . . . Nous étions intéressants parce que avec du talent nous formions une phalange de peintres *convaincus d'un mouvement* et protestant contre la marchandise.'

26 On these shows, see Ward 1996, pp. 22–6.

27 See Jensen 1994, especially pp. 125–31; on the broader implications of marketing individuality, see Green, 'Dealing in Temperaments', 1987.

28 Letter from Caillebotte to Pissarro, 24 January 1881, in Berhaut 1994, pp. 275–6, translated in Rewald 1973, pp. 447–9.

29 Draft letter from Renoir to Durand-Ruel, 26 February 1882, in Venturi 1939, I, p. 122. On the show of 1882, see especially Joel Isaacson, 'The Painters Called Impressionists', in San Francisco 1986.

30 Letter from Gauguin to Pissarro, August/September 1881, Merlhès 1984, letter 17, p. 22: 'Il n'est pas possible de créer un mouvement en dehors de l'Ecole et du Salon sans une estime générale entre les exposants. Vous pouvez vous en expliquer avec Caillebotte lui qui veut une *exposition d'art*; que cet art s'il doit être différent de l'Académie ne doit pas figurer au Salon de l'Académie.' See also letter from Pissarro to Caillebotte, 27 January 1881, in Bailly-Herzberg, I, 1980, letter 86, p. 145.

31 Louis Leroy, *Le Charivari*, 17 March 1882, in Berson 1996, I, p. 402: 'Les frimousses des deux jeunes filles, leurs ajustements, la couleur de l'ensemble ont des qualités bourgeois que l'impressionnisme exècre.'

32 Leroy, ibid.: 'surface hachée, zébrée, tachée'.

33 Letter from Monet to Théodore Duret, 8 March 1880, in Wildenstein, I, 1974, letter 173, p. 438.

34 Letter from Monet to Durand-Ruel, 23 February 1882, in Wildenstein, II, 1979, letter 249, p. 216.

35 See above, p. 19 , and Le Men and Abélès 1993.

36 Letter from Samuel Avery to John Taylor Johnson, 31 July 1872, in Fidell-Beaufort and Welcher 1982, p. 54.

37 It was at this moment that Durand-Ruel initiated the ambitious project of publishing a sequence of etched reproductions of pictures in his gallery stock; the *Recueil d'estampes* was published in monthly instalments of ten prints each, over thirty months from January 1873 to June 1875. The vast majority of prints included were of 'Barbizon School' artists, with a small number of works by the Impressionists. His choice to publish reproductions in the 'fine art' medium of etching was a marker of his determination to differentiate his stock from Goupil's, which was disseminated in the mechanical reproductive media of photography and various forms of engraving (see *Etat des lieux*, 1, 1994, and 2, 2000).

38 See especially Crow 1983.

39 See Roos 1989; Mainardi 1993, Chapter 2.

40 Paris, Salon Catalogue, 1880, p. vii, reprinting Ferry's prize-giving speech of 1879: 'Nous avons toute une école nouvelle . . . toute une génération d'artistes, qui, non contente de rechercher la vérité comme on l'entendait autrefois, la vérité dans l'atelier, poursuit une vérité plus fugitive, mais aussi plus intime, plus difficile à saisir, mais par la même plus saisissante, ce qu'on appelle aujourd'hui la vérité du plein air.'

41 Jules Bastien-Lepage was made a Chevalier de la Légion d'Honneur in 1879; in 1880 Pascal Adolphe Jean Dagnan-Bouveret won a first-class medal and Albert Besnard a second-class medal. Alfred Roll's controversial *Miners' Strike* (Musée des Beaux-Arts, Valenciennes) was purchased by the State in 1880 (on critical responses to this, see Hérold 1924, pp. 41–4). Roll had been awarded a first-class medal in 1877 for his monumental scene of modern-life heroism *The Flood on the Outskirts of Toulouse in June 1875*, but its dramatised, theatrical treatment, reminiscent of Géricault's *Raft of the Medusa*, clearly made it acceptable to the authorities.

42 In 1879 Carolus-Duran won the Médaille d'Honneur and Ernest Duez a first-class medal; Manet won a second-class medal in 1881. Henri Gervex had won a second-class medal in 1876 for a contemporary subject, but this was an autopsy scene, an image of committed professional work, and thus acceptable to the 'moral order' regime.

43 For a valuable compendium of the 1882 reviews of *La Paye des moissonneurs*, see Le Pelley Fonteny 1991.

44 See Dunkerque 2001–2, especially pp. 95–113.

45 On the celebrations of 14 July, see Amalvi 1984.

46 The *gamin* is described in many texts of the mid-century, among others an essay by Jules Janin in *Les Français peints par eux-mêmes* of 1840–42; his most famous literary incarnation was Gavroche in Victor Hugo's *Les Misérables* of 1862.

47 The masculine pronouns are intended here; this notion of creative individuality paraded through the artist's technique was fundamentally masculine-gendered.

48 Mainardi 1989 and Mainardi 1993.

49 Paris, Salon Catalogue, 1884, pp. ix–xi, reprinting Ferry's speech of 1883.

50 Paris, Salon Catalogue, 1882, pp. vii–ix, reprinting Ferry's speech of 1881.

51 See e.g. Bernard 1881.

52 Paris, Galerie Georges Petit, 1883, p. 5: 'une caractère purement artistique'; on Petit's exhibitions, see Ward 1991, pp. 614–16; House, 'Renoir', 1992, pp. 578–9.

53 For a brief summary of evidence about the development

of Pissarro's political beliefs, see House, 'Pissarro', 1986, pp. 161–4; Clark 1999, pp. 95–109, is an important account of Pissarro's political beliefs and their contexts (Pissarro's 'pacifism' is questioned on p. 101).

54 For Monet at Etretat and his interest in Courbet there, see Herbert 1994, pp. 61 ff.

55 Letter from Monet to Alice Hoschedé, 1 February 1883, in Wildenstein, II, 1979, letter 312, p. 223: 'Je compte faire une grande toile de la falaise d'Etretat, bien que ce soit terriblement audacieux de ma part de faire cela après Courbet qui l'a faite admirablement, mais je tâcherai de la faire autrement . . .'.

56 These are listed at length in the Joanne guidebooks of the 1880s (see Joanne 1887, p. 151).

57 A distinctive feature of Etretat, they are described in Joanne 1887, p. 150.

58 On Renoir's Guernsey paintings, see House [1988].

59 Letter from Renoir to Durand-Ruel, 27 September 1883, in Venturi 1939, I, pp. 125–6: 'Ici l'on se baigne dans les rochers qui servent de cabine, puisqu'il n'y a rien autre chose; rien de joli comme ce mélange de femmes et d'hommes serrés sur les rochers. On se croirait beaucoup plus dans un paysage de Watteau que dans la réalité. . . . comme à Athènes les femmes ne craignent nullement le voisinage d'hommes sur les rochers voisins. Rien de plus amusant, en circulant dans ces rochers, que de surprendre des jeunes filles en train de s'apprêter pour le bain, et qui, quoique anglaises, ne s'effarouchent pas autrement.'

60 On these issues in the context of Renoir's *Bathers* of 1887 (Philadelphia Museum of Art), see House, 'Renoir', 1992.

61 On Pissarro's peasant paintings of this period, see especially Ward 1996, pp. 33–48; Clark 1999, Chapter 2 (focusing on *Two Young Peasant Women* of 1892, Metropolitan Museum of Art, New York); House, 'Pissarro', 1986.

62 Letter from Pissarro to Lucien Pissarro, 12 March 1882, in Bailly-Herzberg, I, 1980, letter 100, p. 157: 'C'est le type qui m'intéresse comme recherche, ce n'est pas gai par exemple, mais que voulez-vous, je suis la pente de mes sensations, je m'y laisse rouler.'

63 Sentimentality, see letter from Pissarro to Lucien Pissarro, 28 December 1883, in Bailly-Herzberg, I, 1980, letter 203, p. 266: 'Le sentiment, ou plutôt la sentimentalité ne peut sans danger être de mise dans une société pourrie et en voie de décomposition.' 'Romance', see letter from Pissarro to Octave Mirbeau, 22 November 1891, in Bailly-Herzberg, III, 1988, letter 713, p. 149: 'Je hais la romance! – comment ne pas tomber en ce crime?'

64 See above, p. 185 and p. 234 notes 77 and 78.

65 For a salutary discussion of the complexities of the category 'peasant', see Pollock 1984, pp. 361–3.

66 See above, p. 185 and p. 234 note 78.

Coda

1 John Rewald, 'Foreword', in London, Hayward Gallery, 1980–81, pp. 9–10, reprinted as 'Pissarro, Nietzsche and Kitsch', in Rewald 1985; this polemic was triggered in part by the *Post-Impressionism* exhibition at the Royal Academy of Arts, London, in 1979–80, of which I was co-director (London, Royal Academy, 1979–80), and by the revised version of the show presented at the National Gallery of Art, Washington, in 1980. Rewald's *The History of Impressionism*, first published by the Museum of Modern Art, New York, in 1946, is the seminal presentation of this view of Impressionism. On this, see House, 'Rewald Legacy', 1986.

2 See Fried 1996, e.g. pp. 6–9, and especially pp. 455–6 (note 18); quotation from p. 456.

3 See Pool 1967; Smith 1995; Rubin 1999; Thomson 2000.

4 Mark Steven Walker, 'Bouguereau au travail', in Paris, Petit Palais, 1984–5, p. 71: 'A ces marcheurs émerveillés s'ouvriront les portes des tabernacles. A eux sera dévoilée . . . toute la magie d'un monde mystérieux qui se nomme l'illusion. Aux jeunes d'esprit, aux idéalistes, à ceux qui refusent de cultiver le mépris pour masquer leur fatigue, sera donné le pouvoir de pénétrer dans l'univers de William Adolphe Bouguereau . . .'. This passage was not included in the English-language edition of the catalogue. This position has, through the 1990s, been developed in the *Classical Realism Journal*, published by the American Society of Classical Realism. On these issues, see House 1984, and McWilliam 1989.

5 See Rosenblum 1984; Minneapolis 1969.

6 London, Royal Academy, 2000

7 See especially Nochlin 1971; Clark 1973.

8 Shiff 1978; Shiff 1984; Shiff, 'The End of Impressionism', in San Francisco 1986.

9 See Herbert 1988; Tucker 1982; Brettell 1990.

10 London, Hayward Gallery, 1995–6; on the organisation of this show, with its two titles, see John House, 'Possibilities for a Revisionist Blockbuster: *Landscapes/Impressions of France*', in Haxthausen 2002.

11 See e.g. Clark 1984/5, pp. 70–72 (on this, see also Chapter Four above).

12 Clark 1984/5, pp. 111–31.

13 Eisenman 1994, p. 13.

14 See e.g. Clayson 1991; Higonnet 1992; Callen 1995.

15 See e.g. Pollock 1988; Adler 1989.

16 See e.g. Garb 1998, Chapter Five, on Renoir; Solomon-Godeau 1989, on Gauguin. For more nuanced, though still controversial, readings of Gauguin, see Brooks 1993; Eisenman 1997.

17 Green 1990.

18 Green, 'Dealing in Temperaments', 1987; Green, 'All the Flowers', 1987; Green 1989.

19 Vaisse 1995.

20 See e.g. Mainardi 1987; Mainardi 1993; Jensen 1994; Roos 1996.

21 See e.g. Garb 1994.

22 Louise d'Argencourt, 'Bouguereau et le marché de l'art en France', in Paris, Petit Palais, 1984–5, pp. 95–103.

23 Ward 1991.

24 Stephen F. Eisenman, 'The Instransigent Artist or How the Impressionists Got Their Name', in San Francisco 1986; Nord 2000.

25 See e.g. Bouillon 1989, Orwicz 1994.

26 Spate 1992, pp. 92–9; Clayson in San Francisco 1986.

27 Armstrong 1991.
28 Parsons and Ward 1986.
29 Riout 1989; Bouillon 1990.
30 Berson 1996.
31 See Callen 1982; House, *Monet*, 1986; London, National Gallery, 1990–91.
32 Callen 2000.
33 See e.g. Renoir in London, Paris and Boston (London, Hayward Gallery, 1985–6); Degas in Paris, Ottawa and New York (Paris, Grand Palais, 1988–9), and Caillebotte in Paris, Chicago and Los Angeles (Paris, Grand Palais, 1994–5); for an illuminating debate about recent Impressionist exhibitions, see Haxthausen 2002.
34 In San Francisco and Washington (San Francisco 1986).
35 See above, note 10.
36 In London, Amsterdam and Williamstown (London, National Gallery, 2000–01); for a detailed discussion of the problems raised by this show and its catalogue, see House 2001.
37 On the Musée d'Orsay, see House 1987 and Schneider 1998.

Chronology

1863
- March: Louis Martinet mounts exhibition of modern painting in Paris, including Corot, Courbet, Diaz de la Peña, Rousseau and fourteen works by Manet.
- May onwards: State-organised Salon des Refusés shows works excluded by jury from Salon, including Harpignies, Jongkind, Manet, Pissarro, Whistler and perhaps Cézanne.
- November–December: Publication of Baudelaire's 'Le Peintre de la vie moderne'.

1864

1865
- Manet's *Olympia* at the Salon; Monet exhibits two seascapes.

1866
- Monet shows *Camille* at the Salon; Manet rejected.

1867
- January: Zola publishes pamphlet on Manet.
- January: Plans for political liberalisation announced.
- February: French military withdrawal from Mexico.
- April–November: Exposition Universelle in Paris; eight Medals of Honour awarded, most to genre painters; Théodore Rousseau the only landscapist among recipients.
- April–May: First plan for group exhibition fails owing to lack of funds.
- May onwards: Courbet and Manet hold one-artist exhibitions.
- 19 June: Execution of Emperor Maximilian in Mexico.
- June: Studies by Théodore Rousseau exhibited at Cercle des Arts (the paintings owned by the dealers Durand-Ruel and Brame).

1868
- May–June: Zola's Salon reviews focus on young artists, including the future Impressionists.
- May–June: Some relaxation of laws on press and public meetings.

1869
- May: Duranty's Salon review describes young painters, including future Impressionists, as the 'école des Batignolles'.
- May: Opening of Folies-Bergère, the first music hall in Paris.
- Late summer: Monet and Renoir working at La Grenouillère.
- Construction of Bon Marché, the first purpose-built department store in Paris

1870
- January: 'Liberal Empire' created with Léon Ollivier as chief minister.
- January: Dismissal of Baron Haussmann as Prefect of Paris.
- 19 July: Outbreak of Franco-Prussian War.
- August: Fall of Ollivier.
- 30 August–2 September: French defeat at Sédan.
- September: Fall of Napoleon III; Third Republic proclaimed, with General Trochu as President.
- September–January 1871: Siege of Paris.
- Autumn: Daubigny, Monet and Pissarro take refuge from Franco-Prussian War in London.
- November: Bazille killed in action.
- November: Charles Blanc appointed Director of Fine Arts.
- December: Durand-Ruel opens London gallery, meets Monet and Pissarro.

1871
- 28 January: Armistice and capitulation of Paris.
- February: Elections; Adolphe Thiers becomes Prime Minister after fall of Trochu; seat of government moved to Versailles.
- March: Commune takes control of Paris, in opposition to national government at Versailles.
- April: Courbet assumes responsibility for fine arts under the Commune.
- 16 May: Destruction of Vendôme Column.
- 21–8 May: Versailles government overthrows Commune and massacres Communards in Bloody Week.
- August: Thiers becomes President.
- June: Courbet arrested.
- September: Courbet jailed.

1872

- Durand-Ruel buys extensively from Manet, Monet, Pissarro and Sisley.

1873

- January: Durand-Ruel begins to publish etchings of his stock; continues to buy from Monet, Pissarro and Sisley.
- January: *Loi Roussel* against public drunkenness.
- May: Marshal MacMahon replaces Thiers as President, institutes 'moral order' regime.
- May onwards: State-organised Salon des Refusés, including Renoir.
- May: Paul Alexis writes article supporting independently organised exhibitions; Monet replies describing plans to form exhibiting society.
- July: Courbet goes into exile in Switzerland.
- July: Law passed authorising the building of a basilica to the Sacred Heart (the Sacré Coeur) on hill of Montmartre to expiate for France's recent disasters.
- Repression of cafés and Republican press; commemoration of 14 July banned.
- Autumn: Failure of plan to reintroduce monarchy.
- December: Founding charter of Société anonyme des artistes peintres, sculpteurs, graveurs, etc.
- December: Marquis de Chennevières appointed Director of Fine Arts.

1874

- Early: Financial difficulties force Durand-Ruel to stop buying.
- April–May: First group exhibition of Sociéte anonyme, leads to group being named 'Impressionists'; exhibition includes Boudin, Cézanne, Degas, Monet, Morisot, Pissarro, Renoir and Sisley.

1875

- March: Monet, Morisot, Renoir and Sisley mount auction sale of their work.

1876

- January–March: Elections return right-wing majority in Senate, Republican majority in Chamber of Deputies.
- April: Second group exhibition includes Caillebotte, Degas, Monet, Morisot, Pissarro, Renoir and Sisley.
- Duranty publishes *La nouvelle peinture*.

1877

- April: Third group exhibition includes Caillebotte, Cézanne, Degas, Monet, Morisot, Pissarro, Renoir and Sisley.
- Spring: Georges Rivière edits short-lived periodical *L'Impressionniste*.
- May: Second auction sale of works by Caillebotte, Pissarro, Renoir and Sisley.

- May: MacMahon seeks to extend presidential authority and power of the right; nominates right-wing government under duc de Broglie.
- Further repression of cafés and other sites of potential political opposition.
- October: Elections: Republicans retain majority in Chamber of Deputies.
- December: Death of Courbet.

1878

- April–June: Durand-Ruel mounts exhibition of paintings and drawings by Daumier.
- Renoir returns to Salon.
- May onwards: Exposition Universelle in Paris; Medals of Honour mostly awarded to history painters; only one landscapist among fifteen recipients.
- 30 June: *Fête nationale*.
- Théodore Duret publishes *Les Peintres impressionnistes*.

1879

- January: Elections return firm Republican majority in Senate; MacMahon resigns as President, replaced by Jules Grévy.
- April–May: Fourth group exhibition includes Caillebotte, Degas, Gauguin, Monet and Pissarro.
- June: Parliament returns from Versailles to Paris.
- July: At Salon prize-giving, Jules Ferry announces major change in State art policy, in favour of open-air painting and modern life subjects.

1880

- April: Manet exhibits at offices of magazine *La Vie moderne*.
- April: Fifth group exhibition includes Caillebotte, Gauguin, Morisot and Pissarro.
- Monet submits again, for last time, to Salon.
- June: Monet exhibits at offices of *La Vie moderne*.
- July: Amnesty for former Communards and relaxation of laws controlling cafés.
- July: First revived celebration of 14 July.
- Durand-Ruel begins to buy again from Sisley and Pissarro.

1881

- Durand-Ruel begins to buy again from Monet and Renoir.
- January: Salon passes from State control to Société des artistes français.
- April: Sixth group exhibition includes Degas, Gauguin, Morisot and Pissarro.
- Sisley exhibits at offices of *La Vie moderne*.
- June: Free primary education instituted and public meetings legalised.
- July: Relaxation of press censorship.

- November: Léon Gambetta takes office as Prime Minister; Antonin Proust appointed Minister for the Arts.

1882
- January: Fall of Gambetta government; Antonin Proust leaves office.
- March: Seventh group exhibition, organised by Durand-Ruel, includes Caillebotte, Gauguin, Monet, Morisot, Pissarro, Renoir and Sisley.
- Spring: First Exposition Internationale organised by dealer Georges Petit.
- May: Courbet retrospective exhibition at Ecole des Beaux-Arts.

1883
- January–May: Series of one-artist shows, of Boudin, Renoir, Monet, Pissarro and Sisley, mounted by Durand-Ruel.
- April: Death of Manet.
- Publication of Huysmans's *L'Art moderne*.

1884
- January: Manet retrospective exhibition at Ecole des Beaux-Arts.

- May–July: Exhibition of jury-free Salon des Indépendants.
- December: First exhibition of jury-free Société des Indépendants (mounts annual exhibitions from 1886 onwards).

1885
- May–June: Monet included in Georges Petit's Exposition Internationale.
- Publication of Duret's *Critique d'avant-garde*.

1886
- May–June: Eighth and final group exhibition includes Degas, Gauguin, Morisot, Pissarro, Seurat and Signac.
- June–July: Monet and Renoir included in Georges Petit's Exposition Internationale.
- Durand-Ruel mounts Impressionist exhibition in New York.

Bibliography

Exhibition catalogues are listed under the exhibition's first, or primary, location.

Abbreviated references to exhibition catalogues in the notes cite only the first or primary location.

Capitalisation of English and French titles follows the standard form for each language.

Publishers are listed for books published since 1950.

References to the press criticism of the Impressionist group exhibitions are given here by their original sources only; all are reprinted in Berson 1996, to which reference is made in the relevant footnotes.

Abbeel, Paul van den, and Juliet Wilson-Bareau, 'Manet's "Au Café" in a Banned Brussels Paper', *Burlington Magazine*, April 1989, pp. 283–8

About, Edmond, 'Le Salon de 1868', *Revue des deux mondes*, 1 June 1868, pp. 714–45

——, 'Le Salon de 1869', *Revue des deux mondes*, 1 June 1869, pp. 725–58

Adler, Kathleen, 'The Suburban, the Modern and "une Dame de Passy"', *Oxford Art Journal*, vol. 12, no. 1, 1989, pp. 3–13

——, 'Stuttgart: Camille Pissarro', exhibition review, *Burlington Magazine*, April 2000, pp. 256–7

Aimé-Martin, L., *Education des mères de famille*, second edition, Paris, 1838

Amalvi, Christian, 'Le 14-Juillet: Du *Dies irae à Jour de fête*', in Pierre Nora (ed.), *Les Lieux de mémoire, I: La République*, Paris: Gallimard, 1984

Ann Arbor, University of Michigan Museum of Art, *The Crisis of Impressionism 1878–1882*, exhibition catalogue by Joel Isaacson and others, 1979–80

Anon., *Progrès de la France sous le gouvernement impérial d'après les documents officiels*, Paris, 1869

——, 'L'Eternel Jury', *Cahiers d'aujourd'hui*, January 1921

Armstrong, Carol, *Odd Man Out: Readings in the Work and Reputation of Edgar Degas*, Chicago: University of Chicago Press, 1991

——, 'Facturing Femininity: Manet's *Before the Mirror*', *October*, no. 74, Fall 1995, pp. 75–104

Astruc, Zacharie, 'Salon de 1868 aux Champs-Elysées: Le grand style – II', *L'Etendard*, 27 June 1868

——, 'Le Salon de 1870, I, IV, VI', *L'Echo des beaux-arts*, 1, 29 May, 12 June 1870

Audouard, Olympe, *Le Luxe des femmes: réponse d'une femme à Monsieur le Procureur Général Dupin*, Paris, 1865

Babou, Hippolyte, 'Les Dissidents de l'exposition', *Revue libérale*, vol. 2, 1867, pp. 284–9

Bailly-Herzberg, Janine (ed.), *Correspondance de Camille Pissarro*, I, Paris: Presses Universitaires de France, 1980; II–V, Paris: Editions du Valhermeil, 1986–91

Baltimore Museum of Art/Museum of Fine Arts, Houston/Cleveland Museum of Art, *Faces of Impressionism: Portraits from American Collections*, exhibition catalogue by Sona Johnston with essay 'Impressionism and the Modern Portrait' by John House, 1999–2000

Balze, R., *Ingres: son école, son enseignement du dessin*, Paris, 1880

Barron, Louis, *La Seine*, Paris, 1889

Barrows, Susanna, 'After the Commune: Alcoholism, Temperance, and Literature in the Early Third Republic', in John M. Merriman (ed.), *Consciousness and Class Experience in Nineteenth-Century Europe*, New York and London: Holmes and Meier, 1979

——, *Distorting Mirrors: Visions of the Crowd in Late Nineteenth-Century France*, New Haven and London: Yale University Press, 1981

——, 'Nineteenth-Century Cafés: Arenas of Everyday Life', in Boston, Museum of Fine Arts, *Pleasures of Paris: Daumier to Picasso*, exhibition catalogue, 1991

——, '"Parliaments of the People": The Political Culture of Cafés in the Early Third Republic', in Susanna Barrows and Robin Room (eds), *Drinking: Behavior and Belief in Modern History*, Berkeley: University of California Press, 1991

Baudelaire, Charles, 'Exposition Universelle 1855: Beaux-Arts, I: Méthode de critique. De l'idée moderne du progrès appliquée aux beaux-arts', *Le Pays*, 26 May 1855, reprinted in Baudelaire 1971, I

——, 'Le Peintre de la vie moderne', *Figaro*, 26, 28 November, 1 December 1863; reprinted in Baudelaire 1971, II

——, *Oeuvres complètes*, Paris: Gallimard, 1961

——, *Ecrits sur l'art*, 2 volumes, Paris: Le Livre de Poche, 1971

Bazille, Frédéric, *Correspondance*, ed. Didier Vatuone, Montpellier: Les Presses du Languedoc, 1992

Berhaut, Marie, 'Le legs Caillebotte, vérités et contre-vérités', *Bulletin de la Société de l'Histoire de l'Art français*, Année 1983, 1985, pp. 209–39

——, *Gustave Caillebotte: catalogue raisonné des peintures et pastels*, new edition, Paris: Wildenstein Institute, 1994

Bernard, Daniel, 'La Peinture de genre', in *L'Exposition des beaux-arts (Salon de 1881)*, Paris: Ludovic Baschet, 1881

Berson, Ruth (ed.), *The New Painting: Impressionism 1874–1886, Documentation*, 2 volumes, San Francisco and Seattle: Fine Arts Museums of San Francisco and Washington University Press, 1996

Bigot, Charles, 'Causerie artistique: L'Exposition des "impressionnistes"', *La Revue politique et littéraire*, 28 April 1877, pp. 1045–8

Blanc, Charles, 'Salon de 1846, IV', *La Réforme*, 19 April 1846

——, 'Salon de 1866 (2e article)', *Gazette des beaux-arts*, 1 July 1866, pp. 28–71

——, *Grammaire des arts du dessin*, Paris, 1867

——, *Rapport au Ministre de l'Instruction Publique, des Cultes et des Beaux-Arts, sur l'Exposition Nationale de 1872*, December 1871, reprinted in catalogue of the Salon of 1872

Blanche, Jacques-Emile, 'Renoir portraitiste', *L'Art vivant*, July 1933

Bodelsen, Merete, 'Early Impressionist Sales 1874–94 in the Light of Some Unpublished "Procès-verbaux"', *Burlington Magazine*, June 1968, pp. 331–48

Boime, Albert, *The Academy and French Painting in the Nineteenth Century*, London: Phaidon, 1971

——, *Art and the French Commune: Imagining Paris after War and Revolution*, Princeton: Princeton University Press, 1995

Bordeaux, Galerie des Beaux-Arts/Paris, Musée Carnavalet/Nice, Musée des Beaux-Arts, *Henri Gervex 1852–1929*, exhibition catalogue, 1992–3

Boston, Museum of Fine Arts, *Pleasures of Paris: Daumier to Picasso*, exhibition catalogue by Barbara Stern Shapiro, 1991

Bouillon, Jean-Paul (ed.), *La Critique d'art en France 1850–1900*, Saint-Etienne: CIEREC, 1989

——, Nicole Dubreuil-Blondin, Antoinette Ehrard and Constance Naubert-Riser (eds), *La Promenade du critique influent: anthologie de la critique d'art en France 1850–1900*, Paris: Hazan, 1990

Bourget, Paul, 'Paradoxe sur la couleur', *Le Parlement*, 14 April 1881; reprinted in Riout 1989

Brettell, Richard R., *Pissarro and Pontoise*, New Haven and London: Yale University Press, 1990

——, *Modern Art 1851–1929: Capitalism and Representation*, Oxford: Oxford University Press, 1999

Brisbane, Queensland Art Gallery, *Renoir: Master Impressionist*, exhibition catalogue by John House, with essays by Kathleen Adler and Anthea Callen, 1994

Brooks, Peter, 'Gauguin's Tahitian Body', in *Body Work: Objects of Desire in Modern Narrative*, Cambridge, MA: Harvard University Press, 1993

Broude, Norma, *Impressionism: A Feminist Reading*, New York: Rizzoli, 1991

Brown, Marilyn R., *Gypsies and Other Bohemians: The Myth of the Artist in Nineteenth-Century France*, Ann Arbor: UMI Research Press, 1985

Bürger, Peter, *Theory of the Avant-Garde*, Manchester: Manchester University Press, and Minneapolis: University of Minnesota Press, 1984

Burty, Philippe, 'L'Hôtel des ventes et le commerce de tableaux', in *Paris Guide*, 1867, II

——, 'Le Salon, I, III, V, IX', *Le Rappel*, 2, 11, 20 May, 12 June 1870

[——], 'Chronique du jour', *La République française*, 16 April 1874

[——], 'Exposition de la société anonyme des artistes', *La République française*, 25 April 1874

——, preface to sale catalogue, *Tableaux et aquarelles par Claude Monet, Berthe Morisot, A. Renoir, A. Sisley*, Hôtel Drouot, Paris, 24 March 1875, reprinted in Riout 1989

——, preface to sale catalogue, *Tableaux et dessins par M. Amand Gautier*, Hôtel Drouot, Paris, 1 April 1875

——, 'Les Paysages de M. Claude Monet', *La République française*, 27 March 1883

Calinescu, Matei, *Five Faces of Modernity*, Durham, NC: Duke University Press, 1987

Callen, Anthea, *Techniques of the Impressionists*, London: Orbis, 1982

——, 'Impressionist Techniques and the Politics of Spontaneity', *Art History*, December 1991, pp. 599–608

——, *The Spectacular Body: Science, Method and Meaning in the Work of Degas*, New Haven and London: Yale University Press, 1995

——, *The Art of Impressionism: Painting Technique and the Making of Modernity*, New Haven and London: Yale University Press, 2000

Carel, Alfred, *Les Brasseries à femmes de Paris*, Paris, 1884

Castagnary, Jules-Antoine, 'Exposition du boulevard des Capucines: les impressionnistes', *Le Siècle*, 29 April 1874

——, *Salons (1857–1879)*, Paris, 1892

Cézanne, Paul, *Correspondance*, ed. John Rewald, Paris: Grasset, 1978

Chambers, Ross, *Loiterature*, Lincoln and London: University of Nebraska Press, 1999

Champier, Victor, *L'Année artistique, 1879*, Paris, 1880

Chapus, Eugène, *De Paris au Havre*, Paris, 1855

Chaumelin, Marius, 'Salon de 1868, III', *La Presse*, 11 June 1868

——, 'Le Salon de 1869, V', *L'Indépendance belge*, 21 June 1869

——, 'Salon de 1870, VII', *La Presse*, 17 June 1870

Chennevières, Philippe de, *Souvenirs d'un Directeur des Beaux-Arts*, new edition with preface by Jacques Foucart and Louis-Antoine Prat, Paris: Arthena, 1979

Chesneau, Ernest, 'A côté du Salon, II', *Paris-Journal*, 7 May 1874

Chevalier, Frédéric, 'Les Impressionnistes', *L'Artiste*, 1 May 1877, pp. 329–33

Chicago, Art Institute of Chicago/Los Angeles County Museum of Art, *Gustave Caillebotte: Urban Impressionist*, exhibition catalogue, 1995

Chu, Petra ten-Doesschate (ed.), *Correspondance de Courbet*, Paris: Flammarion, 1996

Claretie, Jules, *L'Art et les artistes français contemporains*, Paris, 1876

Clark, T. J., *Image of the People: Gustave Courbet and the 1848 Revolution*, London: Thames and Hudson, 1973

——, *The Painting of Modern Life: Paris in the Art of Manet and his Contemporaries*, New York: Knopf, 1984; London: Thames and Hudson, 1985

——, *Farewell to an Idea: Episodes from a History of Modernism*, New Haven and London: Yale University Press, 1999

Clayson, Hollis, *Painted Love: Prostitution in French Art of the Impressionist Era*, New Haven and London: Yale University Press, 1991

Clemenceau, Georges, *Claude Monet: les nymphéas*, Paris, 1928

Clément, Charles, *Gleyre: étude biographique et critique*, Paris, 1878

Collins, Bradford R. (ed.), *12 Views of Manet's* Bar, Princeton: Princeton University Press, 1996

Collins, John B., *Seeking* l'esprit gaulois: *Renoir's* Bal du Moulin de la Galette *and Aspects of French Social History and Popular Culture*, unpublished PhD thesis, McGill University, Montreal, 2001

Comment, Bernard, *Le XIXe siècle des panoramas*, Paris: Adam Biro, 1993 (enlarged English edition published as *The Panorama*, London: Reaktion, 1999; as *The Painted Panorama*, New York: Abrams, 1999)

Cottington, David, *Cubism in the Shadow of War: The Avant-Garde and Politics in Paris 1905–1914*, New Haven and London: Yale University Press, 1998

Courthion, Pierre (ed.), *Courbet raconté par lui-même et par ses amis*, Geneva: Cailler, 1950

—— (ed.), *Manet raconté par lui-même et par ses amis*, Geneva: Cailler, 1953

Cousin, Victor, *Du vrai, du beau et du bien*, new edition, Paris, 1855

Couture, Thomas, *Couture, par lui-même et par son petit-fils*, Paris, 1933

Crouzet, Marcel, *Un Méconnu du Réalisme: Duranty*, Paris: Nizet, 1964

Crow, Thomas, 'Modernism and Mass Culture in the Visual Arts', in Benjamin H. D. Buchloh, Serge Guilbaut and David Solkin (eds), *Modernism and Modernity: The Vancouver Conference Papers*, Nova Scotia: The Nova Scotia College of Art and Design, 1983 (revised version in Thomas Crow, *Modern Art in the Common Culture*, New Haven and London: Yale University Press, 1996)

Daulte, François, *Auguste Renoir: Catalogue raisonné de l'oeuvre peint, I: Figures 1860–1890*, Lausanne: Durand-Ruel, 1971

Dawkins, Heather, *The Nude in French Art and Culture 1870–1910*, Cambridge and New York: Cambridge University Press, 2002

Delacroix, Eugène, *Journal 1822–1863*, ed. André Joubin, Paris: Plon, 1980

[Delord, Taxile, Arnould Frémy and Edmond Texier], *Paris-Bohème*, par les auteurs des Mémoires de Bilboquet, Paris, 1854

Denis, Maurice, *Théories, 1890–1910*, Paris, 1912

Diderot, Denis, *Salons, III: 1767*, ed. Jean Seznec, second edition, Oxford: Clarendon Press, 1983

Distel, Anne, *Impressionism: The First Collectors*, New York: Abrams, 1990

Dorra, Henri, and John Rewald, *Seurat*, Paris: Les Beaux-Arts, 1959

Dunkerque, Musée des Beaux-Arts, *Des plaines à l'usine: images du travail dans la peinture française de 1870 à 1914*, exhibition catalogue, 2001–2

Dupanloup, Mgr, *La Femme studieuse*, Paris, 1869

Du Pays, A. J., 'Salon de 1859 (neuvième article)', *L'Illustration*, 2 July 1859, pp. 19–22

Duranty, 'Sur le physionomie', *Revue libérale*, 10 July 1867

——, 'Le Salon de 1870, III, XII', *Paris-Journal*, 5, 19 May 1870

——, *La nouvelle peinture*, Paris, 1876; reprinted in San Francisco, *The New Painting*, 1986 and Berson 1996

Duret, Théodore, *Critique d'avant-garde*, Paris, 1885; reprinted with introduction by Denys Riout, Paris: Ecole nationale supérieure des Beaux-Arts, 1998

Duvergier de Hauranne, Ernest, 'Le Salon de 1874', *Revue des deux mondes*, 1 June 1874

Edelstein, T. J. (ed.), *Perspectives on Morisot*, New York: Hudson Hills Press, 1990

Eisenman, Stephen F., *Gauguin's Skirt*, London: Thames and Hudson, 1997

——, and others, *Nineteenth-Century Art: A Critical History*, London: Thames and Hudson, 1994

Elder, Marc, *A Giverny chez Claude Monet*, Paris, 1924

Enault, Louis, 'Mouvement artistique: L'Exposition des intransigeants', *Le Constitutionnel*, 10 April 1876

Ephrussi, Charles, 'Exposition des artistes indépendants', *Gazette des beaux-arts*, 1 May 1880, pp. 485–8

Etat des lieux, Bordeaux: Musée Goupil, I, 1994, and II, 2000

Fénéon, Félix, *Oeuvres plus que complètes*, 2 volumes, Geneva: Droz, 1970

Ferguson, Priscilla Parkhurst, *Paris as Revolution: Writing the Nineteenth-Century City*, Berkeley and Los Angeles: University of California Press, 1994

Feydeau, Ernest, *Du luxe, des femmes, des moeurs, de la littérature et de la vertu*, Paris, 1866

Fidell-Beaufort, Madeleine, and Jeanne K. Welcher, 'Some Views of Art Buying in New York in the 1870s and 1880s', *Oxford Art Journal*, vol. 5, no. 1, 1982, pp. 48–55

Fournel, Victor, *Ce qu'on voit dans les rues de Paris*, Paris, 1858

Fowle, Frances, and Richard Thomson (eds), *Soil and*

Stone: Impressionism, Urbanism, Environment, Aldershot: Ashgate, 2003

Frascina, Francis, and others, *Modernity and Modernism: French Painting in the Nineteenth Century,* New Haven and London: Yale University Press, 1993

Fried, Michael, 'Manet's Sources', *Artforum,* March 1969, pp. 1–82

——, *Absorption and Theatricality: Painting and Beholder in the Age of Diderot,* Berkeley and Los Angeles: University of California Press, 1980

——, *Manet's Modernism; or, The Face of Painting in the 1860s,* Chicago: University of Chicago Press, 1996

——, 'Caillebotte's Impressionism', *Representations,* Spring 1999, pp. 1–51

Fromentin, Eugène, *Les Maîtres d'autrefois,* Paris, 1876

Gantès, F. de, 'Courrier artistique: L'Exposition du boulevard', *La Semaine parisienne,* 23 April 1874

Garb, Tamar, *Sisters of the Brush: Women's Artistic Culture in Late Nineteenth-Century Paris,* New Haven and London: Yale University Press, 1994

——, *Bodies of Modernity: Figure and Flesh in Fin-de-siècle France,* London: Thames and Hudson, 1998

Gautier, Théophile, 'La Rue Laffitte', *L'Artiste,* 3 January 1858, pp. 10–13

——, *Abécédaire du Salon de 1861,* Paris, 1861

——, *Tableaux à la plume,* Paris, 1880

Gavarni and others, *Le Diable à Paris: Paris et les Parisiens à la plume et au crayon,* 2 volumes, Paris, 1845–6

Geffroy, Gustave, *La Vie artistique,* 1, Paris, 1892

——, *Pays d'ouest,* Paris, 1897

Goncourt, Edmond, and Jules de Goncourt, *Journal: mémoires de la vie littéraire,* ed. Robert Ricatte, 3 volumes, Paris: Robert Laffont, 1989

Goodman, Nelson, *Languages of Art,* 1968; second edition, Indianapolis: Hackett, 1976

Grate, Pontus, *Deux critiques d'art de l'époque romantique,* Stockholm: Almquist & Wiksell, 1959

Green, Nicholas, 'Dealing in Temperaments: Economic Transformation of the Artistic Field in France in the Second Half of the Nineteenth Century', *Art History,* March 1987, pp. 59–78

——, '"All the Flowers of the Field": The State, Liberalism and Art in France under the Early Third Republic', *Oxford Art Journal,* vol. 10, no. 1, 1987, pp. 71–84

——, 'Circuits of Production, Circuits of Consumption: The Case of Mid-Nineteenth-Century French Art Dealing', *Art Journal,* Spring 1989, pp. 29–34

——, *The Spectacle of Nature: Landscape and Bourgeois Culture in Nineteenth-Century France,* Manchester: Manchester University Press, 1990

Greenberg, Clement, *The Collected Essays and Criticism, I: Perceptions and Judgments 1939–1944,* ed. John O'Brian, Chicago and London: University of Chicago Press, 1986

Gronberg, Theresa Ann, 'Femmes de brasserie', *Art History,* September 1984, pp. 329–44

Guillemot, Maurice, 'Claude Monet', *Revue illustré,* 15 March 1898

Hadjinicolaou, Nicos, 'Sur l'idéologie de l'avant-gardisme', *Histoire et critique des arts,* no. 6, 1978 (2), pp. 49–76

Hanson, Anne Coffin, *Manet and the Modern Tradition,* New Haven and London: Yale University Press, 1977

Harvey, Benjamin, 'Cézanne and Zola: A Reassessment of "L'Eternel féminin"', *Burlington Magazine,* May 1998, pp. 312–22

Haxthausen, Charles W. (ed.), *The Two Art Histories,* Williamstown: Sterling and Francine Clark Art Institute, 2002

Hefting, Victorine, *Jongkind d'après sa correspondance,* Utrecht: Haentjens Dekker & Gumbert, 1968

Henriet, Frédéric, 'Le Musée des rues, I: Le Marchand de tableaux', *L'Artiste,* 15 November 1854, pp. 113–15, and 1 December 1854, pp. 133–5

——, *Le Paysagiste aux champs,* Paris, 1876

Herbert, Robert L., *Impressionism: Art, Leisure and Parisian Society,* New Haven and London: Yale University Press, 1988

——, *Monet on the Normandy Coast: Tourism and Painting 1867–1886,* New Haven and London: Yale University Press, 1994

Hérold, A.-Ferdinand, *Roll,* Paris, 1924

Higonnet, Anne, *Berthe Morisot: A Biography,* London: Collins, 1990

——, *Berthe Morisot's Images of Women,* Cambridge, MA: Harvard University Press, 1992

Hobbs, Richard (ed.), *Impressions of French Modernity: Art and Literature in France 1850–1900,* Manchester: Manchester University Press, 1998

House, John, 'The New Monet Catalogue', *Burlington Magazine,* October 1978, pp. 678–81

——, 'Pompier Politics: Bouguereau's Art', *Art in America,* October 1984, pp. 140–45

——, 'Renoir and the Earthly Paradise', *Oxford Art Journal,* vol. 8, no. 2, 1985, pp. 21–7

——, *Monet: Nature into Art,* New Haven and London: Yale University Press, 1986

——, 'Camille Pissarro's Seated Peasant Woman: The Rhetoric of Inexpressiveness', in John Wilmerding (ed.), *In Honor of Paul Mellon, Collector and Benefactor,* Washington: National Gallery of Art, 1986

——, 'Impressionism and History: The Rewald Legacy', *Art History,* September 1986, pp. 369–76

——, 'Orsay Observed', *Burlington Magazine,* February 1987, pp. 67–73

——, 'Renoir in Guernsey', in *Artists in Guernsey: Renoir 1841–1919,* Guernsey: Guernsey Museum and Art Gallery, [1988]

——, 'Courbet and Salon Politics', *Art in America,* May 1989, pp. 160–73, 215

——, 'Renoir's "Baigneuses" of 1887 and the Politics of Escapism', *Burlington Magazine,* September 1992, pp. 578–85

——, 'Time's Cycles: Monet and the Solo Show', *Art in America*, October 1992, pp. 126–35, 161

——, and others, *Impressionism for England: Samuel Courtauld as Patron and Collector*, New Haven and London: Yale University Press, 1994

——, *Pierre-Auguste Renoir: La Promenade*, Los Angeles: The J. Paul Getty Museum, 1997

——, 'Manet's *Maximilian*: Censorship and the Salon', in Elizabeth C. Childs (ed.), *Suspended Licence: Censorship and the Visual Arts*, Seattle: University of Washington Press, 1997

——, 'Claude Monet: Le Déjeuner', in *Impressionisten: 6 Französische Meisterwerke/Impressionnistes: 6 chefs d'oeuvre*, Frankfurt: Städel, 1999

——, 'Die französische Landschaft 1877: "Le Village de Lavardin (Loir-et-Cher)" von Charles Busson', in U. Fleckner, M. Schieder and M. F. Zimmermann (eds.), *Jenseits der Grenzen* (festschrift for Thomas W. Gaehtgens), Cologne: Dumont, 2000, II

——, 'The French Nineteenth-Century Landscape', in Kate Flint and Howard Morphy (eds), *Culture, Landscape and the Environment: The Linacre Lectures 1997*, Oxford: Oxford University Press, 2000

——, 'London, Amsterdam and Williamstown: Impression', review of *Impression: Painting Quickly in France*, *Burlington Magazine*, February 2001, pp. 103–7

Houssaye, Arsène, 'Les petites expositions de peinture', *Revue des deux mondes*, 1 March 1880, pp. 193–202

Hugo, Victor, *Les Misérables*, Paris, 1862

Hutton, John, 'The Clown at the Ball: Manet's Masked Ball at the Opera and the Collapse of Monarchism in the Early Third Republic', *Oxford Art Journal*, vol. 10, no. 2, 1987, pp. 76–94

——, *Neo-Impressionism and the Search for Solid Ground: Art, Science and Anarchism in Fin-de-Siècle France*, Baton Rouge and London: Louisiana State University Press, 1994

Huysmans, Joris-Karl, *L'Art moderne*, Paris, 1883

Isaacson, Joel, 'Constable, Duranty, Mallarmé, Impressionism, Plein Air, and Forgetting', *Art Bulletin*, September 1994, pp. 427–50

'Jacques', 'Menus propos: Salon impressionniste', *L'Homme libre*, 11 April 1877 and 12 April 1877

Jean-Aubry, G., *Eugène Boudin d'après des documents inédits*, Paris, 1922

Jeanniot, Georges, 'En souvenir de Manet', *La grande revue*, 10 August 1907

Jensen, Robert, *Marketing Modernism in Fin-de-Siècle Europe*, Princeton: Princeton University Press, 1994

Joanne, Adolphe, *Le Guide parisien*, Paris, 1863

——, *Les Environs de Paris illustrés*, Paris, 1881

Joanne, Paul, *Itinéraire général de la France: Normandie*, Paris, 1887

Jowell, Frances Suzman, *Thoré-Bürger and the Art of the Past*, New York and London: Garland Press, 1977

Kendall, Richard, and Griselda Pollock (eds), *Dealing with Degas: Representations of Women and the Politics of Vision*, London: Pandora, 1992

Kinney, Leila W., 'Genre: A Social Contract?', *Art Journal*, Winter 1987, pp. 267–77

Laforgue, Jules, 'L'Impressionnisme', 1883; first published in *Mélanges posthumes*, Paris, 1903, reprinted in Laforgue 1988 and Riout 1989; translated in London, National Gallery, 2000–01

——, *Textes de critique d'art*, ed. Mireille Dottin, Lille: Presses Universitaires de Lille, 1988

Lagrange, Léon, 'Le Salon de 1865', *Le Correspondant*, May 1865

Larousse, Pierre, *Grand dictionnaire universel du XIXe siècle*, 15 volumes, Paris, 1866–76

Le Men, Ségolène, and Luce Abélès, *Les Français peints par eux-mêmes*, Paris: Réunion des musées nationaux (Musée d'Orsay), 1993

Lemonnier, Camille, *Salon de Paris 1870*, Paris, 1870

Lenoir, Paul, *Le Fayoum, Le Sinaï et Pétra*, Paris, 1872

Le Pelley Fonteny, Monique, *Léon Lhermittte et La Paye des moissonneurs*, Paris: Réunion des musées nationaux (Musée d'Orsay), 1991

Lépinois, E. de, 'L'Art dans la rue', *L'Artiste*, 1 February 1860, pp. 37–40

Le Play, Frédéric, *Les Ouvriers européens: études sur les travaux, la vie domestique et la condition morale des populations ouvrières de l'Europe*, Paris, 1855

Le Roux, Hugues, 'Silhouettes parisiennes: l'exposition Claude Monet', *Gil Blas*, 3 March 1889

Leroy, Louis, 'L'Exposition des impressionnistes', *Le Charivari*, 25 April 1874, pp. 79–80

Lewis, Mary Tompkins, *Cézanne's Early Imagery*, Berkeley: University of California Press, 1989

Lindsay, Suzanne G., 'Berthe Morisot and the Poets: The Visual Language of Woman', *Helicon Nine: The Journal of Women's Arts and Letters*, no. 19, 1988, pp. 8–17

Lipton, Eunice, *Looking into Degas: Uneasy Images of Modern Life*, Berkeley: University of California Press, 1986

London, Hayward Gallery/Grand Palais, Paris/Museum of Fine Arts, Boston, *Pissarro*, exhibition catalogue, 1980–81

London, Hayward Gallery/Grand Palais, Paris/Museum of Fine Arts, Boston, *Renoir*, exhibition catalogue by Anne Distel and John House, 1985–6

London, Hayward Gallery (South Bank Centre)/Museum of Fine Arts, Boston, *Landscapes of France: Impressionism and its Rivals/Impressions of France: Monet, Renoir, Pissarro and their Rivals*, exhibition catalogue by John House, with essays by Ann Dumas, Jane Mayo Roos and James F. McMillan, 1995–6

London, National Gallery, *Art in the Making: Impressionism*, exhibition catalogue, 1990–91

London, National Gallery, *Manet: The Execution of Maximilian: Painting, Politics and Censorship*, exhibition catalogue by Juliet Wilson-Bareau, with essays by John House and Douglas Johnson, 1992

London, National Gallery/Van Gogh Museum, Amsterdam/Sterling and Francine Clark Art Institute, Williamstown, *Impression: Painting Quickly in France 1860–1890*, exhibition catalogue by Richard R. Brettell, 2000–01

London, Royal Academy of Arts, *Post-Impressionism: Cross-Currents in European Painting*, exhibition catalogue, 1979–80

London, Royal Academy of Arts/Musée d'Orsay, Paris/National Gallery of Art, Washington, *Cézanne: The Early Years 1859–1872*, exhibition catalogue by Lawrence Gowing, 1988–9

London, Royal Academy of Arts/Guggenheim Museum, New York, *1900: Art at the Crossroads*, exhibition catalogue, 2000

Los Angeles County Museum of Art/Art Institute of Chicago/Grand Palais, Paris, *A Day in the Country: Impressionism and the French Landscape/L'Impressionnisme et le paysage français*, exhibition catalogue by Richard R. Brettell, Scott Schaefer and others, 1984–5

McMillan, James F., *Napoleon III*, London: Longman, 1991

McWilliam, Neil, 'Limited Revisions: Academic Art History Confronts Academic Art', *Oxford Art Journal*, vol. 12, no. 2, 1989, pp. 71–86

Mainardi, Patricia, *Art and Politics of the Second Empire: The Universal Exhibitions of 1855 and 1867*, New Haven and London: Yale University Press, 1987

——, 'The Double Exhibition in Nineteenth-Century France', *Art Journal*, Spring 1989, pp. 23–8

——, *The End of the Salon: Art and the State in the Early Third Republic*, Cambridge and New York: Cambridge University Press, 1993

Mallarmé, Stéphane, 'The Impressionists and Edouard Manet', *Art Monthly Review*, September 1876; reprinted in San Francisco, *The New Painting*, 1986 and Berson 1996

Manet, Julie, *Journal (1893–1899)*, Paris: Klincksieck, 1979

Mantz, Paul, 'Salon de 1868, v, *L'Illustration*, 6 June 1868

——, 'Salon de 1869, II', *Gazette des Beaux-Arts*, July 1869, pp. 5–23

Marcus, Sharon, *Apartment Stories: City and Home in Nineteenth-Century Paris and London*, Berkeley and Los Angeles: University of California Press, 1999

Martelli, Diego, *Les Impressionnistes et l'Art Moderne*, ed. Francesca Errico, Paris: Vilo, 1979

Massarani, Tullo, *L'Art à Paris*, 2 volumes, Paris, 1880

Mauner, George, *Manet Peintre-Philosophe: A Study of the Painter's Themes*, University Park: Pennsylvania University Press, 1975

Maupassant, Guy de, 'La Vie d'un paysagiste', *Gil Blas*, 28 September 1886; reprinted in Riout 1989

Mayeur, Jean-Marie, and Madeleine Rebérioux, *The Third Republic from its Origins to the Great War 1871–1914*, Cambridge: Cambridge University Press, 1984

Mayne, Jonathan, 'Degas's Ballet Scene from "Robert le Diable"', *Victoria and Albert Museum Bulletin*, October 1966, pp. 148–56

Merlhès, Victor, *Correspondance de Paul Gauguin*, I, Paris: Fondation Singer-Polignac, 1984

Minneapolis, Minneapolis Institute of Arts, *The Past Rediscovered: French Painting 1800–1900*, exhibition catalogue by Robert Rosenblum, 1969

Montifaud, Marc de, 'Exposition du boulevard des Capucines', *L'Artiste*, 1 May 1874, pp. 307–13

Moore, George, 'Degas: The Painter of Modern Life', *Magazine of Art*, September 1890, pp. 416–25

——, *Impressions and Opinions*, London, 1891

Moreau-Nélaton, Etienne, *Bonvin raconté par lui-même*, Paris, 1927

Nead, Lynda, *Victorian Babylon: People, Streets and Images in Nineteenth-Century London*, New Haven and London: Yale University Press, 2000

Nochlin, Linda, 'Gustave Courbet's Meeting: A Portrait of the Artist as a Wandering Jew', *Art Bulletin*, September 1967, pp. 209–22

——, *Realism*, Harmondsworth: Penguin Books, 1971

——, 'A Thoroughly Modern Masked Ball', *Art in America*, November 1983, pp. 188–201; reprinted in Nochlin 1989/91

——, 'Degas and the Dreyfus Affair: Portrait of the Artist as an Anti-Semite', in *The Dreyfus Affair, Art, Truth and Justice*, exhibition catalogue, ed. Norman L. Kleebatt, Jewish Museum, New York, 1987; reprinted in Nochlin 1989/91

——, *Women, Art, and Power and Other Essays*, New York: Harper & Row, 1988; London: Thames and Hudson, 1989

——, *The Politics of Vision: Essays on Nineteenth-Century Art and Society*, New York: Harper & Row, 1989; London: Thames and Hudson, 1991

Nord, Deborah Epstein, *Walking the Victorian Streets: Women, Representation and the City*, Ithaca: Cornell University Press, 1995

Nord, Philip, *Impressionists and Politics: Art and Democracy in the Nineteenth Century*, London: Routledge, 2000

Offenstadt, Patrick, *Jean Béraud 1849–1935: la belle époque, une époque rêvée*, Cologne: Taschen, and Paris: Wildenstein Institute, 1999

Olby, G. d', 'Salon de 1876: avant l'ouverture – exposition des intransigeants', *Le Pays*, 10 April 1876

Orwicz, Michael R. (ed.), *Art Criticism and its Institutions in Nineteenth-Century France*, Manchester: Manchester University Press, 1994

Ottawa, National Gallery of Canada/Art Institute of Chicago/Kimbell Art Museum, Fort Worth, *Renoir's Portraits: Impressions of an Age*, exhibition catalogue by Colin B. Bailey, 1997–8

Paris, Galerie Georges Petit, *Exposition internationale de peinture, deuxième année*, exhibition catalogue, 1883

Paris, Grand Palais, *Le Musée du Luxembourg en 1874*, exhibition catalogue by Geneviève Lacambre, 1974

Paris, Grand Palais, *Hommage à Claude Monet*, exhibition catalogue, 1980

Paris, Grand Palais/National Gallery of Canada, Ottawa/California Palace of the Legion of Honor, San Francisco, *Fantin-Latour*, exhibition catalogue, 1982–3

Paris, Grand Palais/Metropolitan Museum of Art, New York, *Manet*, exhibition catalogue, 1983

Paris, Grand Palais/National Gallery of Canada, Ottawa/New York, Metropolitan Museum of Art, *Degas*, exhibition catalogue, 1988–9

Paris, Grand Palais/Metropolitan Museum of Art, New York, *Impressionnisme: les origines 1859–1869/Origins of Impressionism*, exhibition catalogue by Gary Tinterow and Henri Loyrette, 1994–5

Paris, Grand Palais, *Gustave Caillebotte*, exhibition catalogue, 1994–5

Paris, Grand Palais/Tate Gallery, London/Philadelphia Museum of Art, *Cézanne*, exhibition catalogue by Françoise Cachin and Joseph J. Rishel, 1995–6

Paris Guide, par les principaux écrivains et artistes de la France, Paris, 1867

Paris, Musée d'Orsay/National Gallery of Art, Washington, *Manet, Monet, La Gare Saint-Lazare/Manet, Monet, and the Gare Saint-Lazare*, exhibition catalogue by Juliet Wilson-Bareau, 1998 (English edition published New Haven and London: Yale University Press)

Paris, Musée d'Orsay, *Manet: les natures mortes*, exhibition catalogue, 2000

Paris, Petit Palais/Musée des Beaux-Arts, Montréal/Wadsworth Atheneum, Hartford, *Bouguereau*, exhibition catalogue, 1984–5

Paris, Salons de 1872, 1877, 1880, 1882, 1884, catalogues

Parsons, Christopher, and Martha Ward, *A Bibliography of Salon Criticism in Second Empire Paris*, Cambridge: Cambridge University Press, 1986

Pellerin, Denis, *La Photographie stéréoscopique sous le Second Empire*, Paris: Bibliothèque Nationale de France, 1995

Perrier, Charles, 'Du réalisme', *L'Artiste*, 14 October 1855, pp. 85–90

Perry, Lilla Cabot, 'Reminiscences of Claude Monet from 1889 to 1909', *American Magazine of Art*, March 1927, pp. 119–25

Pissarro, Ludovic-Rodo, and Lionello Venturi, *Camille Pissarro, son art, son oeuvre*, Paris, 1939

Pitman, Dianne W., *Bazille: Purity, Pose and Painting in the 1860s*, University Park: Pennsylvania State University Press, 1998

Planche, Gustave, *Etudes sur l'école française (1831–52)*, Paris, 1855

Poggioli, Renato, *The Theory of the Avant-Garde*, Cambridge: Harvard University Press, 1968

Pollock, Griselda, 'Revising or Reviving Realism?', *Art History*, September 1984, pp. 359–68

——, 'Modernity and the Spaces of Femininity', in *Vision and Difference: Femininity, Feminism and the Histories of Art*, London: Routledge, 1988

——, *Avant-Garde Gambits 1888–1893: Gender and the Colour of Art History*, London: Thames and Hudson, 1992

Pool, Phoebe, *Impressionism*, London: Thames and Hudson, 1967

Prendergast, Christopher, *Paris and the Nineteenth Century*, Oxford: Blackwell, 1992

Privat, Gonzague, *Place aux jeunes! causeries critiques sur le Salon de 1865*, Paris, 1865

Proudhon, Pierre-Joseph, *Du principe de l'art et de sa destination sociale*, Paris, 1865

Proust, Antonin, 'Edouard Manet (Souvenirs)', *Revue blanche*, February–May 1897; reprinted as *Edouard Manet: souvenirs*, Caen: L'Echoppe, 1988

Prouvaire, Jean, 'L'Exposition du boulevard des Capucines', *Le Rappel*, 20 April 1874

Randall, Lilian M. C., *The Diary of George A. Lucas: An American Art Agent in Paris, 1857–1909*, Princeton: Princeton University Press, 1979

Ratcliffe, Robert W., *Cézanne's Working Methods and their Theoretical Background*, unpublished PhD thesis, University of London, 1961

Reclus, Elisée, 'Du sentiment de la nature dans les sociétés modernes', *Revue des deux mondes*, 15 May 1866, pp. 352–81

Reff, Theodore, 'Cézanne's Constructive Stroke', *Art Quarterly*, Autumn 1962, pp. 214–27

——, 'Manet's Sources: A Critical Evaluation', *Artforum*, September 1969, pp. 40–48

——, 'Manet and Blanc's "Histoire des peintres"', *Burlington Magazine*, July 1970, pp. 456–8

——, 'Manet's Portrait of Zola', *Burlington Magazine*, January 1975, pp. 35–44

——, *Manet: Olympia*, London: Penguin, 1976

Reidemeister, Leopold, *Auf den Spuren der Maler der Ile de France*, Berlin: Propyläen, 1963

Renoir, Edmond, 'Cinquième exposition de la Vie moderne', *La Vie moderne*, 19 June 1879, pp. 174–5

Rewald, John, *The History of Impressionism*, fourth edition, New York: Museum of Modern Art, and London: Secker & Warburg, 1973 (first published New York: Museum of Modern Art, 1946)

——, *Paul Cézanne: The Watercolors: A Catalogue Raisonné*, London: Thames and Hudson, 1983

——, *Studies in Impressionism*, London: Thames and Hudson, 1985

——, with Walter Feilchenfeldt and Jayne Warman, *The Paintings of Paul Cézanne: A Catalogue Raisonné*, London: Thames and Hudson, 1996

Riat, Georges, *Gustave Courbet, peintre*, Paris, 1906

Riout, Denys (ed.), *Les Ecrivains devant l'impressionnisme*, Paris: Macula, 1989

Rivière, Georges, 'L'Exposition des impressionnistes', *L'Impressionniste*, 6 May 1877, pp. 2–6, and 14 May 1877, pp. 1–4, 6

——, 'Les Intransigeants et les impressionnistes: souvenirs

du Salon libre de 1877', *L'Artiste*, 1 November 1877, pp. 298–302

——, *Renoir et ses amis*, Paris, 1921

Robinson, Theodore, 'Diary', MS in Frick Art Reference Library, New York

Romieu, Madame (Marie Sincère), *La Femme au XIXe siècle*, Paris, 1858

Roos, Jane Mayo, 'Within the "Zone of Silence": Monet and Manet in 1878', *Art History*, September 1988, pp. 372–407

——, 'Aristocracy and the Arts: Philippe de Chennevières and the Salons of the mid-1870s', *Art Journal*, Spring 1989, pp. 53–62

——, *Early Impressionism and the French State (1866–1874)*, Cambridge and New York: Cambridge University Press, 1996

Roque, Georges, *Art et science de la couleur: Chevreul et les peintres de Delacroix à l'abstraction*, Nîmes: Jacqueline Chambon, 1997

Rosenblum, Robert, *Nineteenth-Century Art*, London: Thames and Hudson, 1984

Rosenfeld, Daniel (ed.), *European Painting and Sculpture ca. 1770–1937 in the Museum of Art, Rhode Island School of Design*, Providence: Rhode Island School of Design, 1991

Roskill, Mark, 'Early Impressionism and the Fashion Print', *Burlington Magazine*, June 1970, pp. 391–5

Rouart, Denis (ed.), *Correspondance de Berthe Morisot avec sa famille et ses amis*, Paris, 1950

Rubin, James H., *Impressionism*, London: Phaidon, 1999

San Francisco, Fine Arts Museums/National Gallery of Art, Washington, *The New Painting: Impressionism 1874–1886*, exhibition catalogue, 1986

Sardou, Victorien, 'Louveciennes, Marly', in *Paris Guide* 1867, II

Scharf, Aaron, *Art and Photography*, London: Allen Lane, The Penguin Press, 1968

Schneider, Andrea Kupfer, *Creating the Musée d'Orsay: The Politics of Culture in France*, University Park: Pennsylvania State University Press, 1998

Schop, Baron, 'La Semaine parisienne: L'Exposition des intransigeants – L'Ecole des Batignolles – Impressionnistes et plein air', *Le National*, 7 April 1876

Ségalen, Martine, *Love and Power in the Peasant Family*, Oxford: Basil Blackwell, and Chicago: University of Chicago Press, 1983 (first published as *Mari et femme dans la société paysanne*, Paris: Flammarion, 1980)

Seigel, Jerrold, *Bohemian Paris: Culture, Politics and the Boundaries of Bourgeois Life, 1830–1930*, New York: Viking, 1986

Sennett, Richard, *The Fall of Public Man*, New York: Knopf, 1977

Sensier, Alfred, *Souvenirs sur Théodore Rousseau*, Paris, 1872

Sheldon, George W., *Recent Ideals in American Art*, New York [1889?]

Shiff, Richard, 'The End of Impressionism', *Art Quarterly*, Autumn 1978, pp. 338–78

——, *Cézanne and the End of Impressionism*, Chicago: University of Chicago Press, 1984

Shikes, Ralph E., and Paula Harper, *Pissarro: His Life and Work*, London: Quartet Books, 1980

Sidlauskas, Susan, 'Resisting Narrative: The Problem of Edgar Degas's *Interior*', *Art Bulletin*, December 1993, pp. 671–96

Siebecker, Edouard, *Cocottes et petits crevés*, Paris, 1867 (in series of *Physionomies parisiennes*)

Silverman, Debora, *Art Nouveau in Fin-de-Siècle France: Politics, Psychology and Style*, Berkeley and Los Angeles: University of California Press, 1989

Silvestre, Théophile, 'Salon de 1874, III', *Le Pays*, 20 May 1874

Simpson, Juliet, 'Bourget, Laforgue and Impressionism's Inside Story', *French Studies*, vol. 55, no. 4, 2001, pp. 467–83

Smith, Bernard, *Modernism's History: A Study in Twentieth-Century Art and Ideas*, New Haven and London: Yale University Press, 1998

Smith, Paul, *Impressionism*, London: Weidenfeld and Nicolson (Everyman Art Library), 1995; as *Impressionism: Beneath the Surface*, New York: Abrams, 1995

——, *Seurat and the Avant-Garde*, New Haven and London: Yale University Press, 1997

Snell, Robert, *Théophile Gautier: A Romantic Critic of the Visual Arts*, Oxford: Clarendon Press, 1982

Solomon-Godeau, Abigail, 'Going Native', *Art in America*, July 1989, pp. 118–29

Spate, Virginia, *The Colour of Time: Claude Monet*, London: Thames and Hudson, 1992

Spencer, Robin, 'Whistler, Manet and the Tradition of the Avant-Garde', in Ruth E. Fine (ed.), *James McNeill Whistler: A Reexamination*, Washington: National Gallery of Art, *Studies in the History of Art*, 19, 1987

Stock, 'Le Salon par Stock', *Album Stock*, 20 March 1870

Tabarant, Adolphe, *Manet et ses oeuvres*, Paris, 1947

Taboureux, Emile, 'Claude Monet', *La Vie moderne*, 12 June 1880, pp. 380–82

Tester, Keith (ed.), *The Flâneur*, London: Routledge, 1994

Thévenin, Evariste, *La Mariage au XIXe siècle: ce qu'il est – ce qu'il doit être*, Paris, 1862

Thomson, Belinda, *Impressionism: Origins, Practice, Reception*, London: Thames and Hudson, 2000

Thomson, Richard, '"Les Quat' Pattes": The Image of the Dog in Late Nineteenth-Century French Art', *Art History*, September 1982, pp. 323–37

—— (ed.), *Framing France: The Representation of Landscape in France 1870–1914*, Manchester: Manchester University Press, 1998

Thoré, Théophile, *Salons de W. Bürger, 1861 à 1868*, 2 volumes, Paris, 1870

Tucker, Paul Hayes, *Monet at Argenteuil*, New Haven and London: Yale University Press, 1982

——, 'The First Impressionist Exhibition and Monet's *Impression, Sunrise*: A Tale of Timing, Commerce and Patriotism', *Art History*, December 1984, pp. 465–76

—— (ed.), *Manet's* Le Déjeuner sur l'herbe, Cambridge and New York: Cambridge University Press, 1998

Vaisse, Pierre, 'Le legs Caillebotte d'après les documents', *Bulletin de la Société de l'Histoire de l'Art français, Année 1983*, 1985, pp. 201–8

——, *La Troisième République et les peintres*, Paris: Flammarion, 1995

Varnedoe, Kirk, 'The Artifice of Candor: Impressionism and Photography Reconsidered, 1', *Art in America*, January 1980, pp. 66–78

——, *Gustave Caillebotte*, New Haven and London: Yale University Press, 1987 (revised version of exhibition catalogue of 1976)

——, *A Fine Disregard: What Makes Modern Art Modern*, London: Thames and Hudson, 1990

[Vassy, Gaston], 'La Journée à Paris: L'Exposition des impressionnistes', *L'Evénement*, 6 April 1877

Venturi, Lionello, *Les Archives de l'impressionnisme*, 2 volumes, Paris, 1939

Vinet, Ernest, 'Correspondence: Letters from Paris', *Fine Arts Quarterly Review*, October 1866, pp. 431–46

Vollard, Ambroise, *En écoutant Cézanne, Degas, Renoir*, Paris, 1938

Wagner, Anne, 'Why Monet Gave Up Figure Painting', *Art Bulletin*, December 1994, pp. 612–29

Ward, Martha, 'Impressionist Installations and Private Exhibitions', *Art Bulletin*, December 1991, pp. 599–622

——, *Pissarro, Neo-Impressionism and the Spaces of the Avant-Garde*, Chicago and London: University of Chicago Press, 1996

Webster, J. C., 'The Technique of Impressionism', *College Art Journal*, November 1944, pp. 3–22

Weinberg, Bernard, *French Realism: The Critical Reaction 1830–1870*, New York: Modern Language Association of America, 1937

White, Barbara Ehrlich, *Impressionists Side by Side: Their Friendships, Rivalries and Artistic Exchanges*, New York: Knopf, 1996

Wildenstein, Daniel, *Monet: biographie et catalogue raisonné*, Lausanne and Paris, Bibliothèque des Arts, I, 1974, II and III, 1979, IV, 1985, V, 1991 (the new, slightly updated edition, Cologne: Taschen, 1996, omits Monet's graphic work as well as the documentary footnotes to the biography and the entire sequence of Monet's correspondence)

Wilhelm, Jacques, 'The Sketch in Eighteenth-Century French Painting', *Apollo*, September 1962, pp. 517–24

Wilson, Elizabeth, *The Sphinx in the City: Urban Life, the Control of Disorder and Women*, London: Virago, 1991

——, *Bohemians: The Glamorous Outcasts*, London: I. B. Tauris, 2000

Wilson Bareau, Juliet, *The Hidden Face of Manet: An Investigation of the Artist's Working Processes*, London: Burlington Magazine, 1986 (catalogue of exhibition held at Courtauld Institute Galleries, London, also published as supplement to *Burlington Magazine*, April 1986)

Wilson-Bareau, Juliet, *Manet by Himself*, London: Macdonald, 1991

Wolff, Albert, 'Le Calendrier parisien', *Le Figaro*, 3 April 1876

Wolff, Janet, 'The Invisible Flâneuse: Women and the Literature of Modernity', in Andrew Benjamin (ed.), *The Problems of Modernity: Adorno and Benjamin*, London: Routledge, 1989

Wood, Paul (ed.), *The Challenge of the Avant-Garde*, New Haven and London: Yale University Press/Open University, 1999

Zola, Emile, 'Le Moment artistique', *L'Evénement*, 4 May 1866; reprinted in Zola 1970

——, 'Les Chutes', *L'Evénement*, 15 May 1866; reprinted in Zola 1970

——, 'Edouard Manet', *Revue du XIXe siècle*, 1 January 1867; reprinted in Zola 1970

——, 'Mon Salon', *L'Evénement illustré*, 2 May – 16 June 1868; reprinted in Zola 1970

——, 'Le Naturalisme au Salon', *Le Voltaire*, 18–22 June 1880; reprinted in Zola 1970

——, *Mon Salon, Manet: Ecrits sur l'art*, ed. A. Ehrard, Paris: Garnier-Flammarion, 1970

Photograph Credits

Index